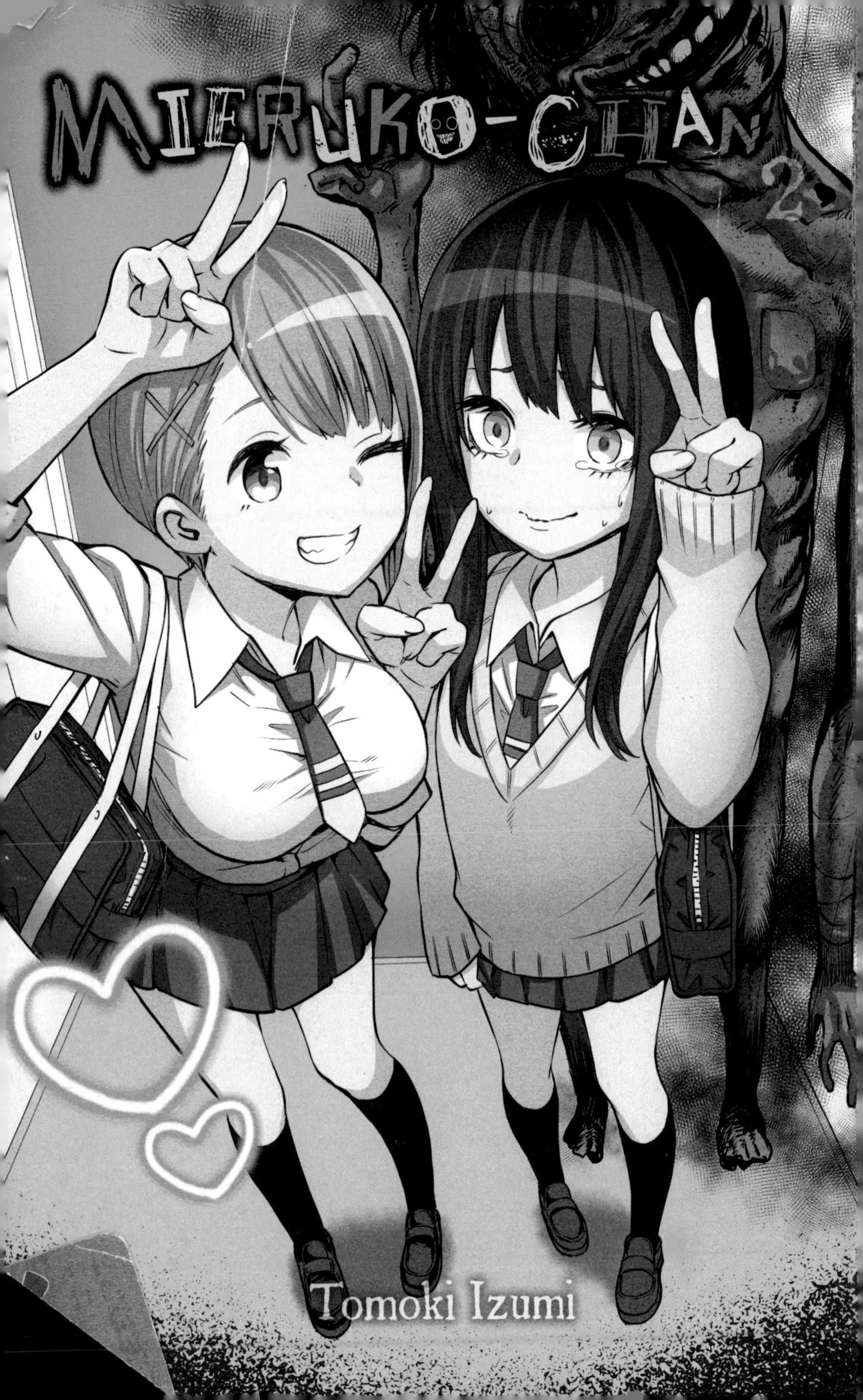
MIERUKO-CHAN
2
Tomoki Izumi

CONTENTS

Chapter 10 003

Chapter 11 018

Chapter 12 037

Chapter 13 055

Chapter 14 · Part 1 073

Chapter 14 · Part 2 089

Chapter 15 107

Chapter 16 129

Side Story 1 148

Side Story 2 152

Extra 156

Special Thanks 161

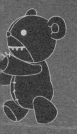
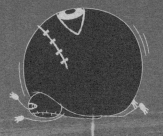
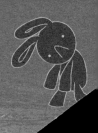

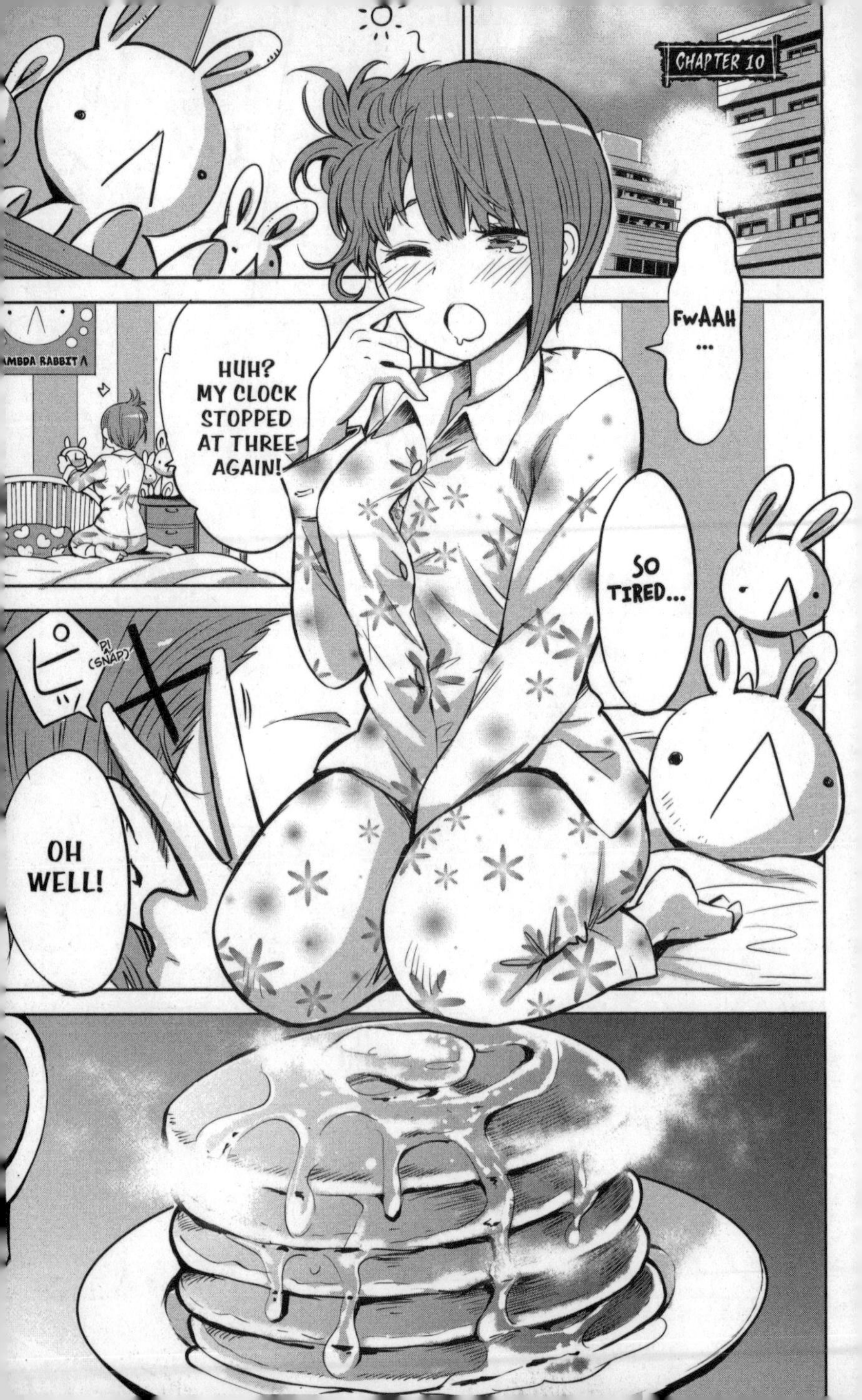
CHAPTER 10
FwAAH ...
AMBDA RABBIT Λ
HUH? MY CLOCK STOPPED AT THREE AGAIN!
SO TIRED...
ピッ
PI (SNAP)
OH WELL!

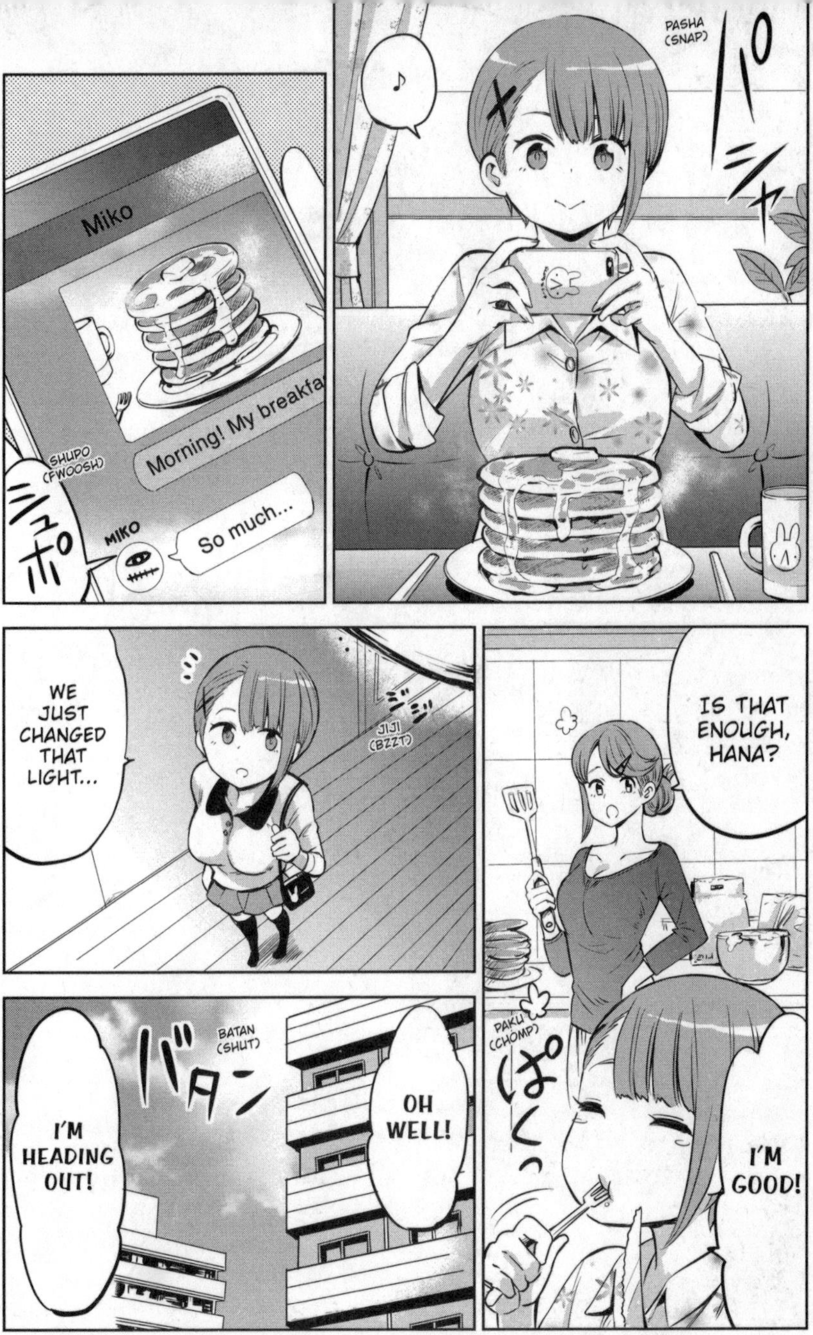

♪
PASHA (SNAP)
パシャ
Miko
Morning! My breakfa
MIKO
So much...
SHUPO (FWOOSH)
シュポ
IS THAT ENOUGH, HANA?
WE JUST CHANGED THAT LIGHT...
JIJI (BZZT)
ジジ
PAKU (CHOMP)
ぱくっ
I'M GOOD!
OH WELL!
BATAN (SHUT)
バタン
I'M HEADING OUT!

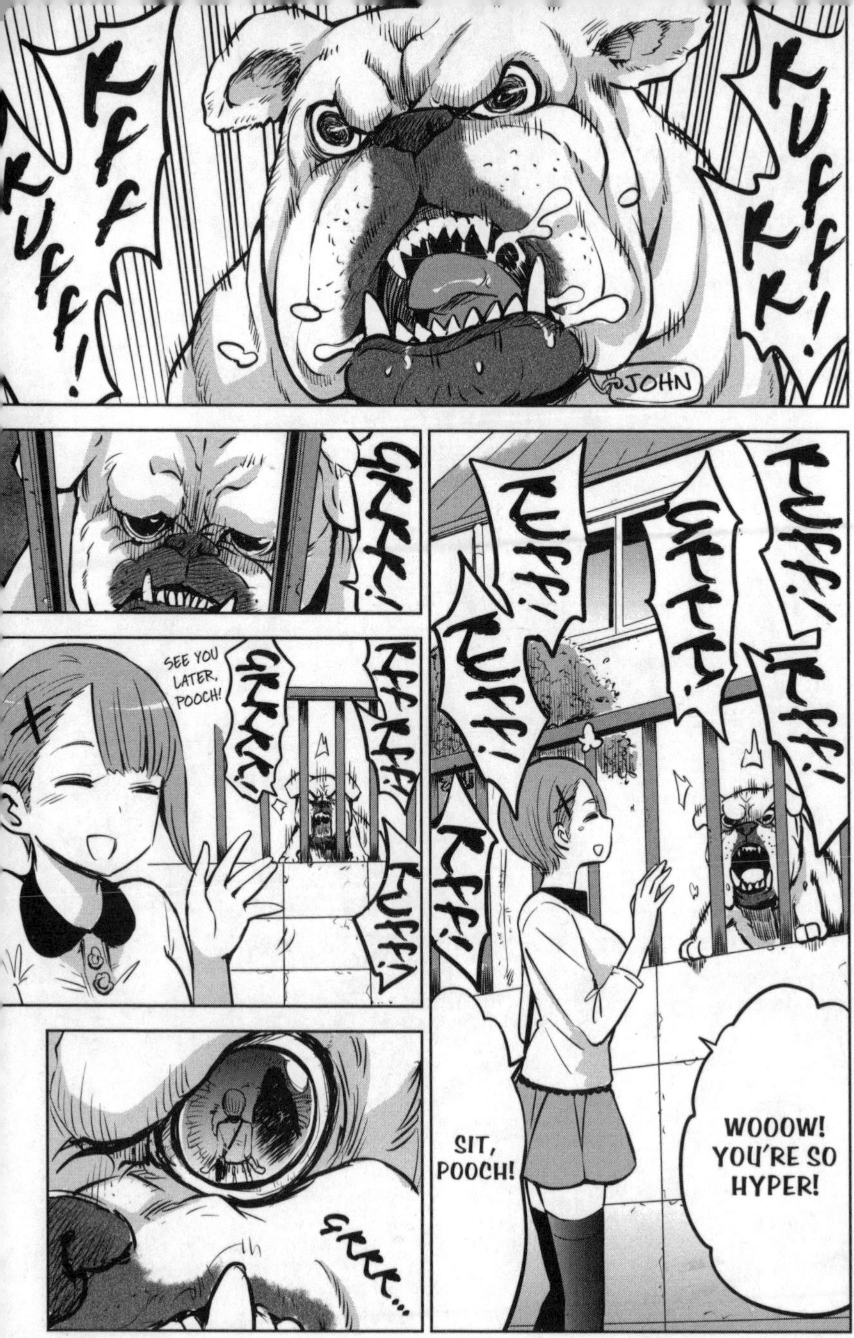
RUFF RR!
RFF RUFF!
JOHN
RUFF! RUFF!
GRRRR!
RUFF! RUFF!
RUFF!
WOOOW! YOU'RE SO HYPER!
SIT, POOCH!
GRRR!
RFF RFF!
RUFF!
GRRRR!
SEE YOU LATER, POOCH!
GRRR...

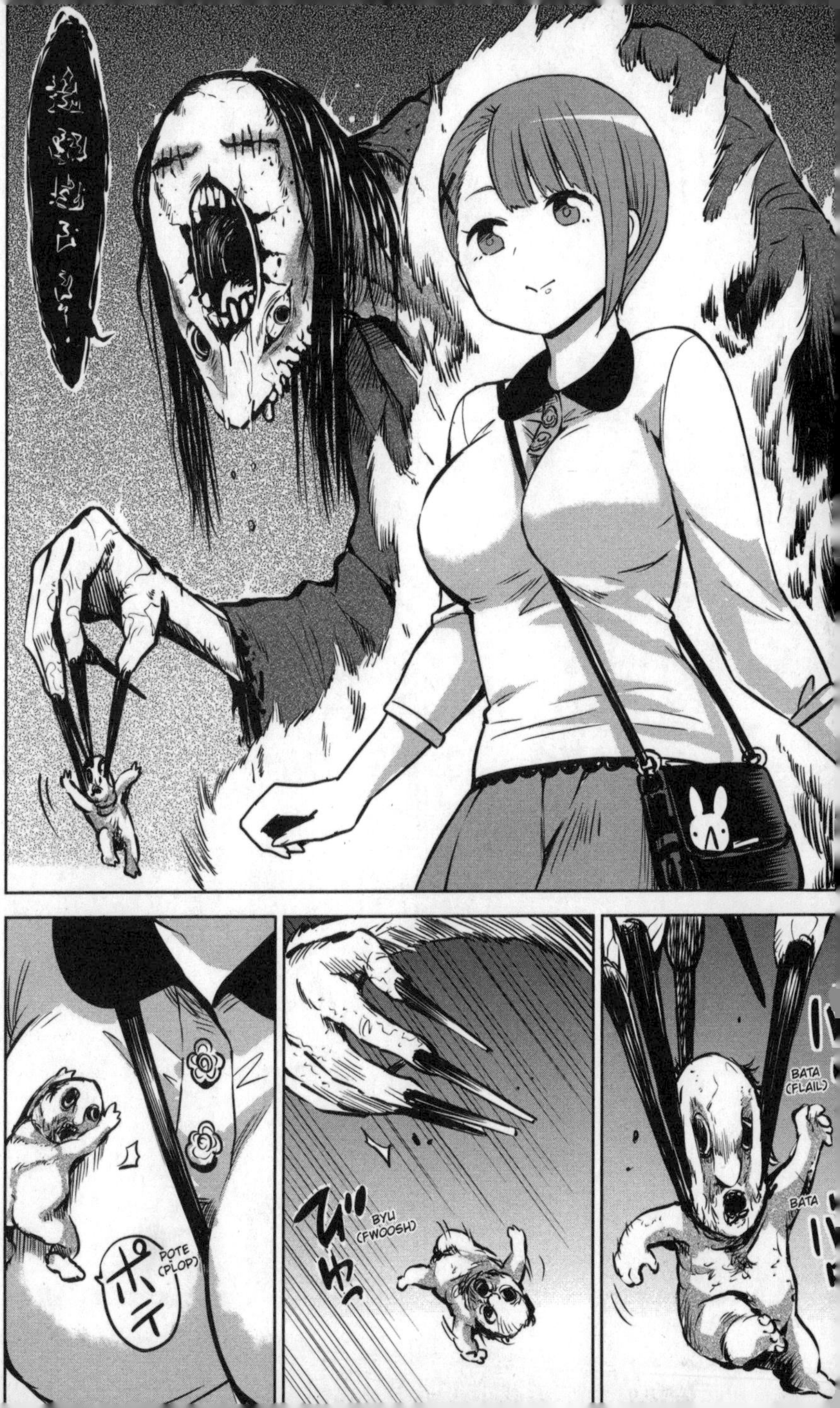
BATA (FLAIL)
BATA
BYU (FWOOSH)
ポテ
POTE (PLOP)

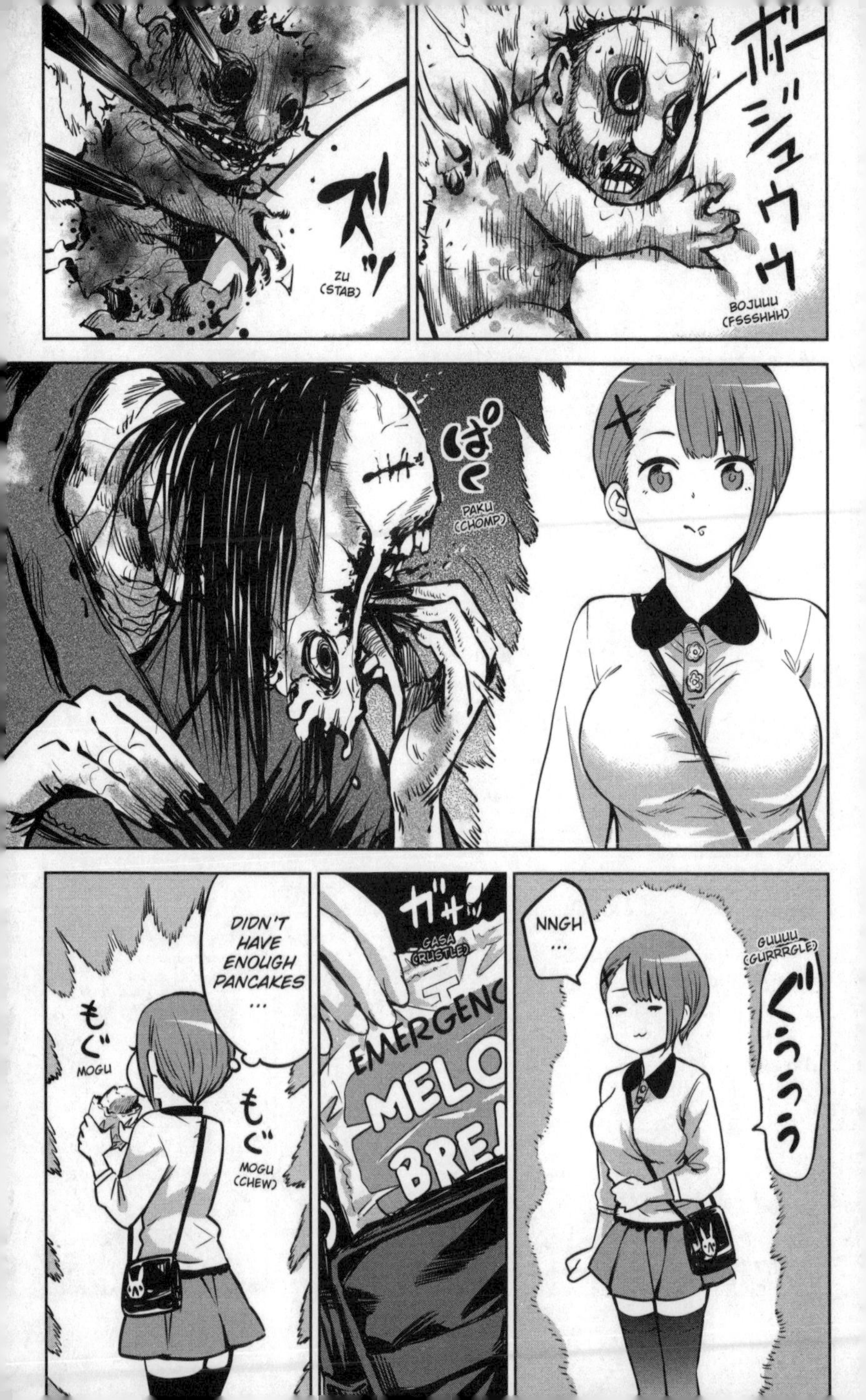
ボジュウウ
BOJUUU (FSSSHHH)
ズッ
ZU (STAB)
ぱく
PAKU (CHOMP)
NNGH ...
ぐううう
GUUUU (GURRRGLE)
ガサ
GASA (RUSTLE)
EMERGENC
MELO
BRE
DIDN'T HAVE ENOUGH PANCAKES ...
もぐ
MOGU
もぐ
MOGU (CHEW)

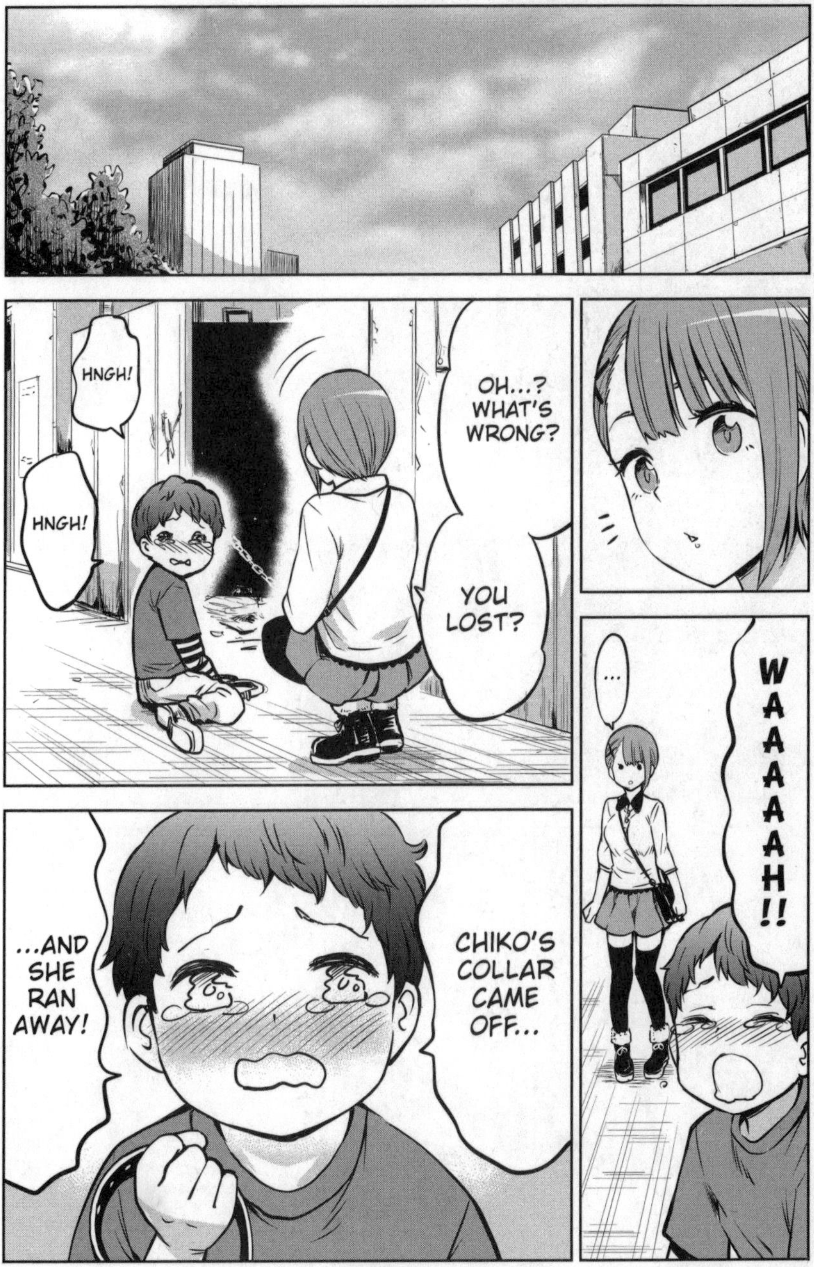
...
WAAAAAAAH!!
OH...? WHAT'S WRONG?
YOU LOST?
HNGH!
HNGH!
CHIKO'S COLLAR CAME OFF...
...AND SHE RAN AWAY!

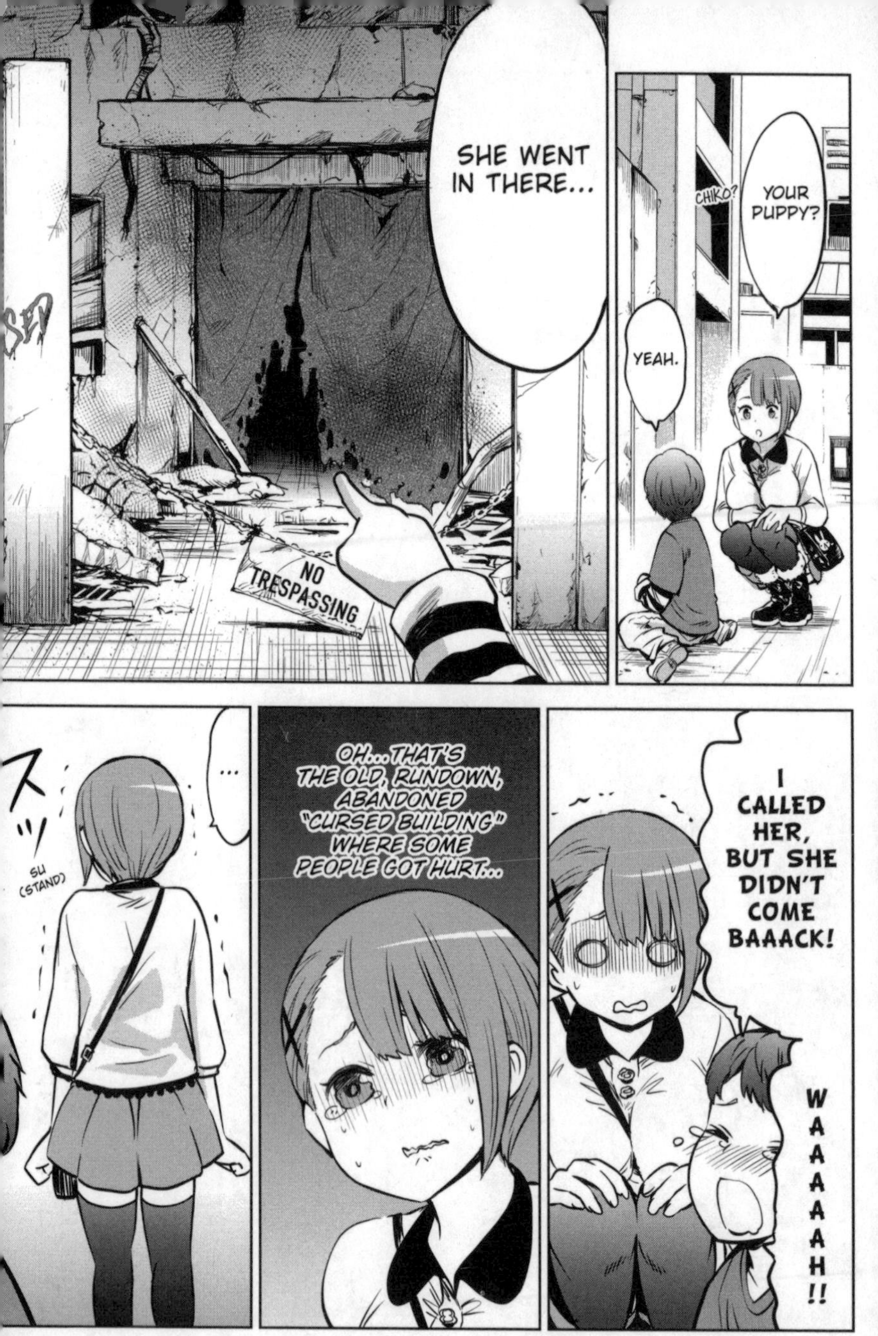
YOUR PUPPY?
CHIKO?
YEAH.
SHE WENT IN THERE...
NO TRESPASSING
I CALLED HER, BUT SHE DIDN'T COME BAAACK!
WAAAAAAAH!!
OH... THAT'S THE OLD, RUNDOWN, ABANDONED "CURSED BUILDING" WHERE SOME PEOPLE GOT HURT...
...
スッ
SU (STAND)

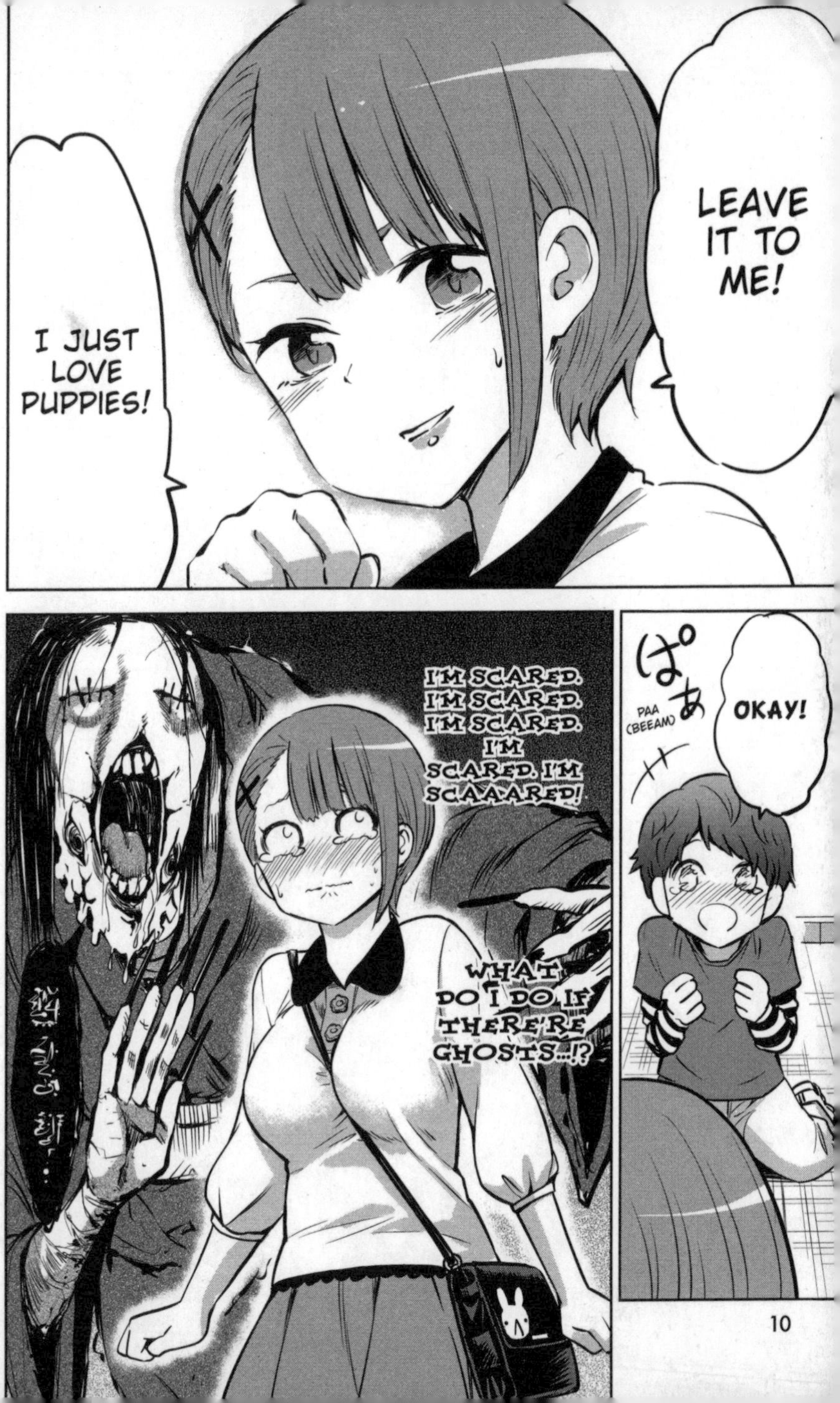
LEAVE IT TO ME!
I JUST LOVE PUPPIES!
ぱあ
PAA (BEEAM)
OKAY!
I'M SCARED. I'M SCARED. I'M SCARED. I'M SCARED. I'M SCAAAARED!
WHAT DO I DO IF THERE'RE GHOSTS...!?

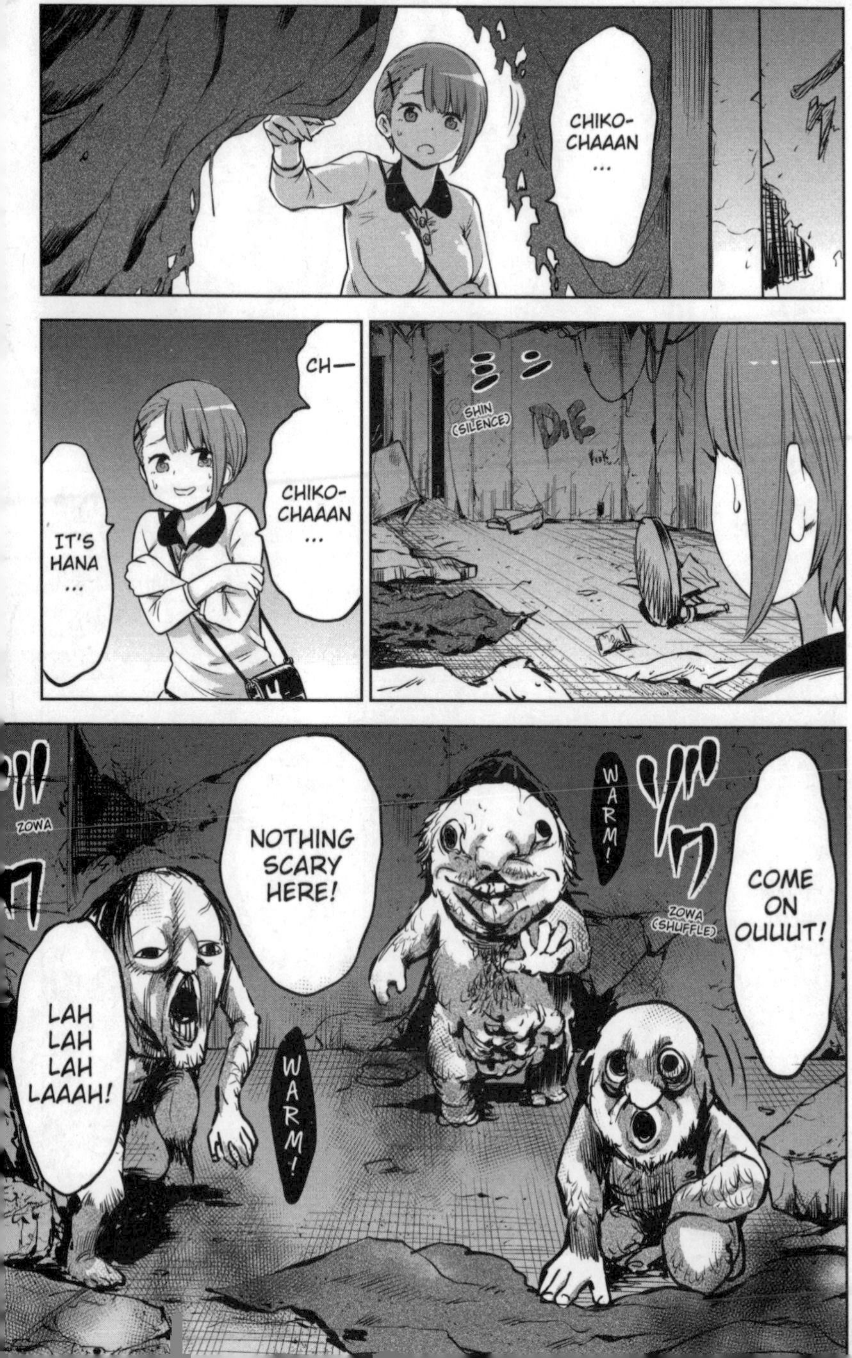
CHIKO-CHAAAN ...
SHIN (SILENCE)
DIE
CH—
CHIKO-CHAAAN ...
IT'S HANA ...
COME ON OUUUT!
ZOWA (SHUFFLE)
WARM!
NOTHING SCARY HERE!
ZOWA
LAH LAH LAH LAAAH!
WARM!

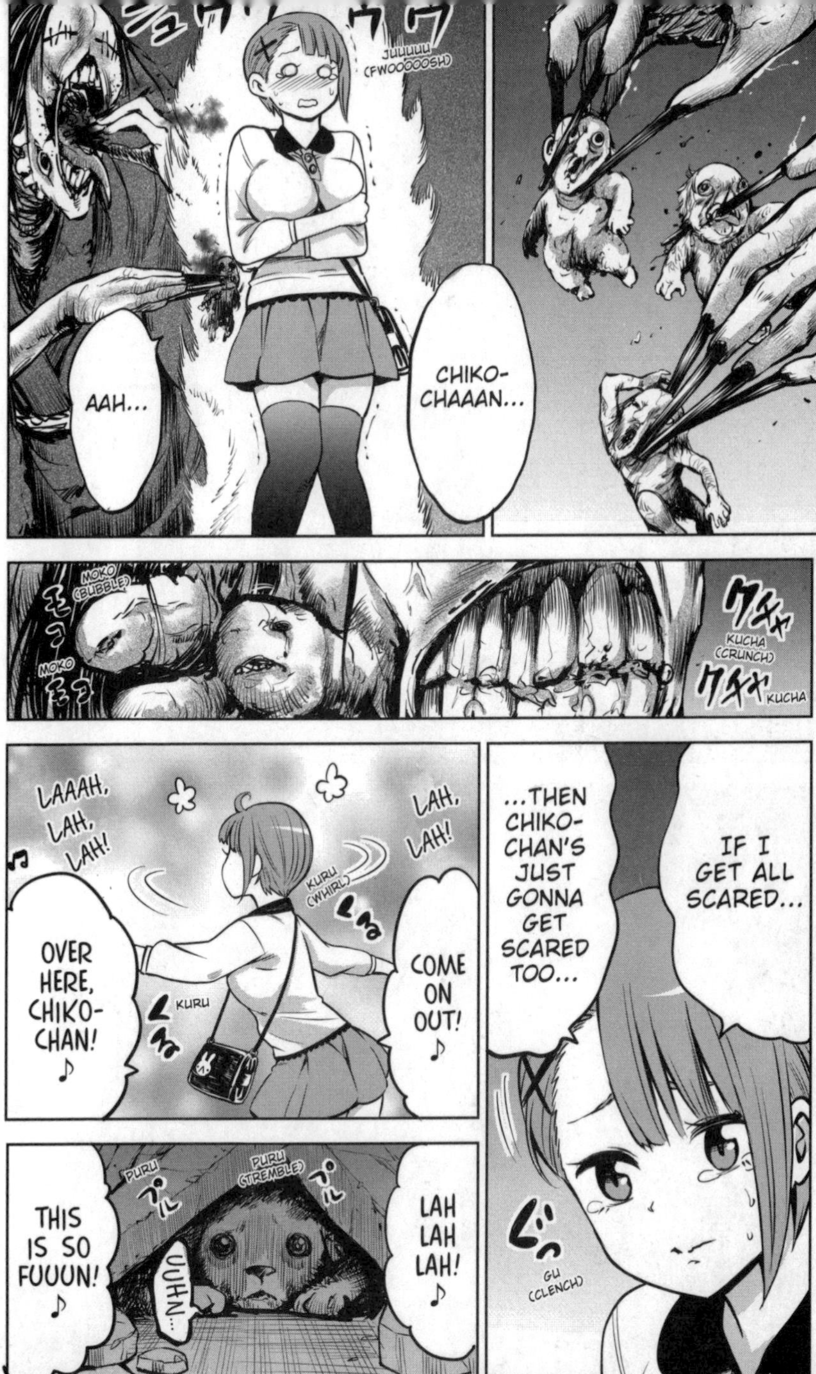
JUUUUUU (FWOOOOOSH)
CHIKO-CHAAAN...
AAH...
KUCHA (CRUNCH)
KUCHA
MOKO (BUBBLE)
MOKO
IF I GET ALL SCARED...
...THEN CHIKO-CHAN'S JUST GONNA GET SCARED TOO...
GU (CLENCH)
LAH, LAH!
LAAAH, LAH, LAH!
KURU (WHIRL)
COME ON OUT! ♪
KURU
OVER HERE, CHIKO-CHAN! ♪
PURU (TREMBLE)
PURU
LAH LAH LAH! ♪
UUHN...
THIS IS SO FUUUN! ♪

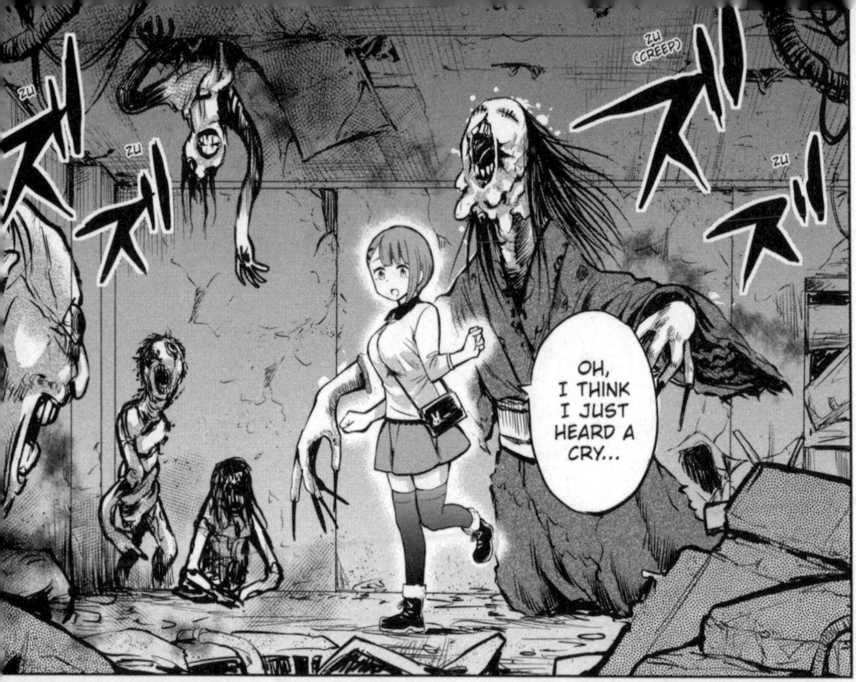
ZU (CREEP)
ZU
OH, I THINK I JUST HEARD A CRY...
ZU
ZU

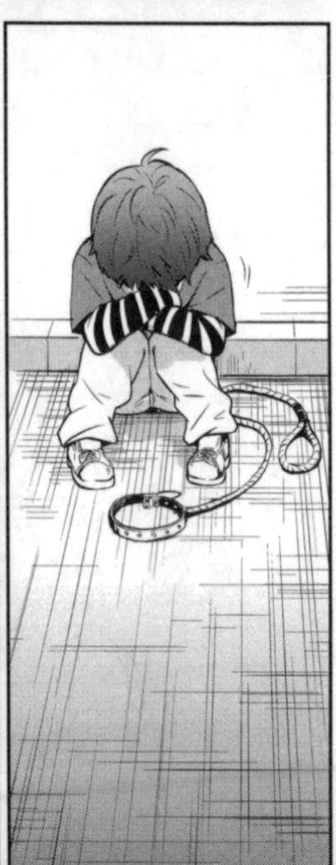

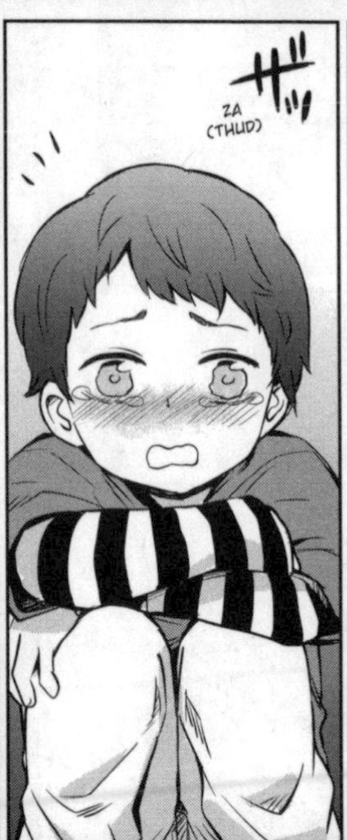
ZA (THUD)

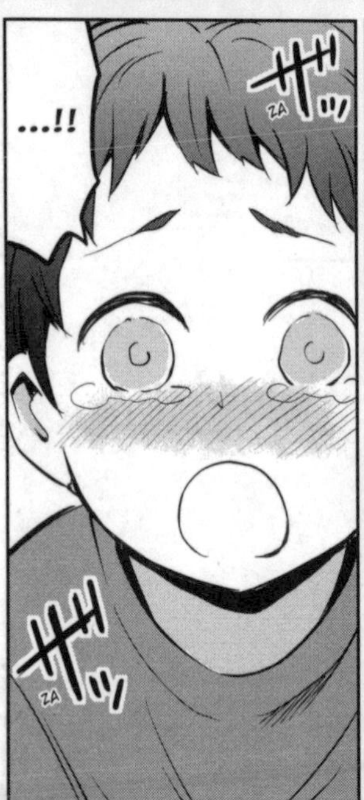
ZA
...!!
ZA

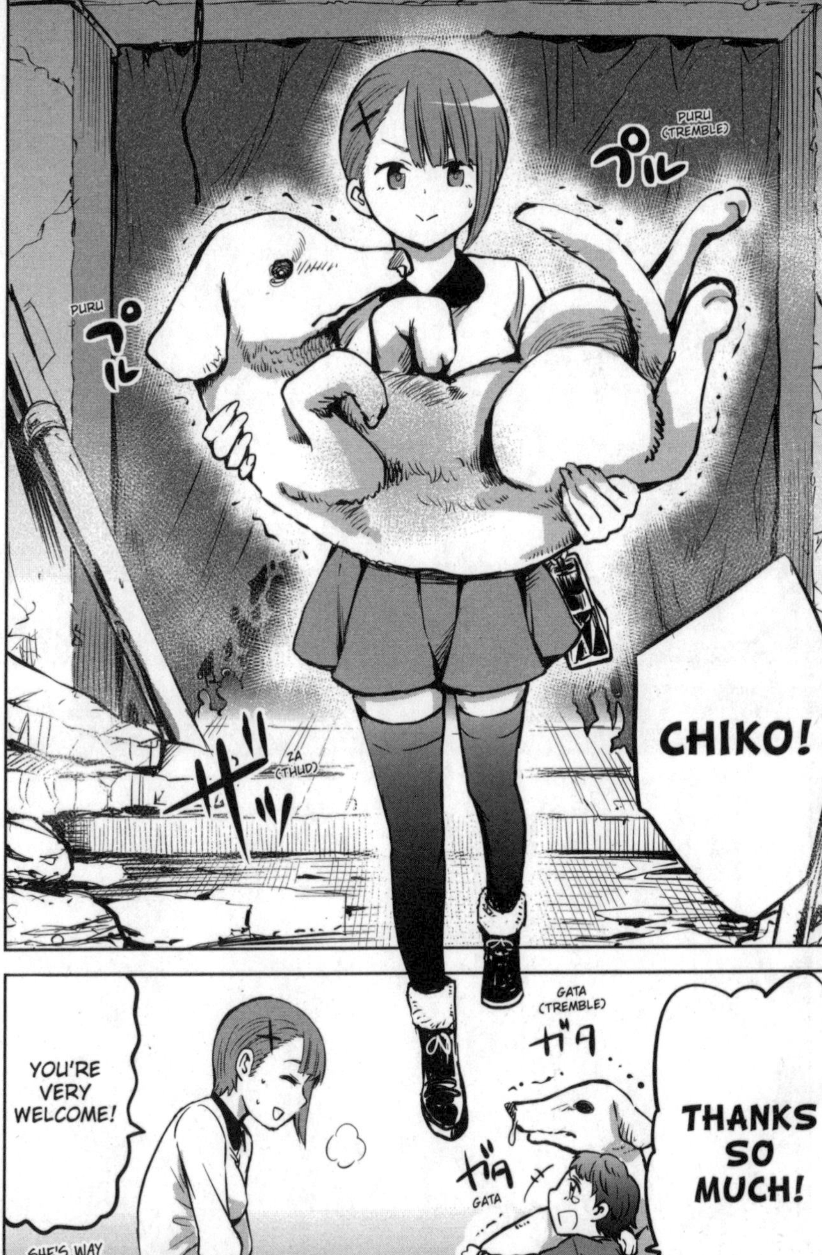

PURU (TREMBLE)
プル
PURU
プル
CHIKO!
ZA (THUD)
ザッ
THANKS SO MUCH!
GATA (TREMBLE)
ガタ
ガタ
GATA
YOU'RE VERY WELCOME!
SHE'S WAY BIGGER THAN I EXPECTED.

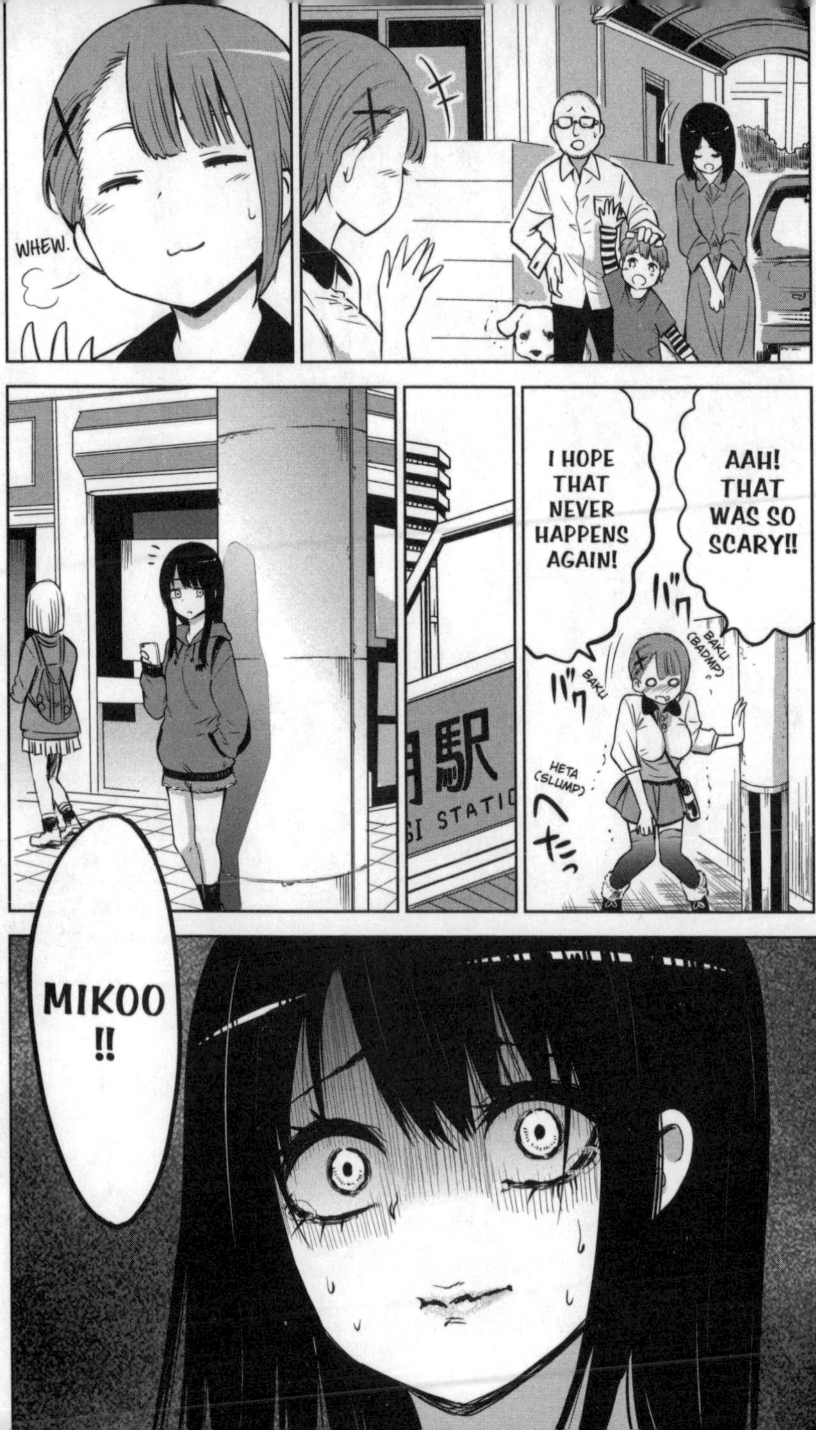
WHEW.
AAH! THAT WAS SO SCARY!!
I HOPE THAT NEVER HAPPENS AGAIN!
BAKU (BADMP)
BAKU
HETA (SLUMP)
SI STATIO
MIKOO !!

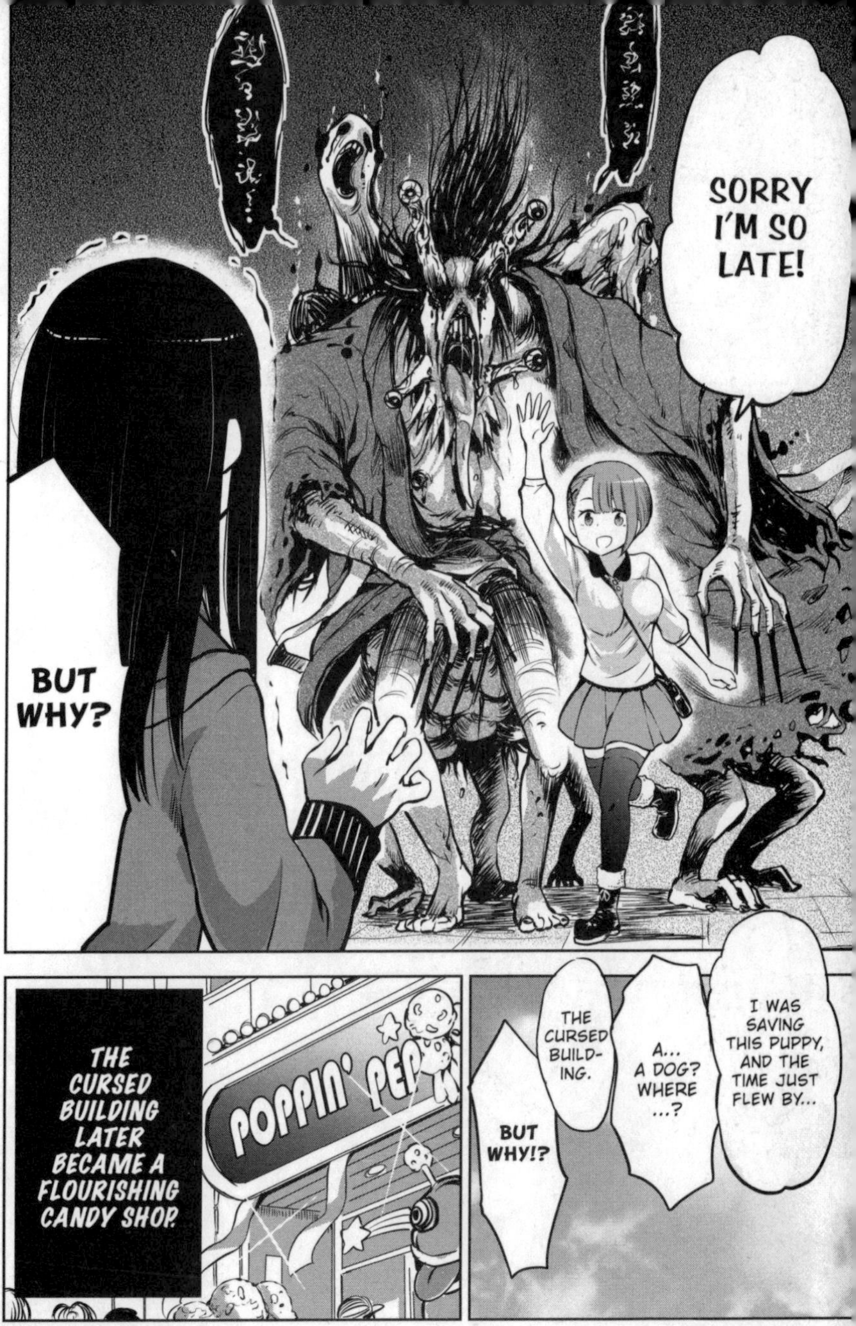
SORRY I'M SO LATE!
BUT WHY?
I WAS SAVING THIS PUPPY, AND THE TIME JUST FLEW BY...
A... A DOG? WHERE ...?
THE CURSED BUILD-ING.
BUT WHY!?
THE CURSED BUILDING LATER BECAME A FLOURISHING CANDY SHOP.
POPPIN' PEP

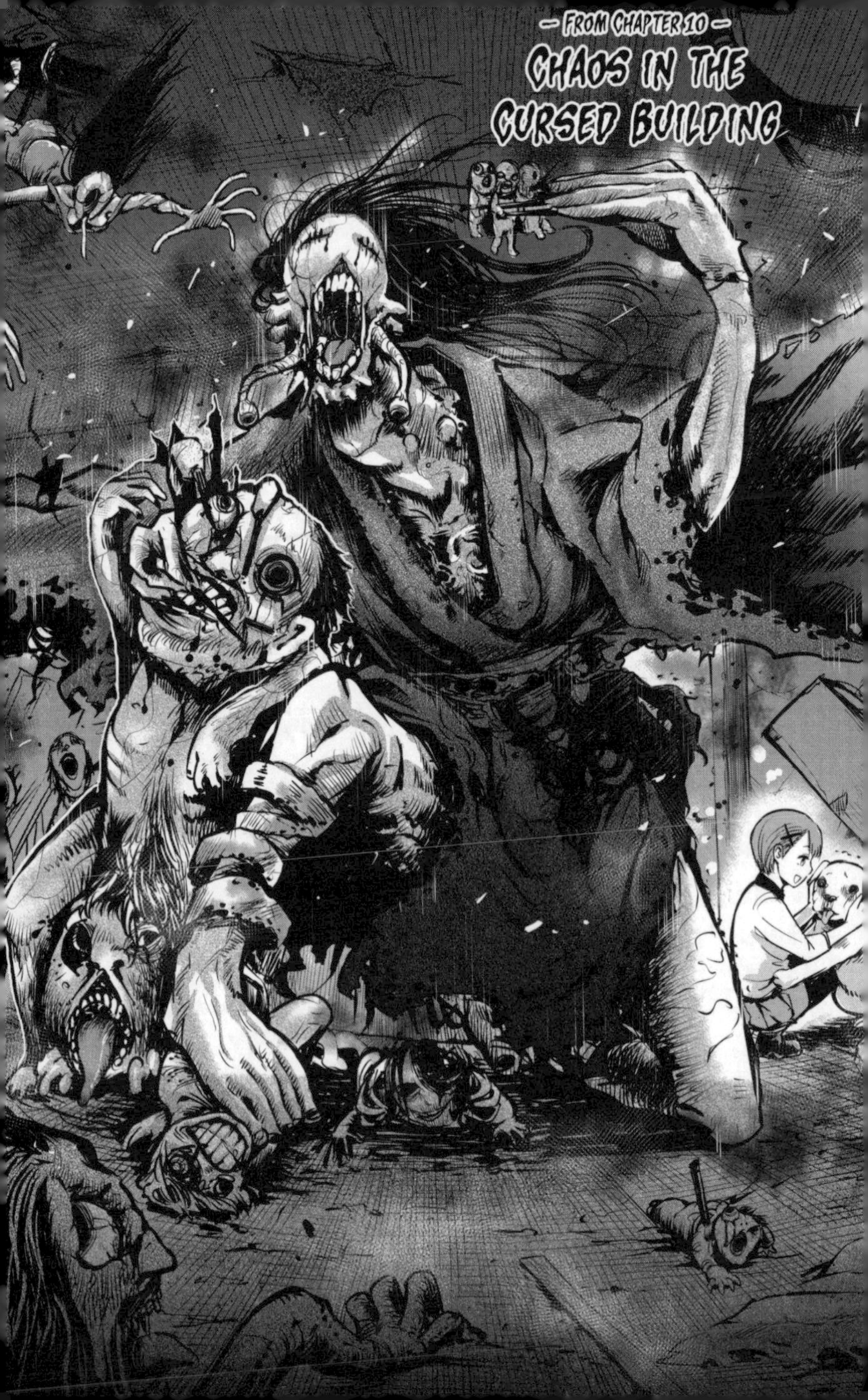
— FROM CHAPTER 10 —
CHAOS IN THE CURSED BUILDING

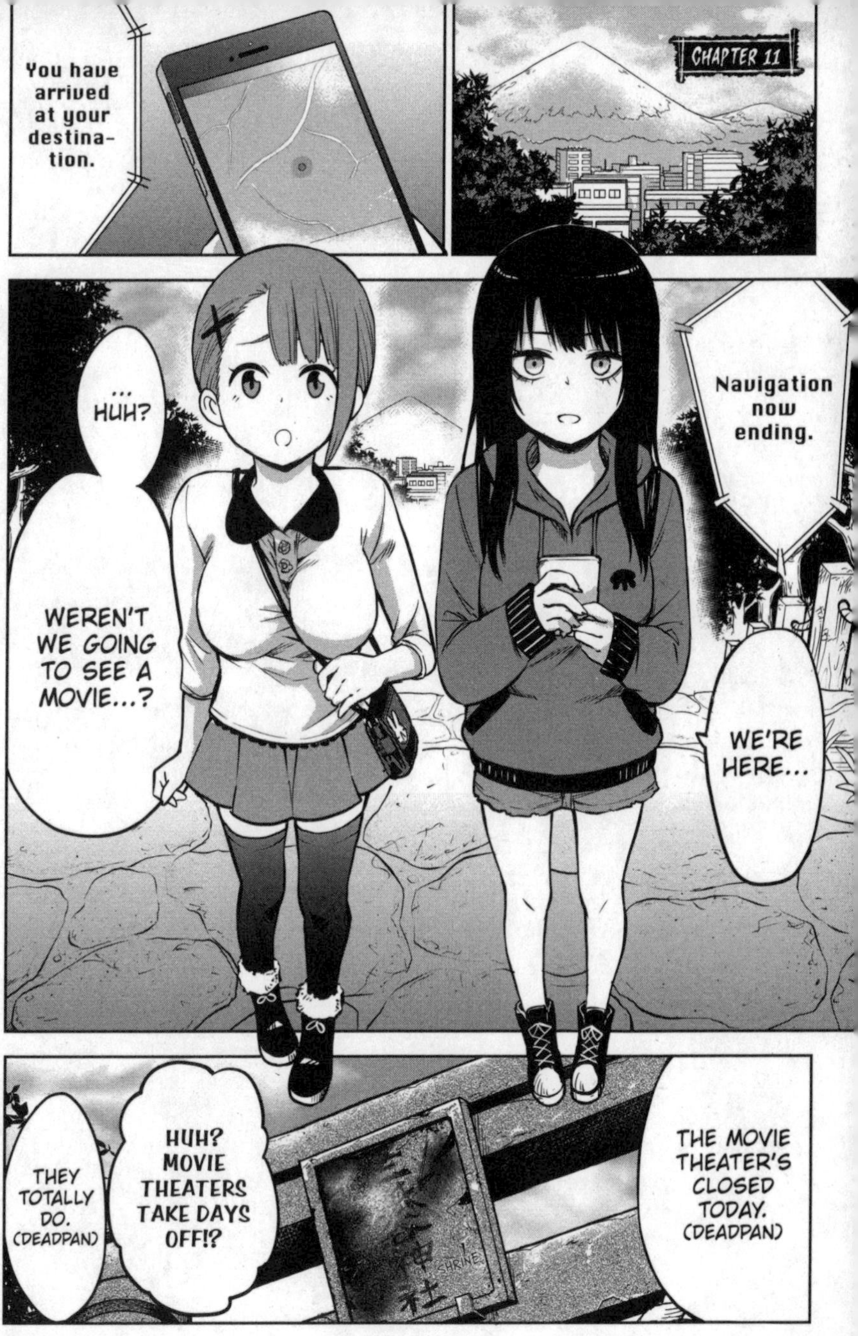
CHAPTER 11
You have arrived at your destination.
Navigation now ending.
... HUH?
WE'RE HERE...
WEREN'T WE GOING TO SEE A MOVIE...?
THE MOVIE THEATER'S CLOSED TODAY. (DEADPAN)
HUH? MOVIE THEATERS TAKE DAYS OFF!?
SHRINE
THEY TOTALLY DO. (DEADPAN)

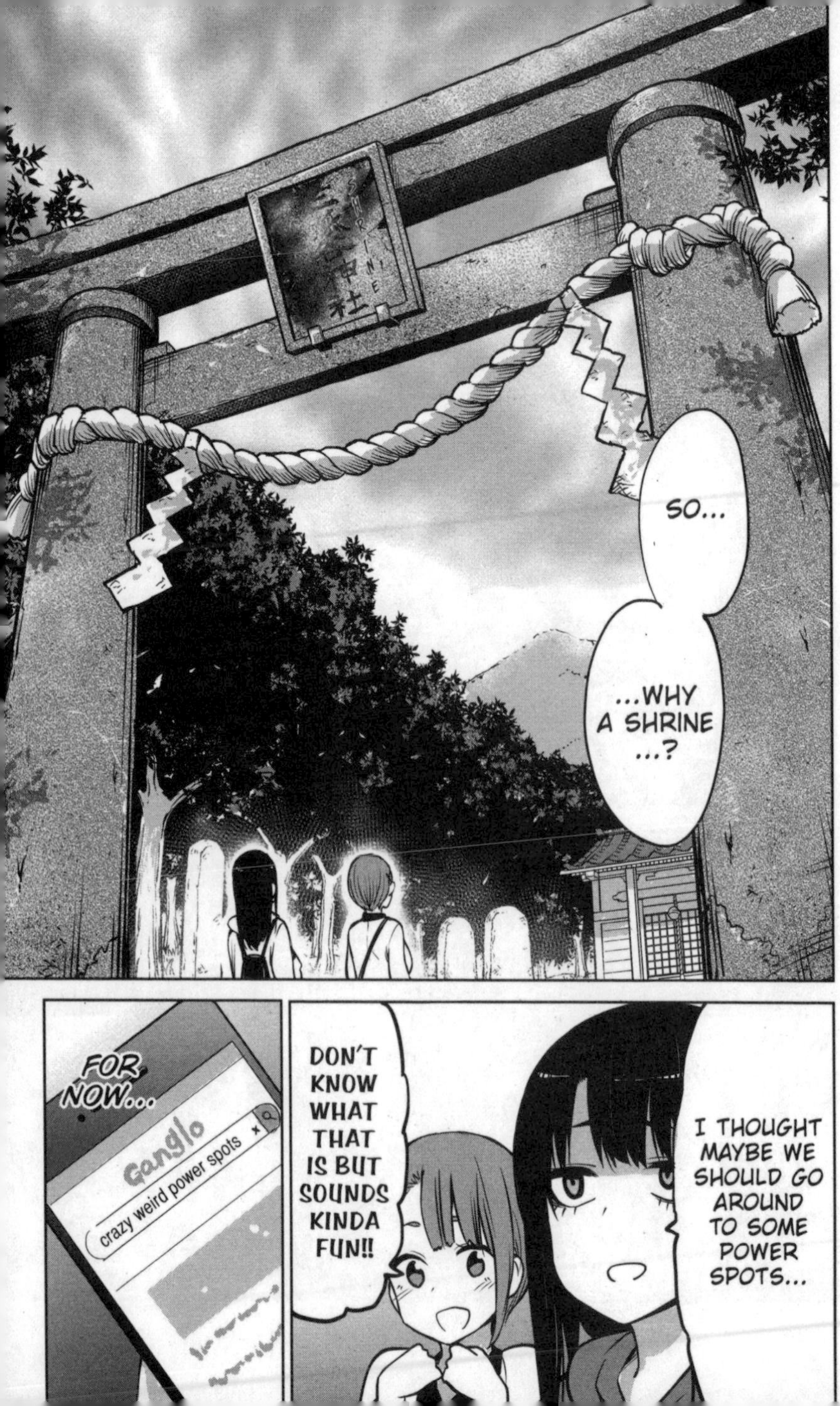
SHRINE
SO...
...WHY A SHRINE ...?
I THOUGHT MAYBE WE SHOULD GO AROUND TO SOME POWER SPOTS...
DON'T KNOW WHAT THAT IS BUT SOUNDS KINDA FUN!!
FOR NOW...
Ganglo
crazy weird power spots

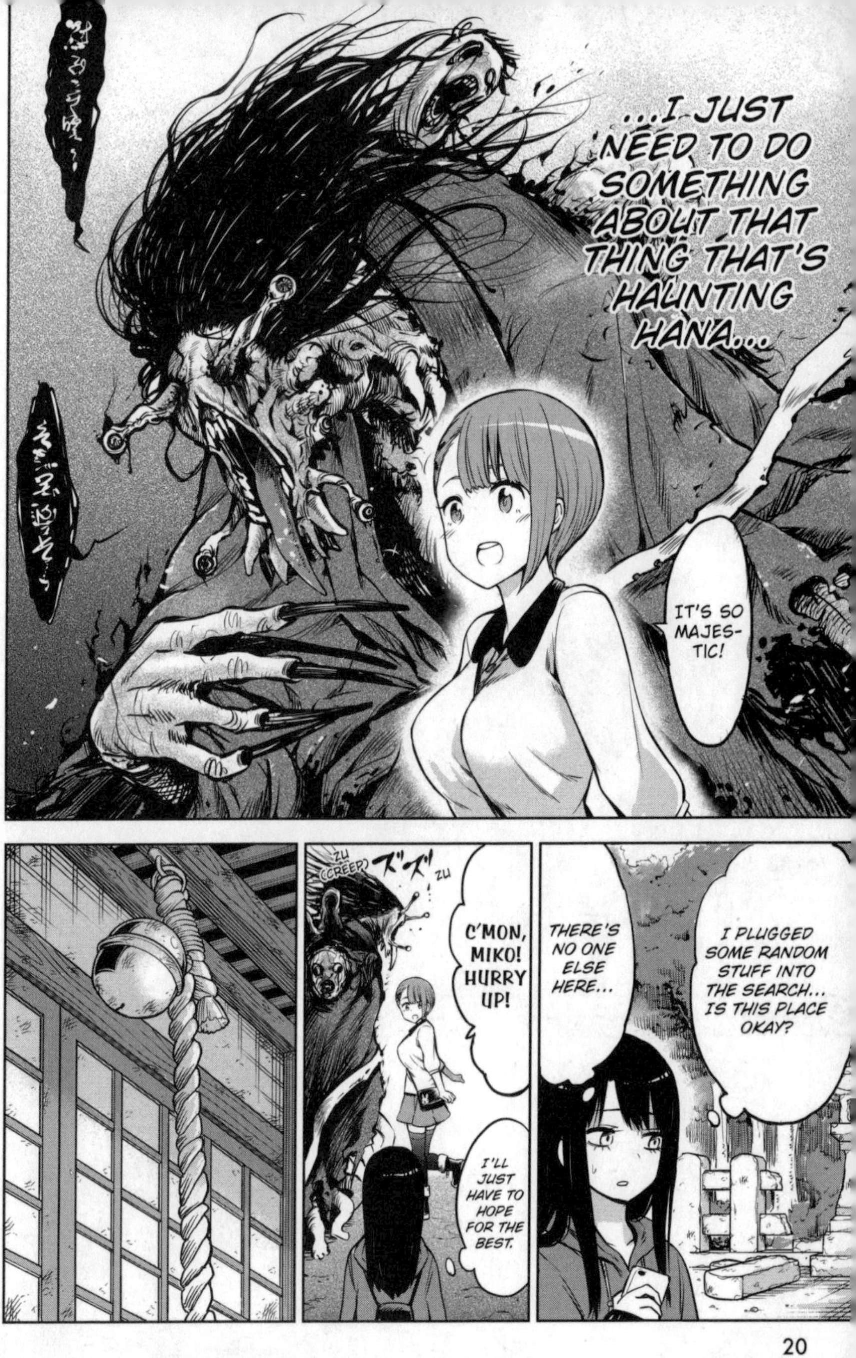
...I JUST NEED TO DO SOMETHING ABOUT THAT THING THAT'S HAUNTING HANA...
IT'S SO MAJES-TIC!
I PLUGGED SOME RANDOM STUFF INTO THE SEARCH... IS THIS PLACE OKAY?
THERE'S NO ONE ELSE HERE...
C'MON, MIKO! HURRY UP!
ZU (CREEP) ズズ ZU
I'LL JUST HAVE TO HOPE FOR THE BEST.

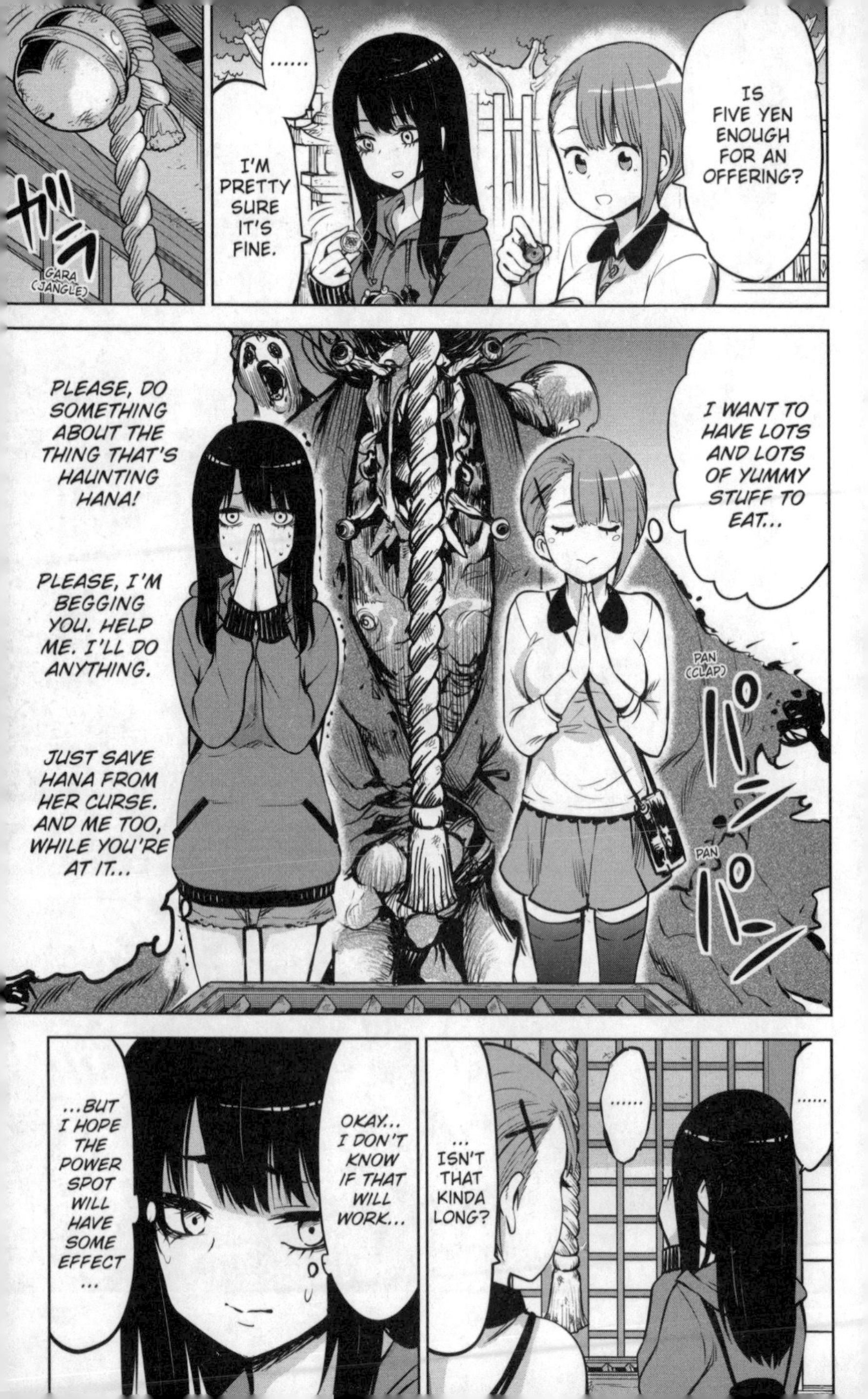
IS FIVE YEN ENOUGH FOR AN OFFERING?
......
I'M PRETTY SURE IT'S FINE.
ガラ
GARA (JANGLE)
I WANT TO HAVE LOTS AND LOTS OF YUMMY STUFF TO EAT...
PAN (CLAP)
パン
PAN
パン
PLEASE, DO SOMETHING ABOUT THE THING THAT'S HAUNTING HANA!
PLEASE, I'M BEGGING YOU. HELP ME. I'LL DO ANYTHING.
JUST SAVE HANA FROM HER CURSE. AND ME TOO, WHILE YOU'RE AT IT...
......
......
...ISN'T THAT KINDA LONG?
OKAY... I DON'T KNOW IF THAT WILL WORK...
...BUT I HOPE THE POWER SPOT WILL HAVE SOME EFFECT...

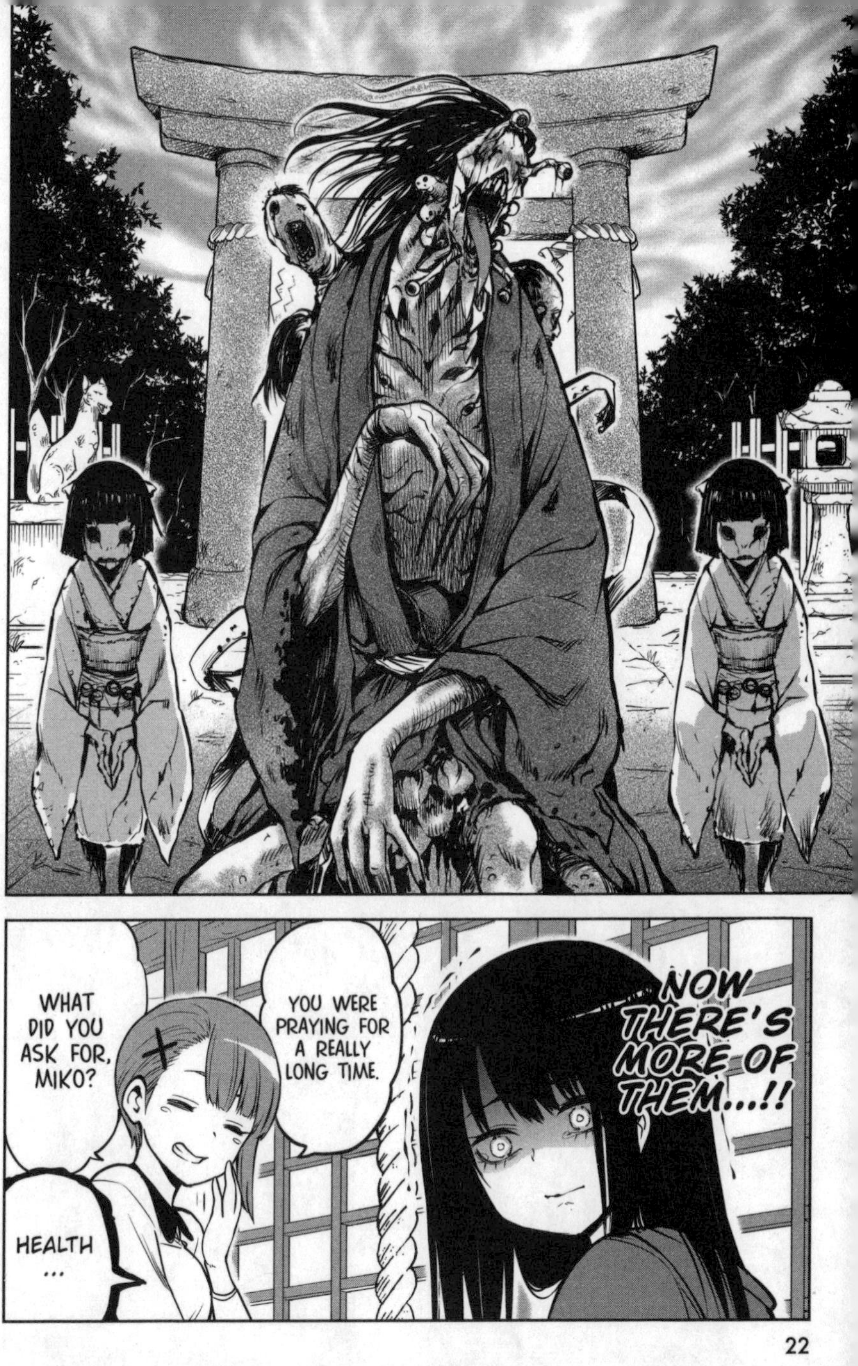
NOW THERE'S MORE OF THEM...!!
YOU WERE PRAYING FOR A REALLY LONG TIME.
WHAT DID YOU ASK FOR, MIKO?
HEALTH ...

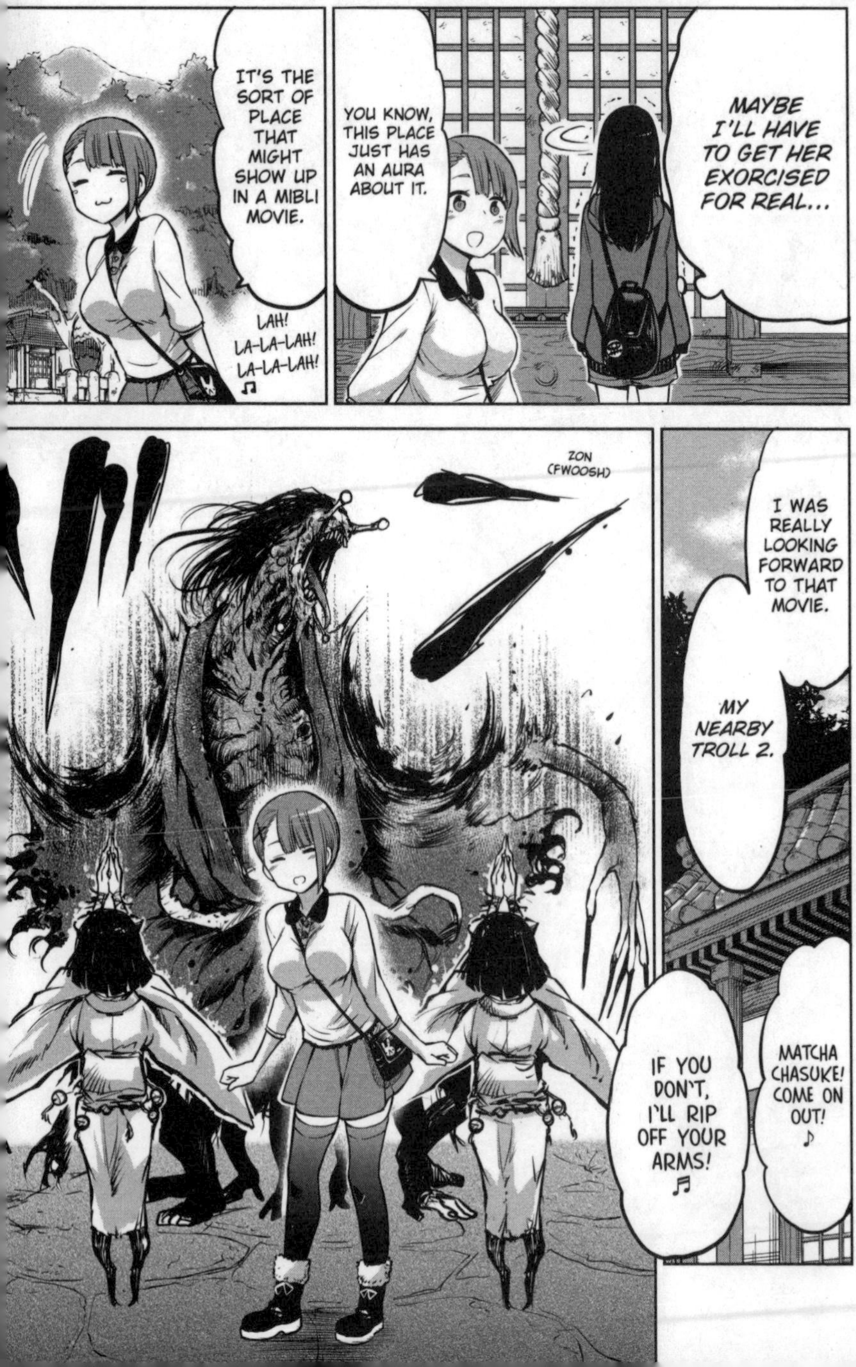
MAYBE I'LL HAVE TO GET HER EXORCISED FOR REAL...
YOU KNOW, THIS PLACE JUST HAS AN AURA ABOUT IT.
IT'S THE SORT OF PLACE THAT MIGHT SHOW UP IN A MIBLI MOVIE.
LAH! LA-LA-LAH! LA-LA-LAH! ♫
I WAS REALLY LOOKING FORWARD TO THAT MOVIE.
MY NEARBY TROLL 2.
MATCHA CHASUKE! COME ON OUT! ♪
IF YOU DON'T, I'LL RIP OFF YOUR ARMS! ♬
ZON (FWOOSH)

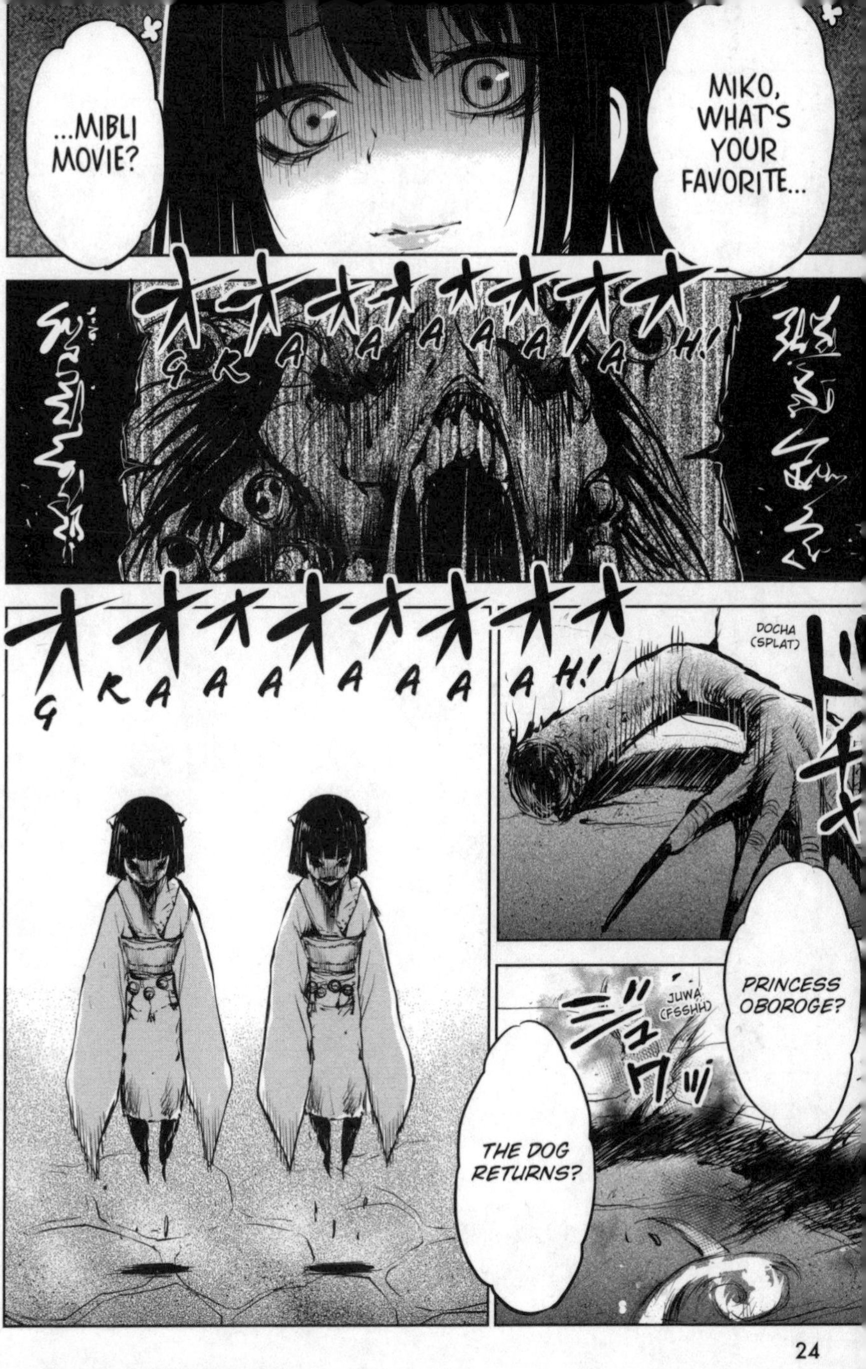
MIKO, WHAT'S YOUR FAVORITE...
...MIBLI MOVIE?
GRAAAAAAH!
DOCHA (SPLAT)
PRINCESS OBOROGE?
JUWA (FSSHH)
THE DOG RETURNS?
GRAAAAAAAH!

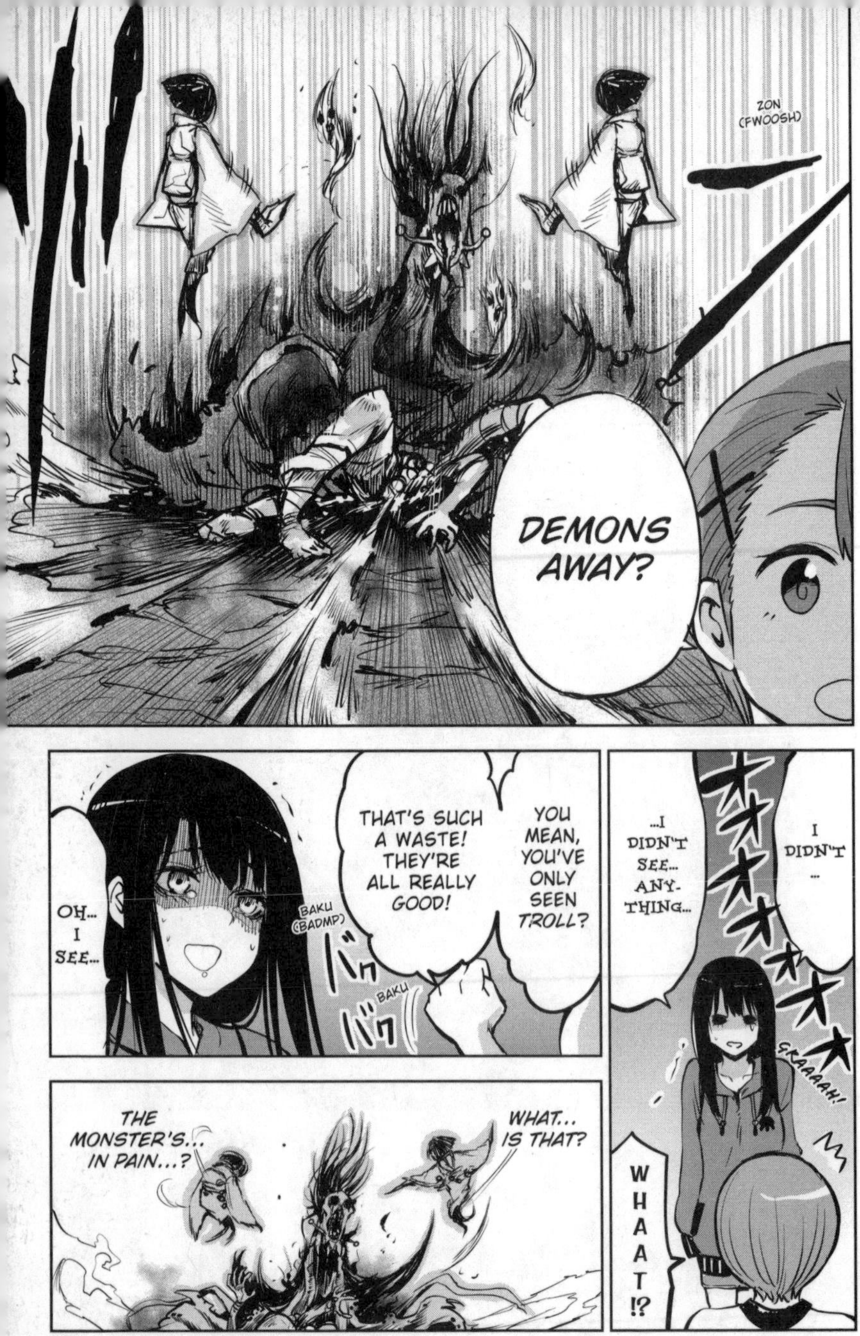
ZON (FWOOSH)
DEMONS AWAY?
I DIDN'T ...
...I DIDN'T SEE... ANY-THING...
GRAAAAH!
WHAAAT!?
YOU MEAN, YOU'VE ONLY SEEN TROLL?
THAT'S SUCH A WASTE! THEY'RE ALL REALLY GOOD!
BAKU (BADMP)
BAKU
OH... I SEE...
WHAT... IS THAT?
THE MONSTER'S... IN PAIN...?

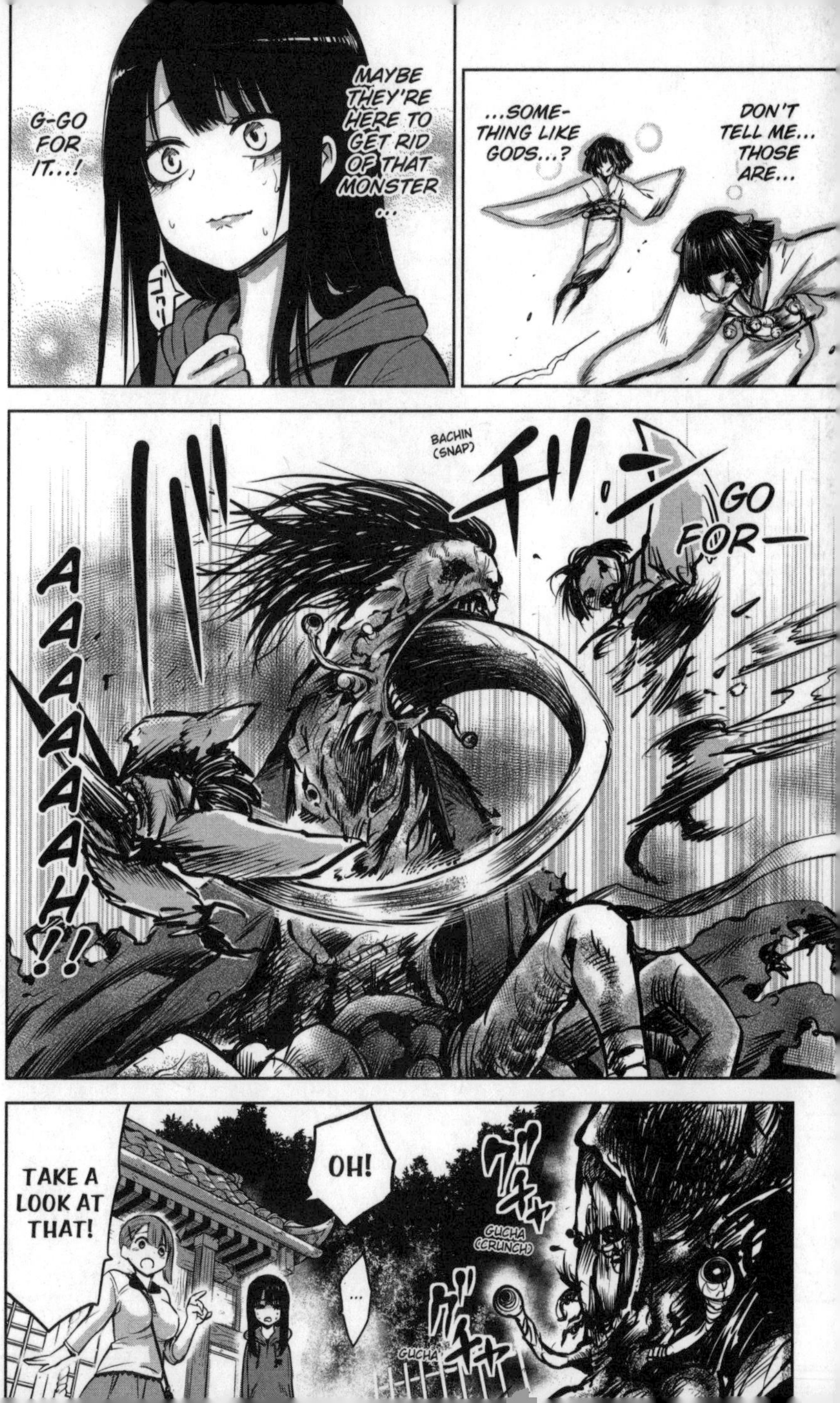
DON'T TELL ME... THOSE ARE...
...SOME-THING LIKE GODS...?
MAYBE THEY'RE HERE TO GET RID OF THAT MONSTER...
G-GO FOR IT...!
GO FOR—
BACHIN (SNAP)
AAAAAAAH!!
GUCHA (CRUNCH)
GUCHA
OH!
...
TAKE A LOOK AT THAT!

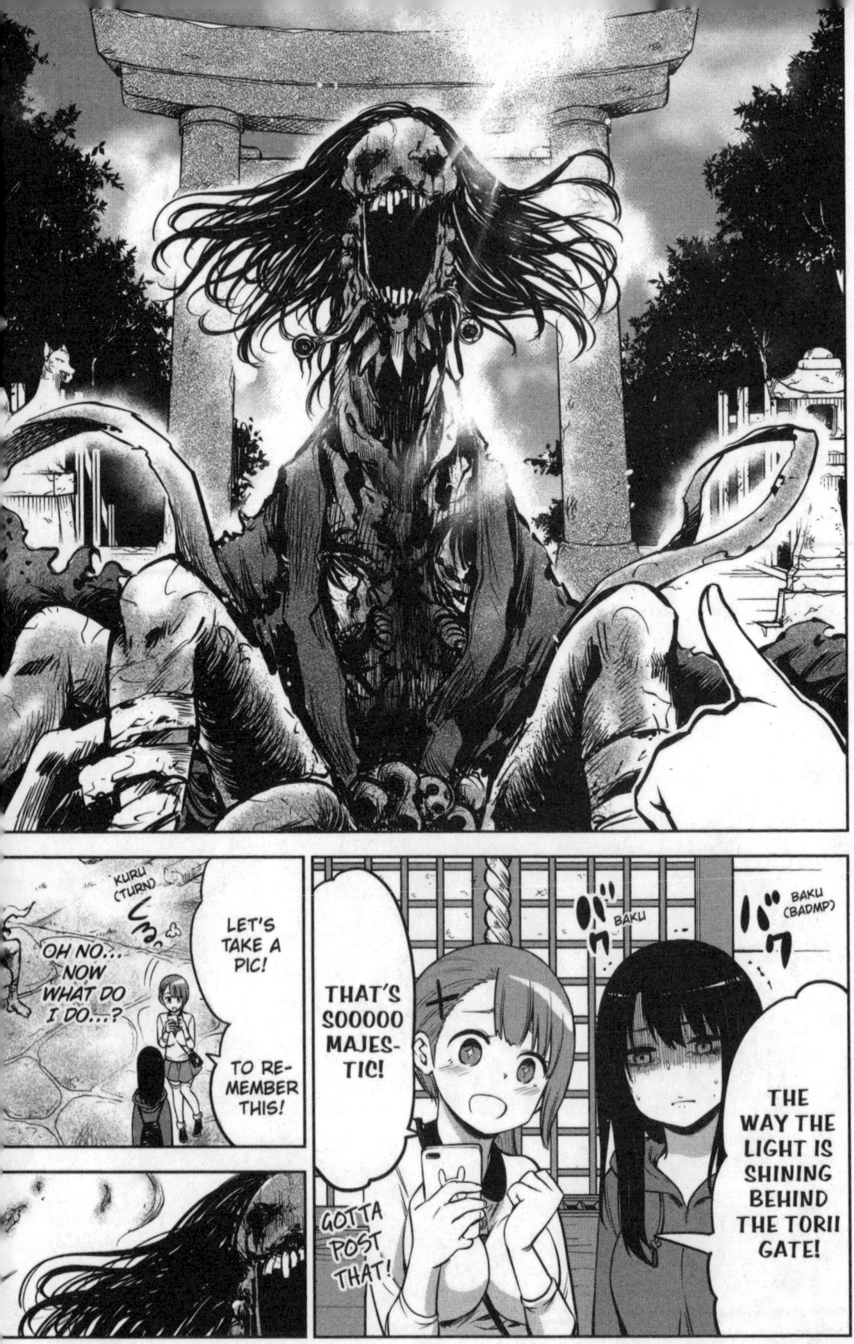
BAKU (BADMP)
BAKU
THAT'S SOOOOO MAJESTIC!
THE WAY THE LIGHT IS SHINING BEHIND THE TORII GATE!
GOTTA POST THAT!
LET'S TAKE A PIC!
TO REMEMBER THIS!
KURU (TURN)
OH NO... NOW WHAT DO I DO...?

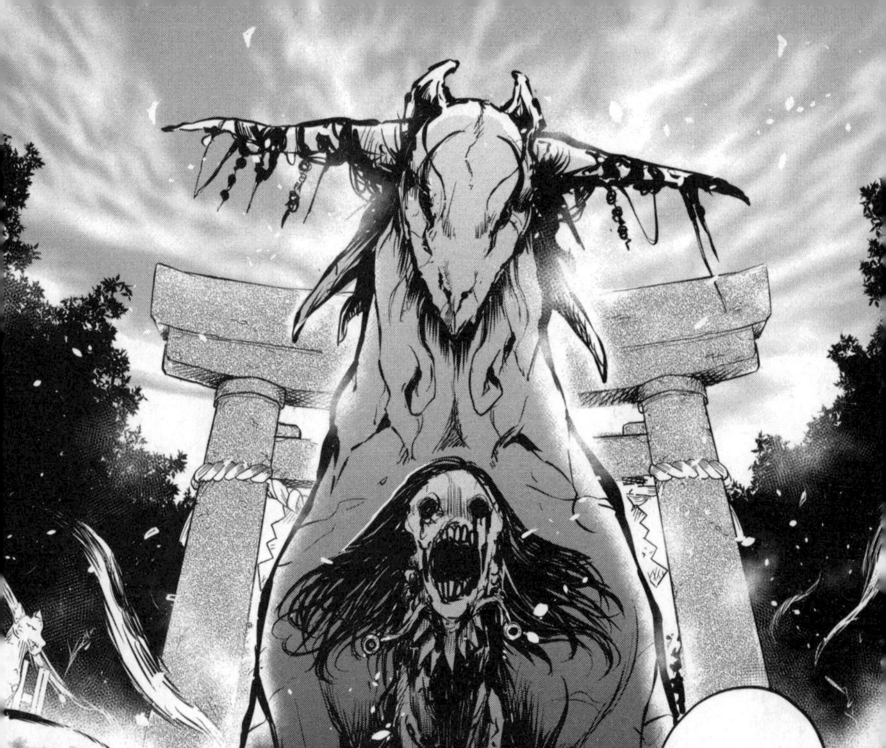
OH, THE LIGHT COULD ACTUALLY BE A PROBLEM, I THINK...

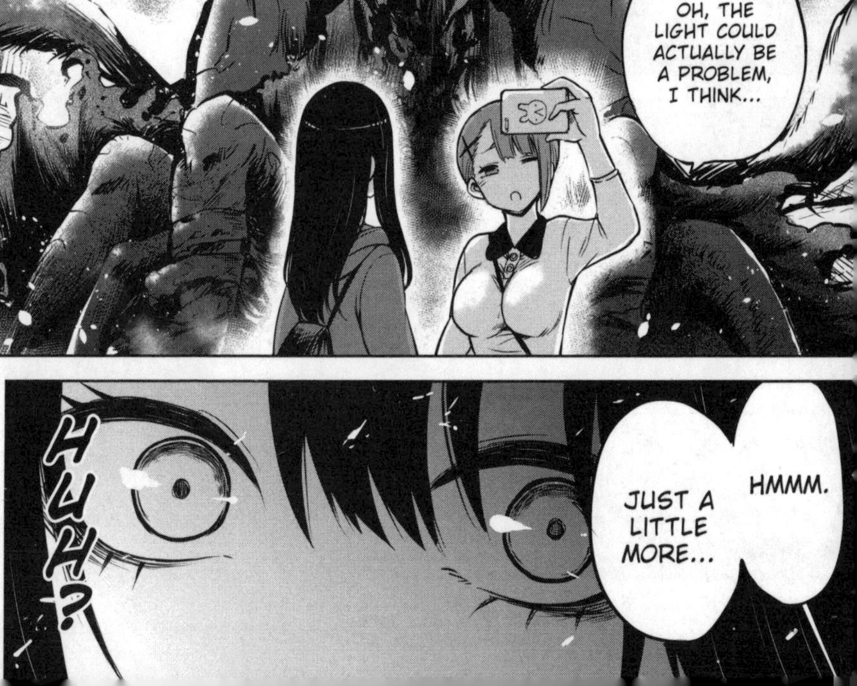
HMMM.
JUST A LITTLE MORE...
HUH?

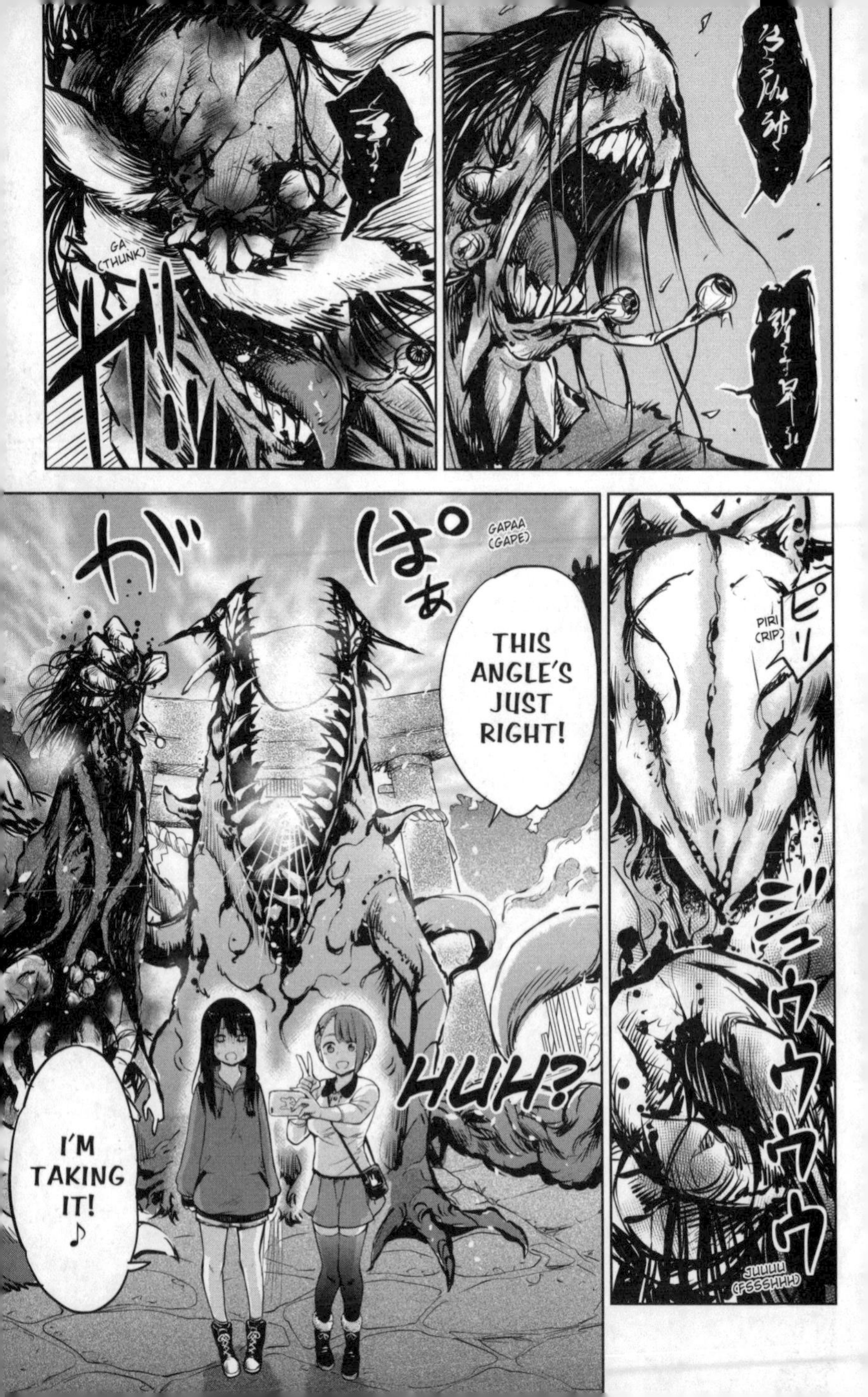
GA (THUNK)
PIRI (RIP)
ピリ
ジュウウウウ
JUUUU (FSSSHHH)
ぱぁ
GAPAA (GAPE)
THIS ANGLE'S JUST RIGHT!
HUH?
I'M TAKING IT! ♪

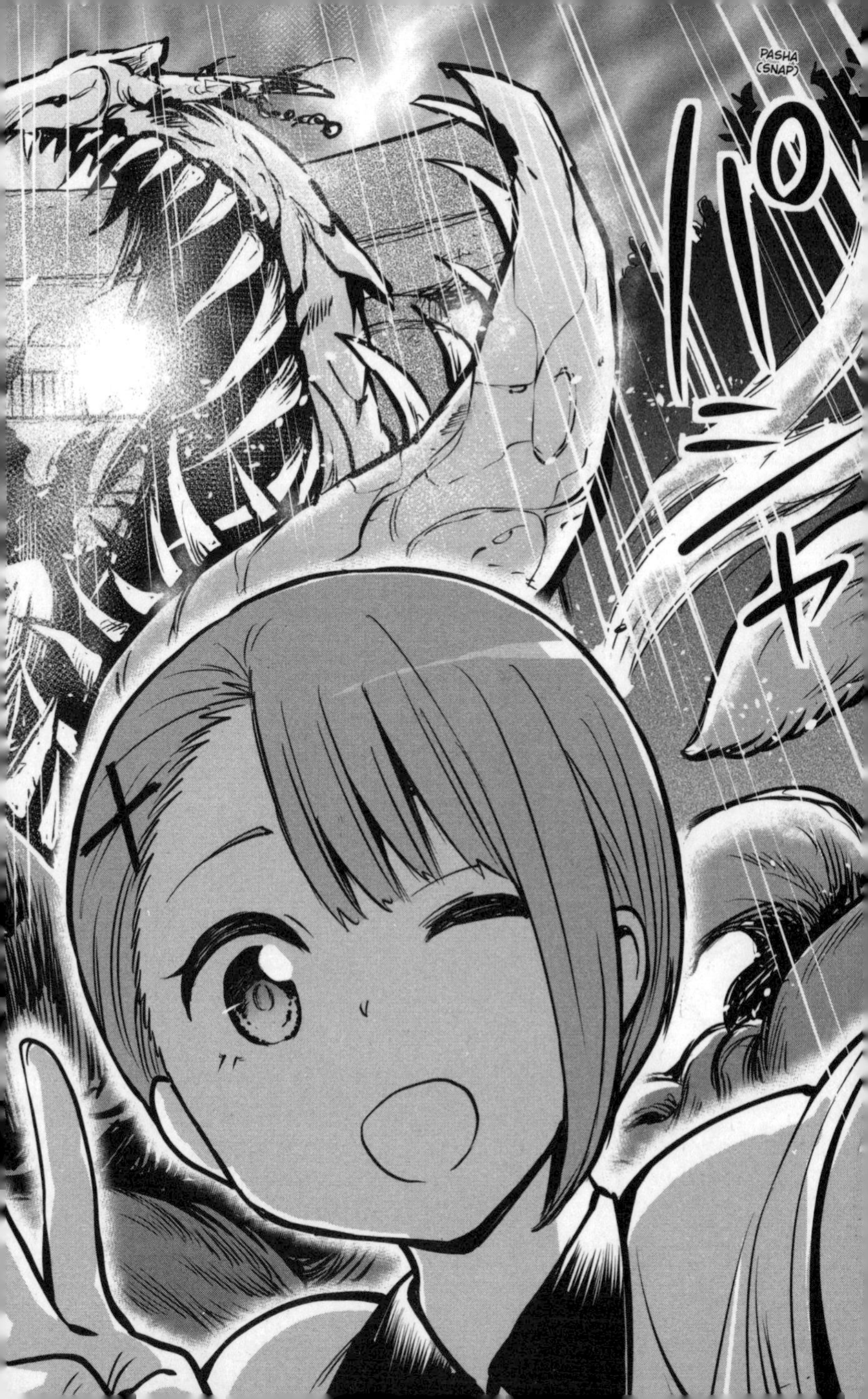
PASHA
(SNAP)

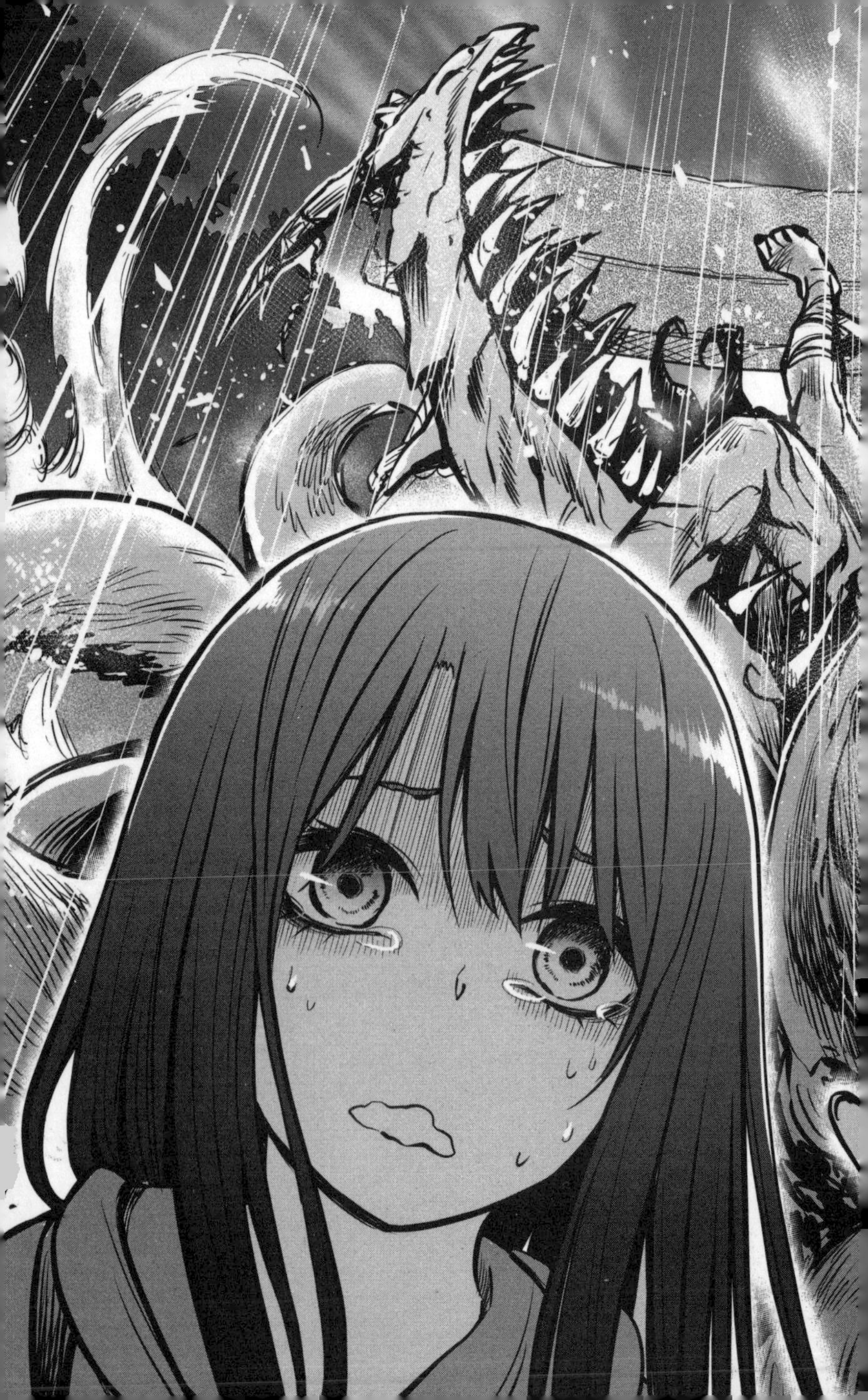

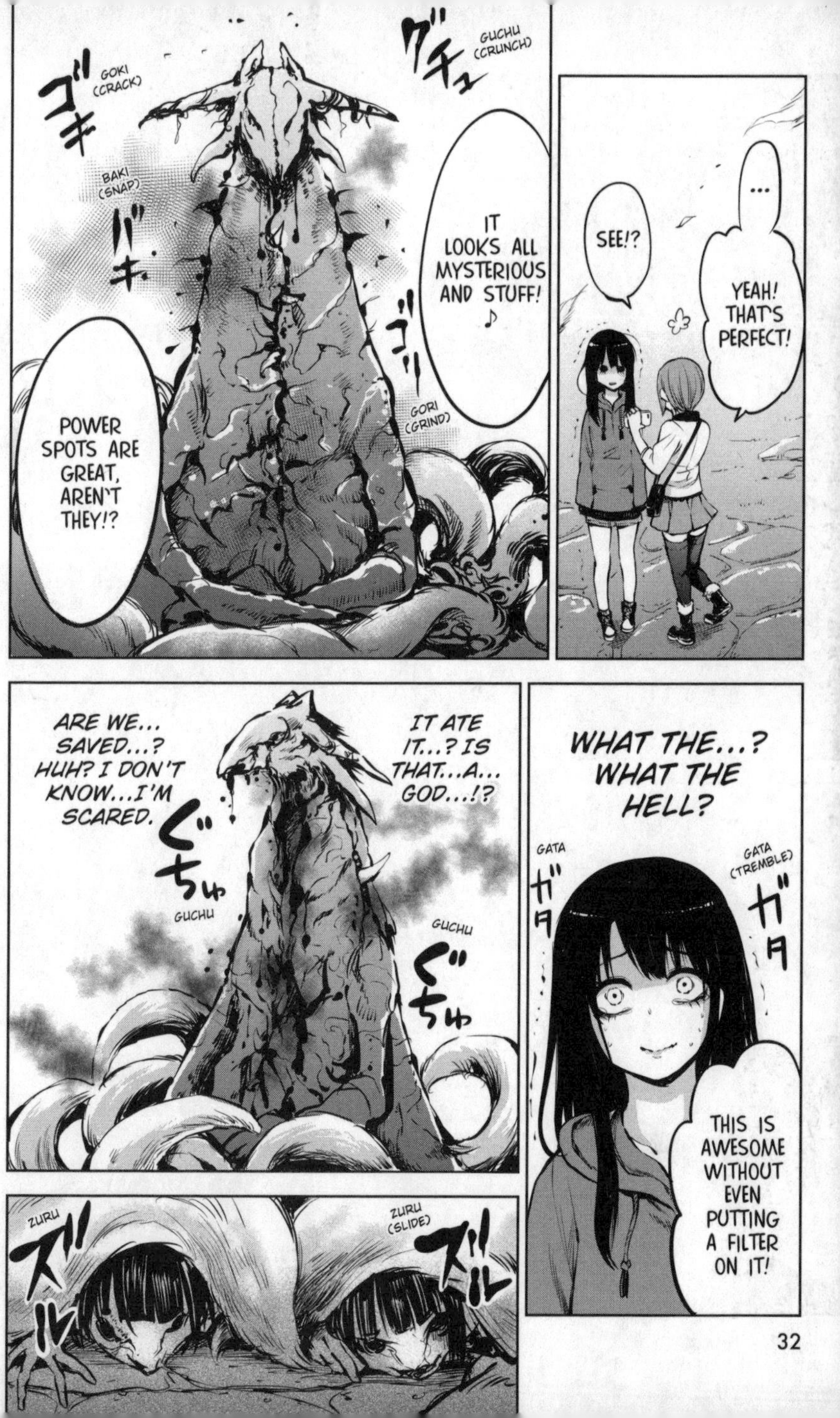
...
YEAH! THAT'S PERFECT!
SEE!?
GUCHU (CRUNCH)
GOKI (CRACK)
IT LOOKS ALL MYSTERIOUS AND STUFF! ♪
BAKI (SNAP)
GORI (GRIND)
POWER SPOTS ARE GREAT, AREN'T THEY!?
WHAT THE...? WHAT THE HELL?
GATA (TREMBLE)
GATA
THIS IS AWESOME WITHOUT EVEN PUTTING A FILTER ON IT!
IT ATE IT...? IS THAT...A... GOD...!?
ARE WE... SAVED...? HUH? I DON'T KNOW...I'M SCARED.
GUCHU
GUCHU
ZURU (SLIDE)
ZURU

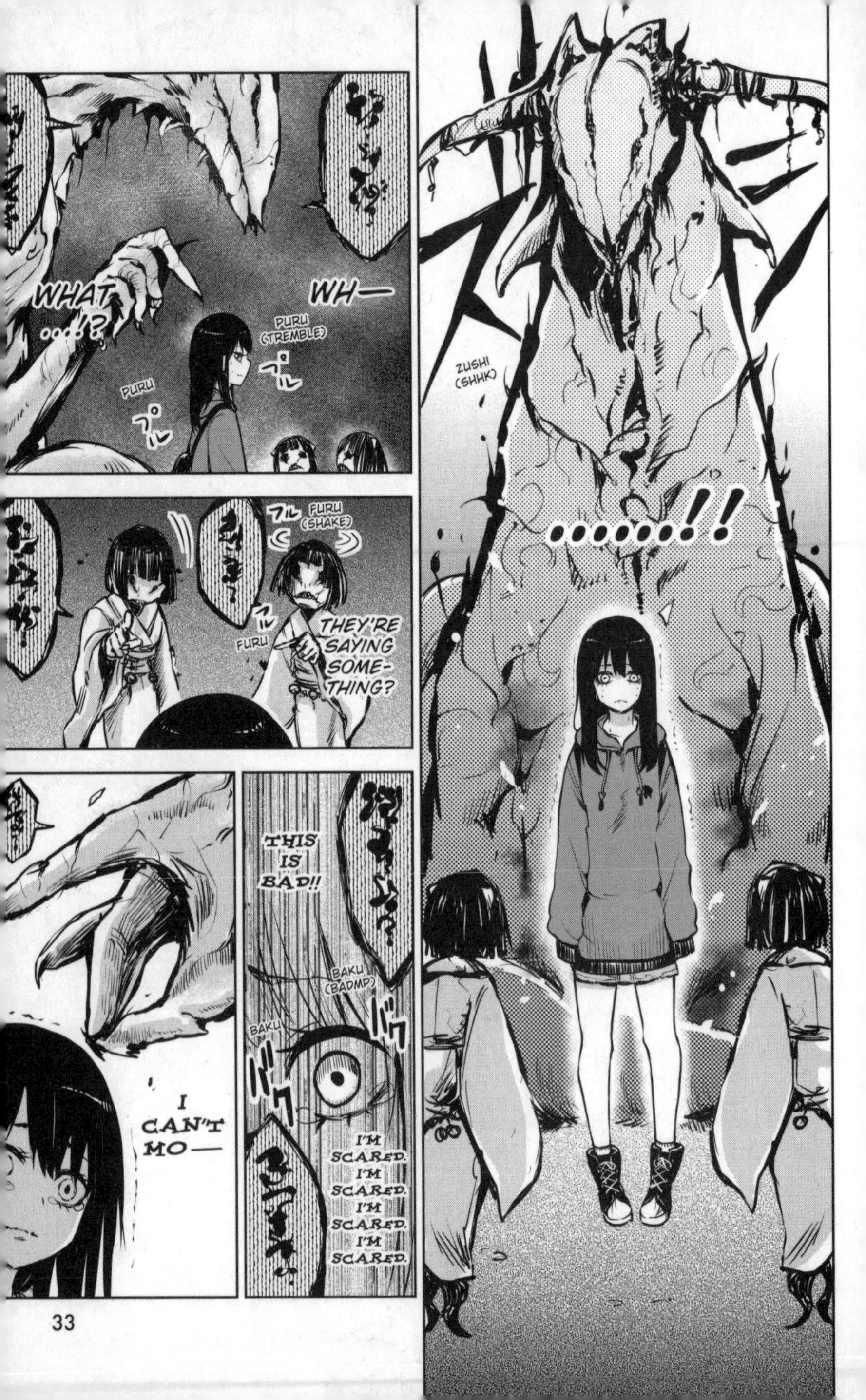
ZUSHI (SHHK)
........!!
WH—
PURU (TREMBLE)
PURU
WHAT ...!?
FURU (SHAKE)
FURU
THEY'RE SAYING SOMETHING?
THIS IS BAD!!
BAKU (BADMP)
BAKU
I'M SCARED. I'M SCARED. I'M SCARED. I'M SCARED.
I CAN'T MO—

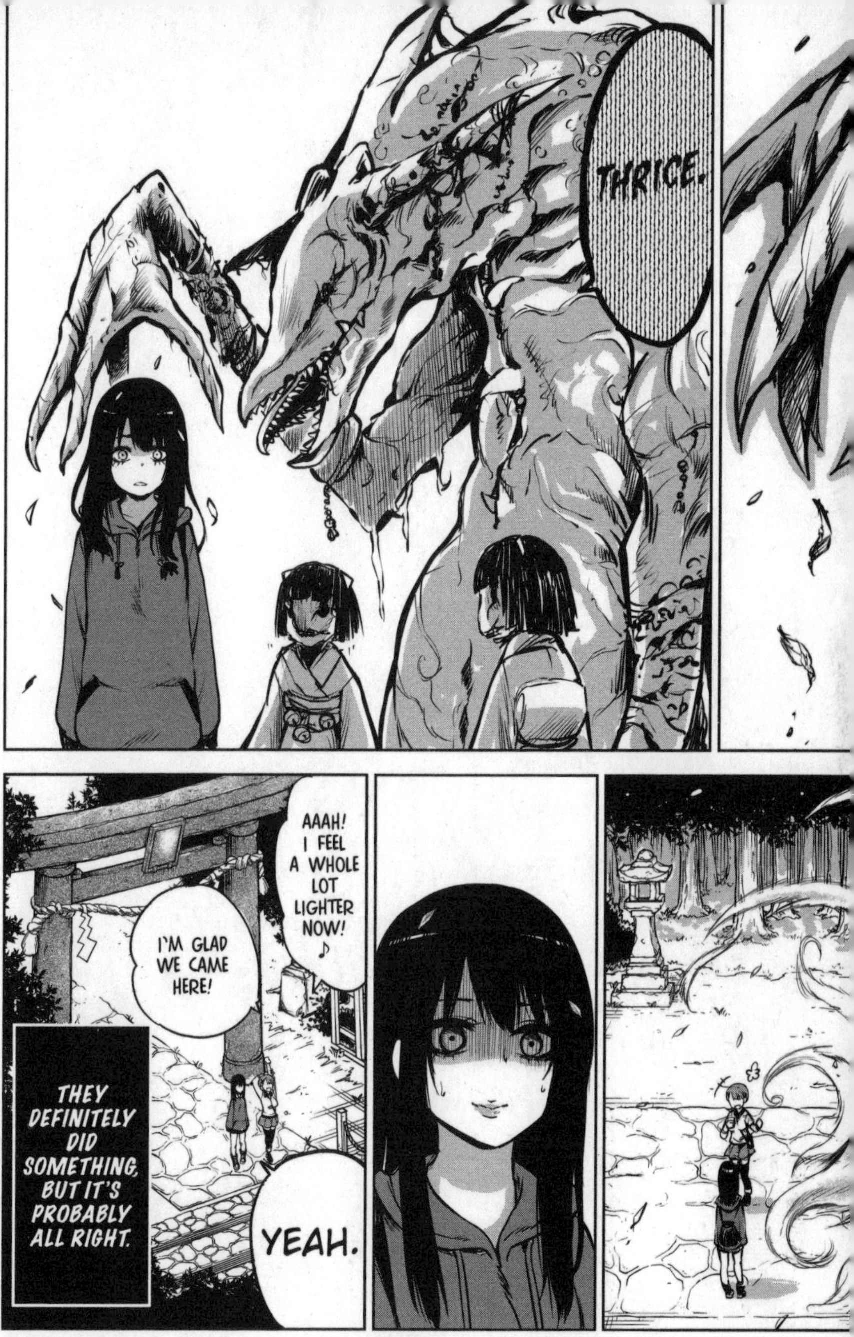
THRICE.
AAAH! I FEEL A WHOLE LOT LIGHTER NOW! ♪
I'M GLAD WE CAME HERE!
YEAH.
THEY DEFINITELY DID SOMETHING, BUT IT'S PROBABLY ALL RIGHT.

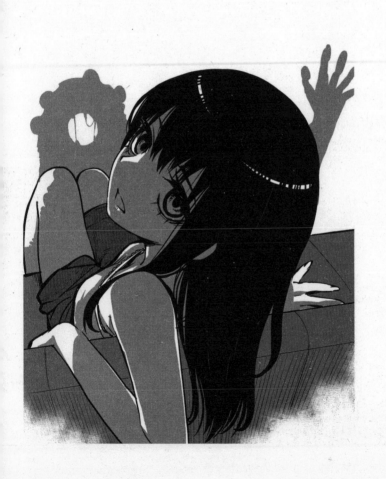

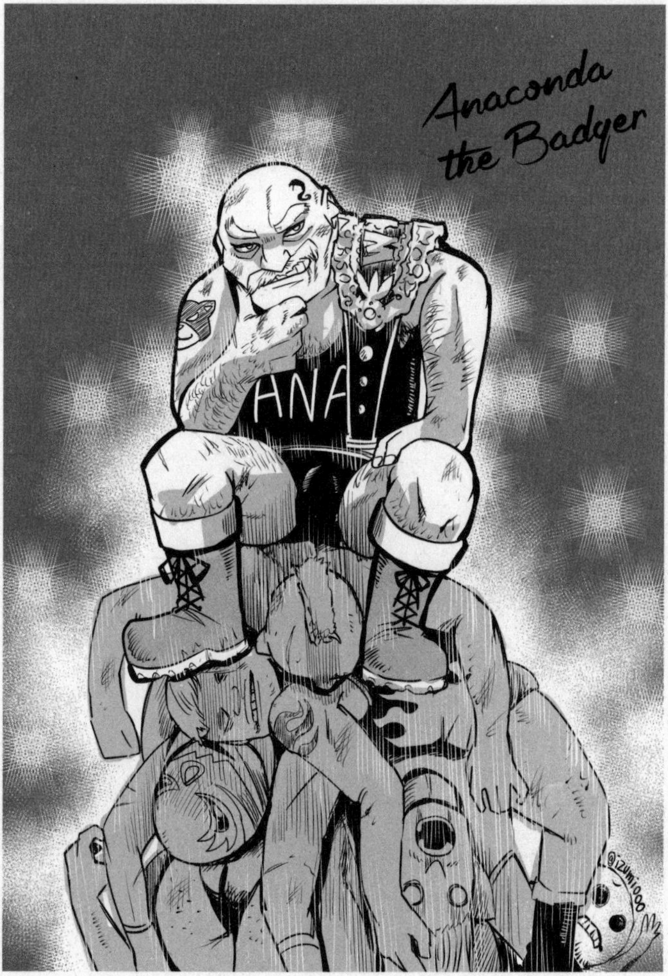
Anaconda the Badger
ANA
@izumi000

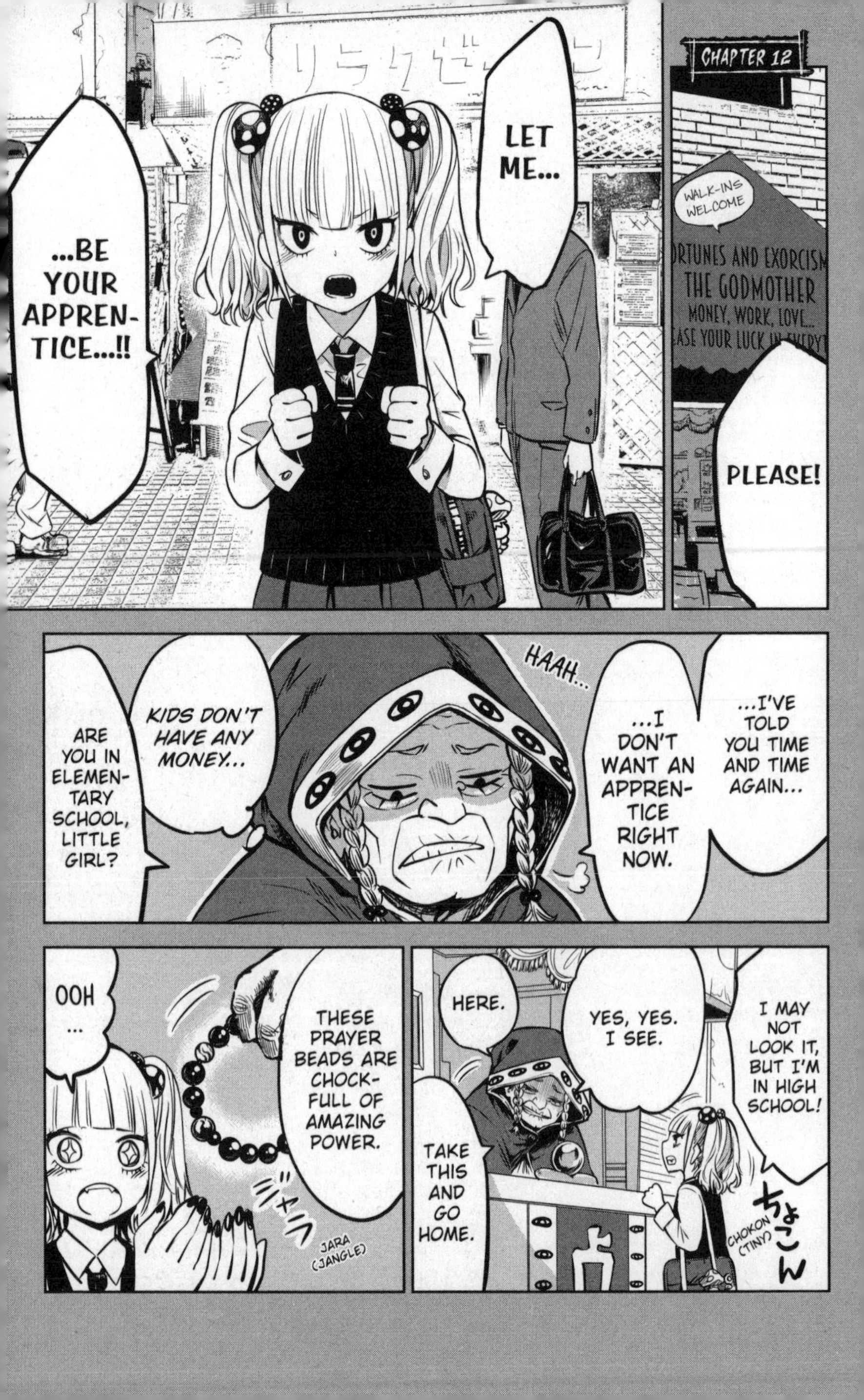
CHAPTER 12
WALK-INS WELCOME
ORTUNES AND EXORCISM
THE GODMOTHER
MONEY, WORK, LOVE...
EASE YOUR LUCK IN EVERY
PLEASE!
LET ME...
...BE YOUR APPRENTICE...!!
...I'VE TOLD YOU TIME AND TIME AGAIN...
HAAH...
...I DON'T WANT AN APPRENTICE RIGHT NOW.
KIDS DON'T HAVE ANY MONEY...
ARE YOU IN ELEMENTARY SCHOOL, LITTLE GIRL?
I MAY NOT LOOK IT, BUT I'M IN HIGH SCHOOL!
YES, YES. I SEE.
HERE.
ちょこん
CHOKON (TINY)
TAKE THIS AND GO HOME.
THESE PRAYER BEADS ARE CHOCK-FULL OF AMAZING POWER.
OOH...
ジャラ
JARA (JANGLE)

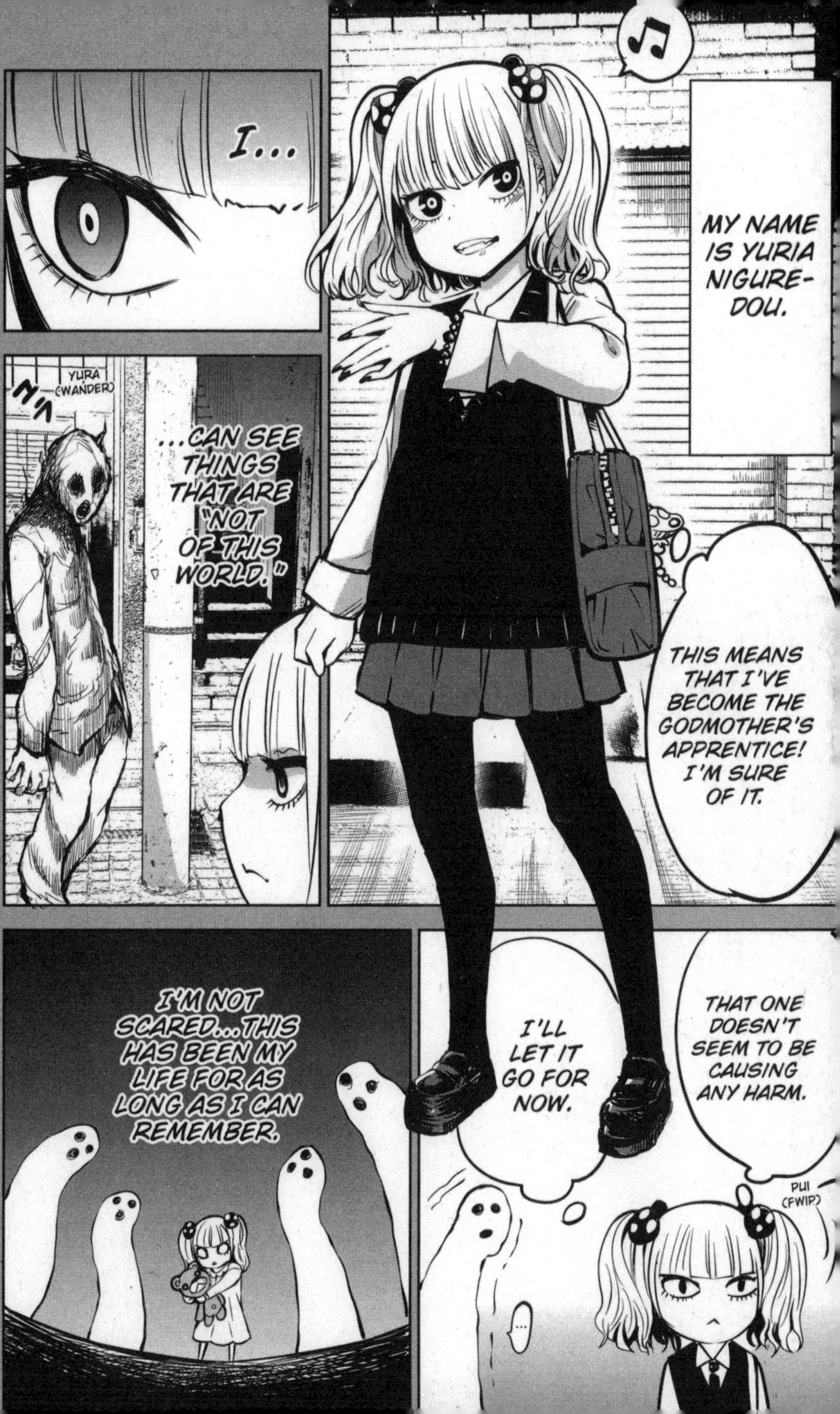
♪
MY NAME IS YURIA NIGURE-DOU.
THIS MEANS THAT I'VE BECOME THE GODMOTHER'S APPRENTICE! I'M SURE OF IT.
I...
YURA (WANDER)
...CAN SEE THINGS THAT ARE "NOT OF THIS WORLD."
THAT ONE DOESN'T SEEM TO BE CAUSING ANY HARM.
I'LL LET IT GO FOR NOW.
PUI (FWIP)
...
I'M NOT SCARED... THIS HAS BEEN MY LIFE FOR AS LONG AS I CAN REMEMBER.

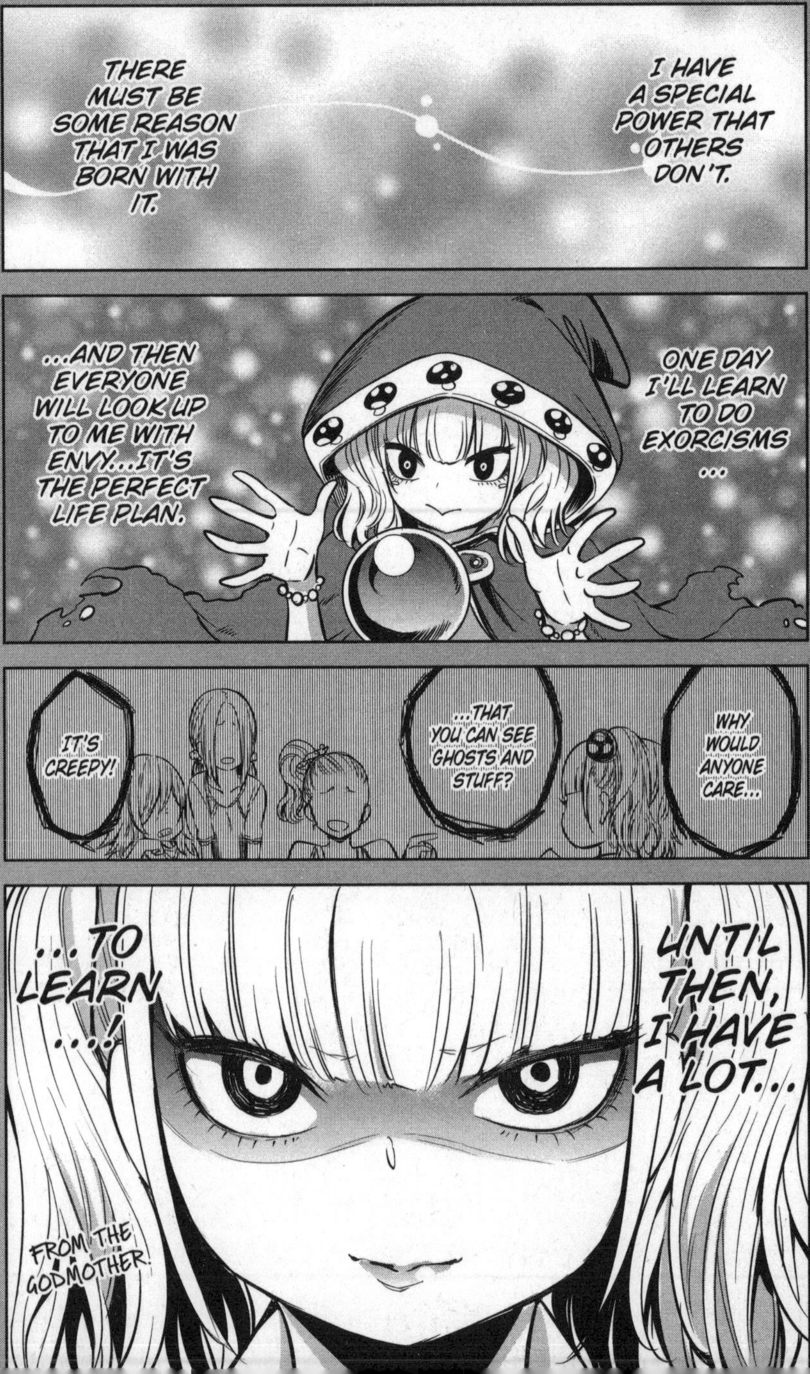
I HAVE A SPECIAL POWER THAT OTHERS DON'T.
THERE MUST BE SOME REASON THAT I WAS BORN WITH IT.
ONE DAY I'LL LEARN TO DO EXORCISMS...
...AND THEN EVERYONE WILL LOOK UP TO ME WITH ENVY...IT'S THE PERFECT LIFE PLAN.
WHY WOULD ANYONE CARE...
...THAT YOU CAN SEE GHOSTS AND STUFF?
IT'S CREEPY!
UNTIL THEN, I HAVE A LOT...
...TO LEARN...!
FROM THE GODMOTHER.

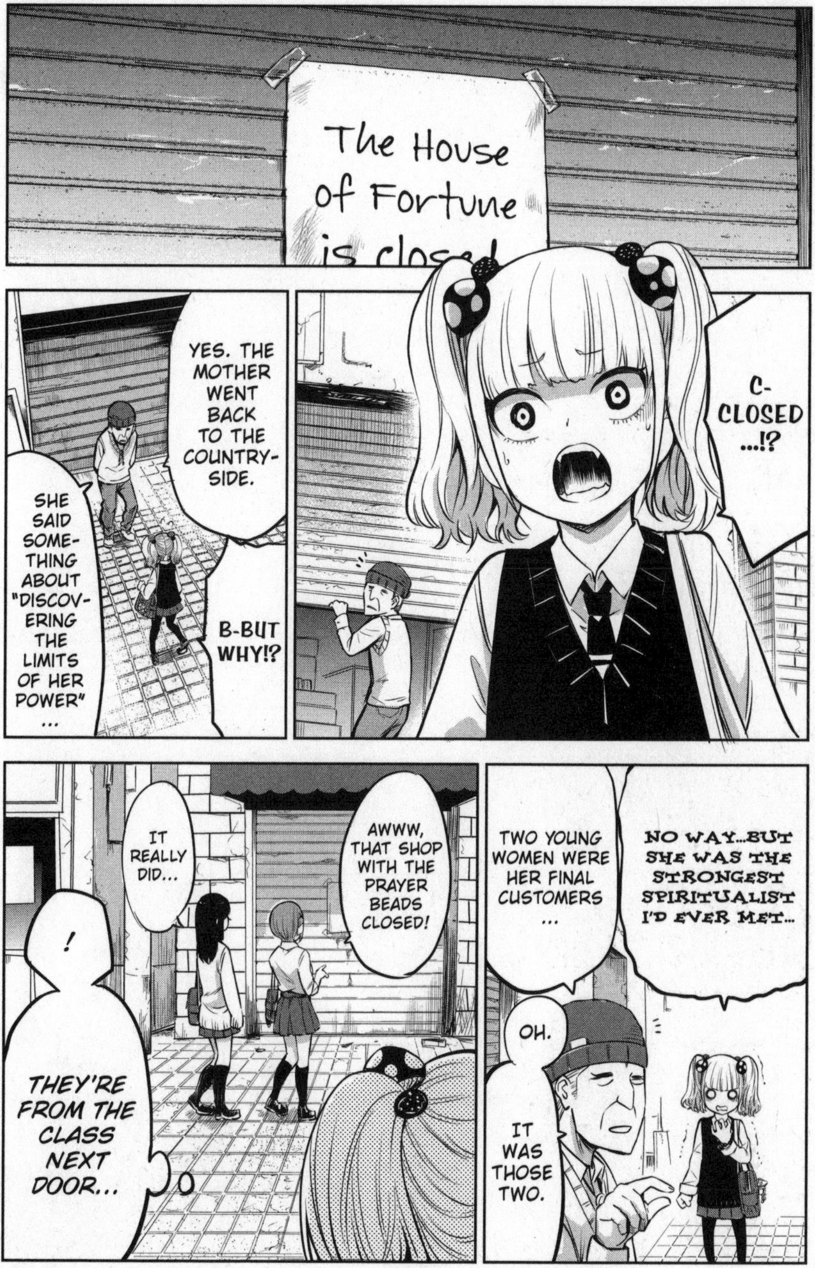
The House of Fortune is closed
C-CLOSED ...!?
B-BUT WHY!?
YES. THE MOTHER WENT BACK TO THE COUNTRYSIDE.
SHE SAID SOMETHING ABOUT "DISCOVERING THE LIMITS OF HER POWER" ...
NO WAY...BUT SHE WAS THE STRONGEST SPIRITUALIST I'D EVER MET...
TWO YOUNG WOMEN WERE HER FINAL CUSTOMERS ...
OH.
IT WAS THOSE TWO.
AWWW, THAT SHOP WITH THE PRAYER BEADS CLOSED!
IT REALLY DID...
!
THEY'RE FROM THE CLASS NEXT DOOR...

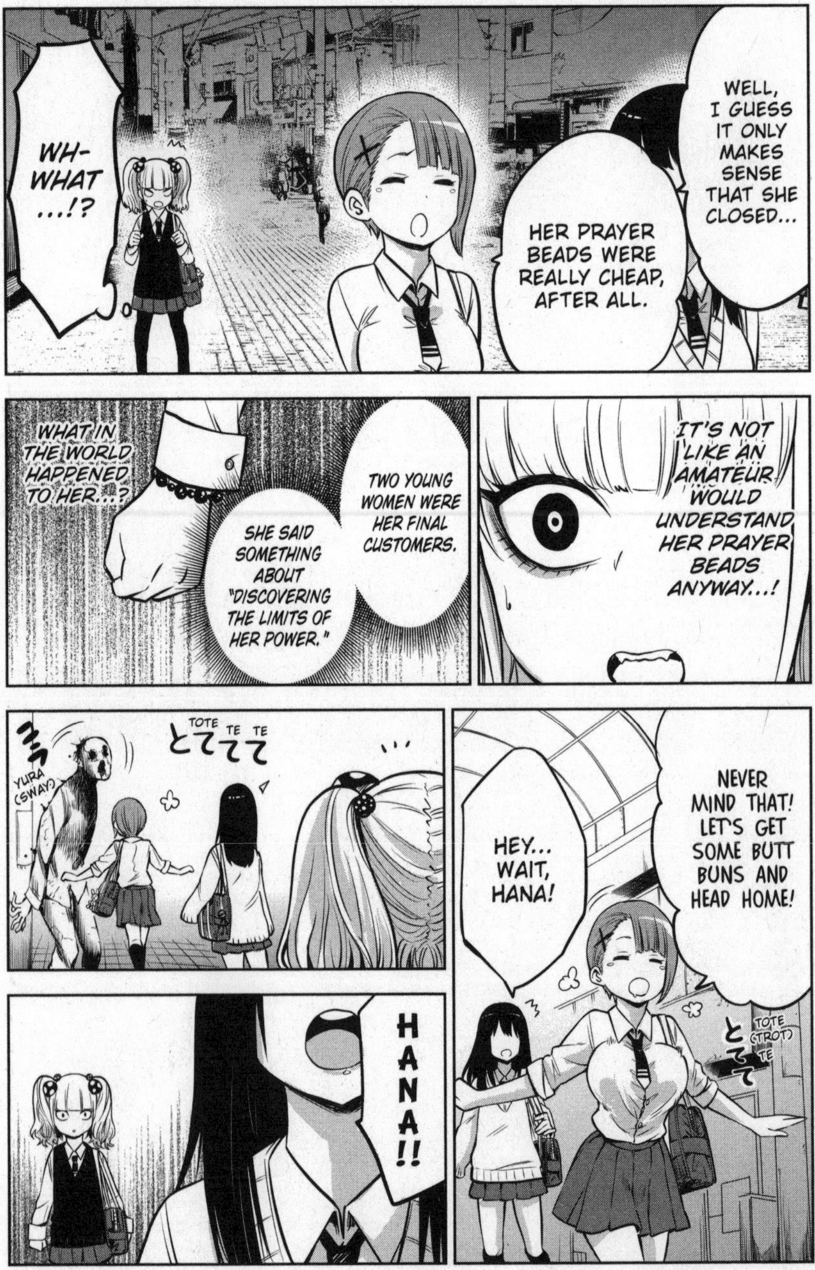
WELL, I GUESS IT ONLY MAKES SENSE THAT SHE CLOSED...
HER PRAYER BEADS WERE REALLY CHEAP, AFTER ALL.
WH-WHAT ...!?
IT'S NOT LIKE AN AMATEUR WOULD UNDERSTAND HER PRAYER BEADS ANYWAY...!
TWO YOUNG WOMEN WERE HER FINAL CUSTOMERS.
SHE SAID SOMETHING ABOUT "DISCOVERING THE LIMITS OF HER POWER."
WHAT IN THE WORLD HAPPENED TO HER...?
NEVER MIND THAT! LET'S GET SOME BUTT BUNS AND HEAD HOME!
HEY... WAIT, HANA!
とてて TOTE (TROT) TE
とててて TOTE TE TE
YURA (SWAY)
HANA!!

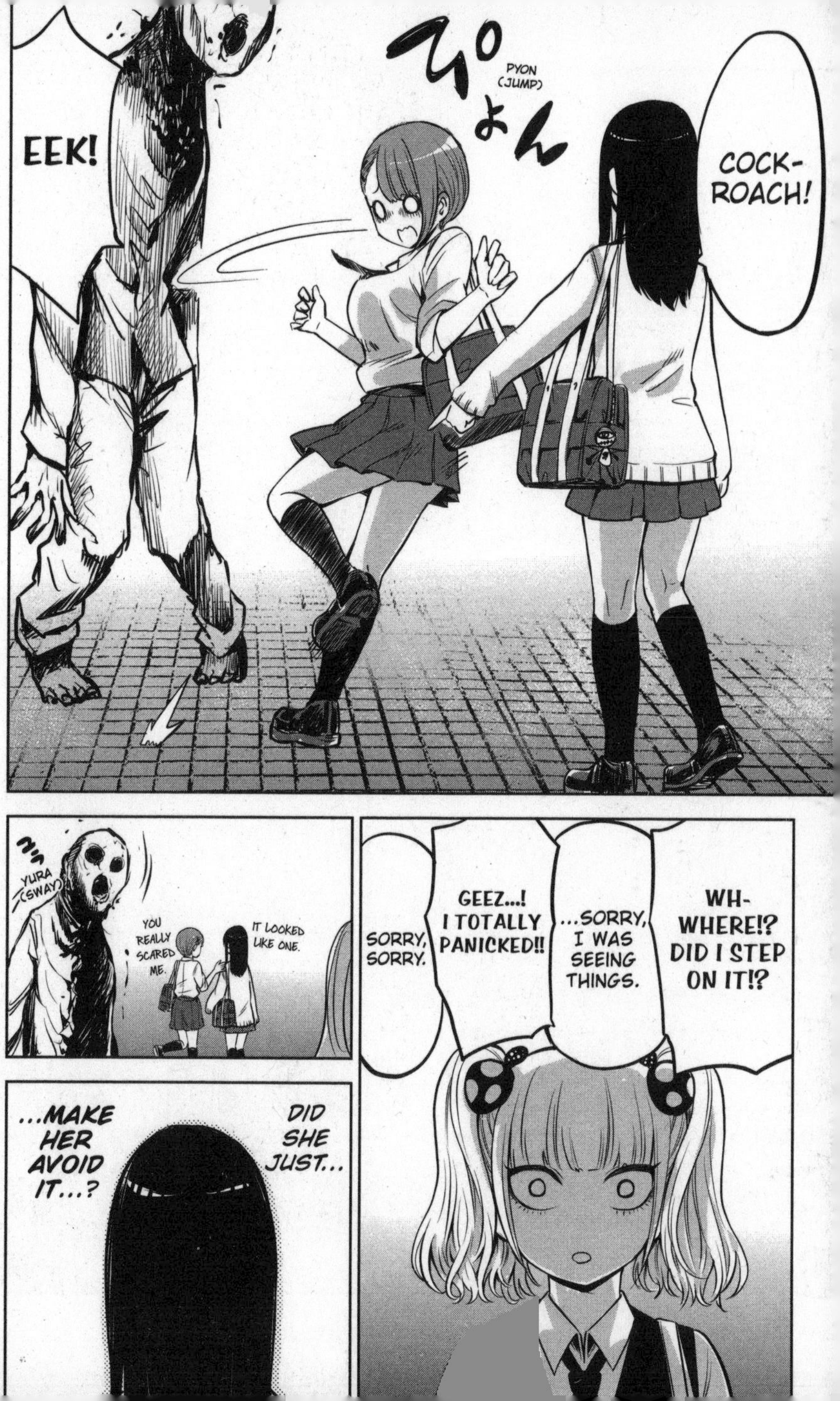
COCK-ROACH!
ぴょん
PYON (JUMP)
EEK!
WH- WHERE!? DID I STEP ON IT!?
...SORRY, I WAS SEEING THINGS.
GEEZ...! I TOTALLY PANICKED!!
SORRY, SORRY.
IT LOOKED LIKE ONE.
YOU REALLY SCARED ME.
YURA (SWAY)
DID SHE JUST...
...MAKE HER AVOID IT...?

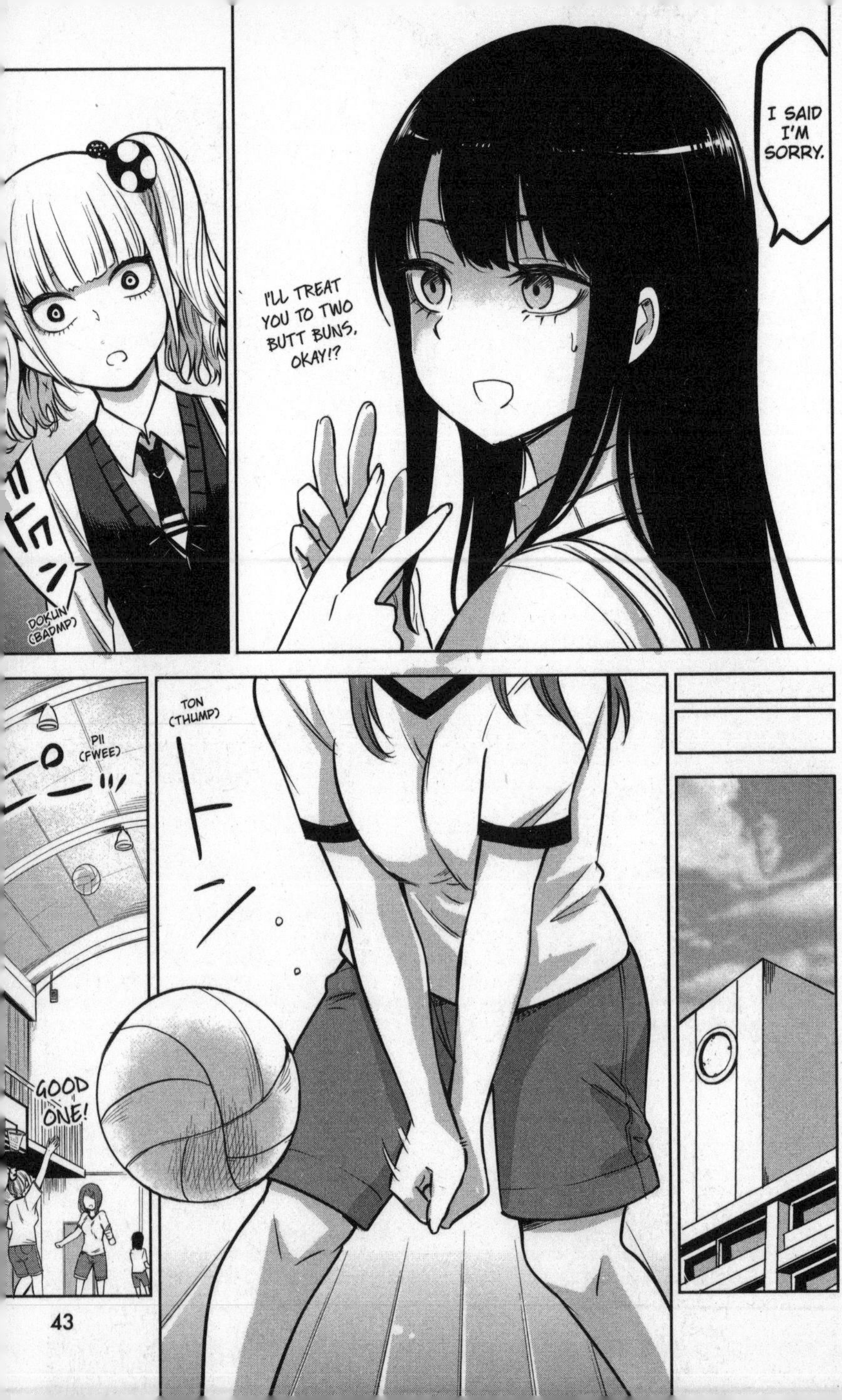
I SAID I'M SORRY.
I'LL TREAT YOU TO TWO BUTT BUNS, OKAY!?
DOKUN (BADMP)
TON (THUMP)
PII (FWEE)
GOOD ONE!

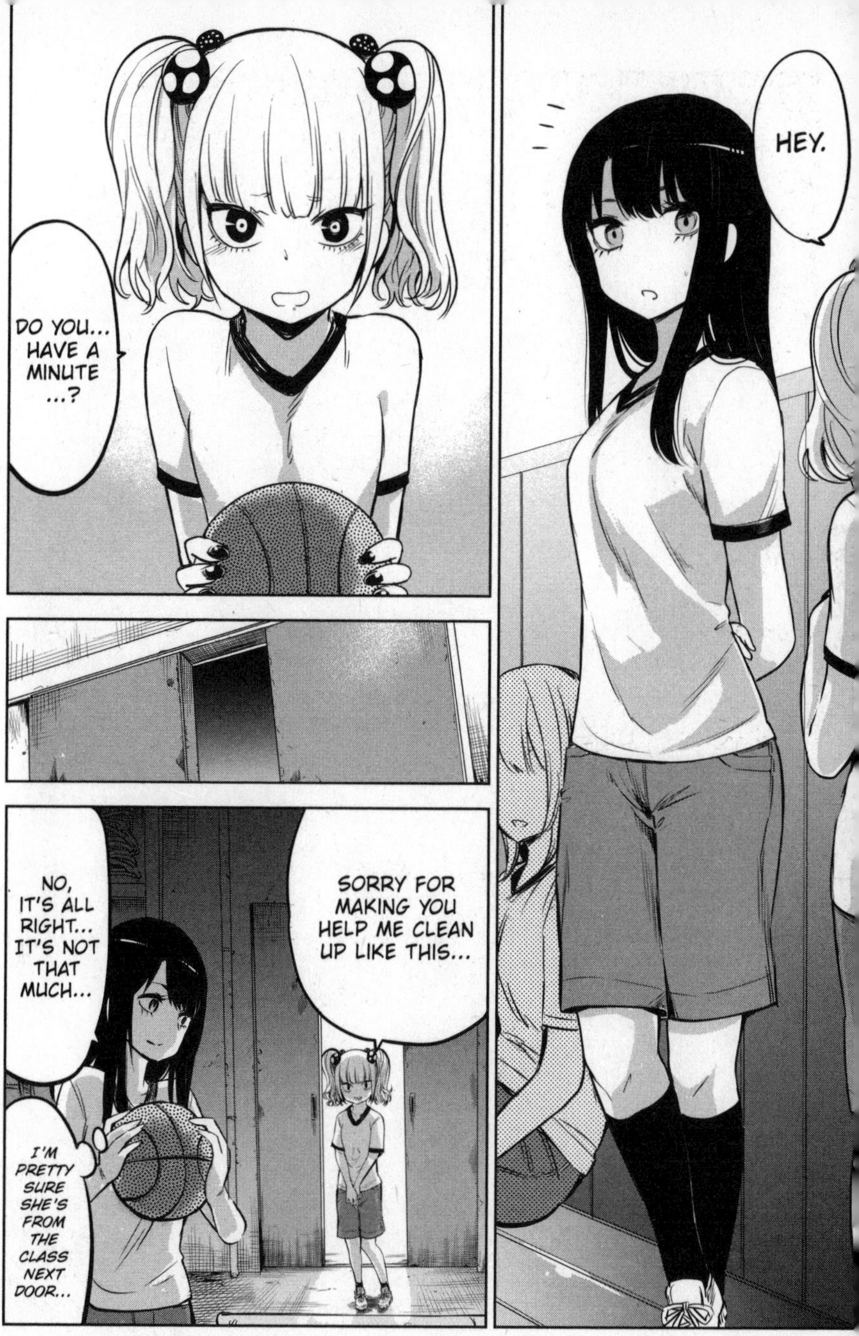
HEY.
DO YOU... HAVE A MINUTE ...?
SORRY FOR MAKING YOU HELP ME CLEAN UP LIKE THIS...
NO, IT'S ALL RIGHT... IT'S NOT THAT MUCH...
I'M PRETTY SURE SHE'S FROM THE CLASS NEXT DOOR...

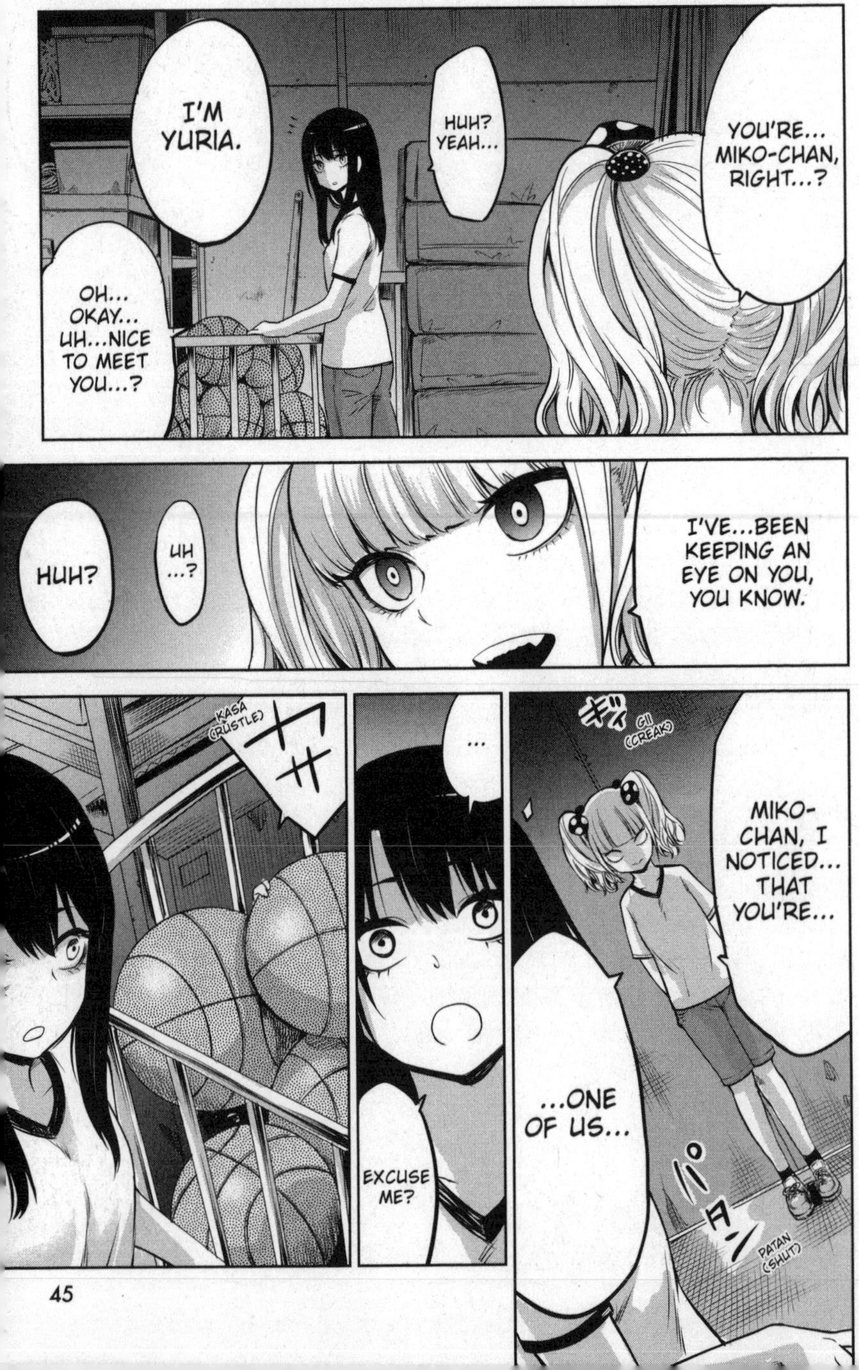
YOU'RE... MIKO-CHAN, RIGHT...?
HUH? YEAH...
I'M YURIA.
OH... OKAY... UH...NICE TO MEET YOU...?
I'VE...BEEN KEEPING AN EYE ON YOU, YOU KNOW.
UH ...?
HUH?
GII (CREAK)
MIKO-CHAN, I NOTICED... THAT YOU'RE...
...ONE OF US...
PATAN (SHUT)
...
EXCUSE ME?
KASA (RUSTLE)

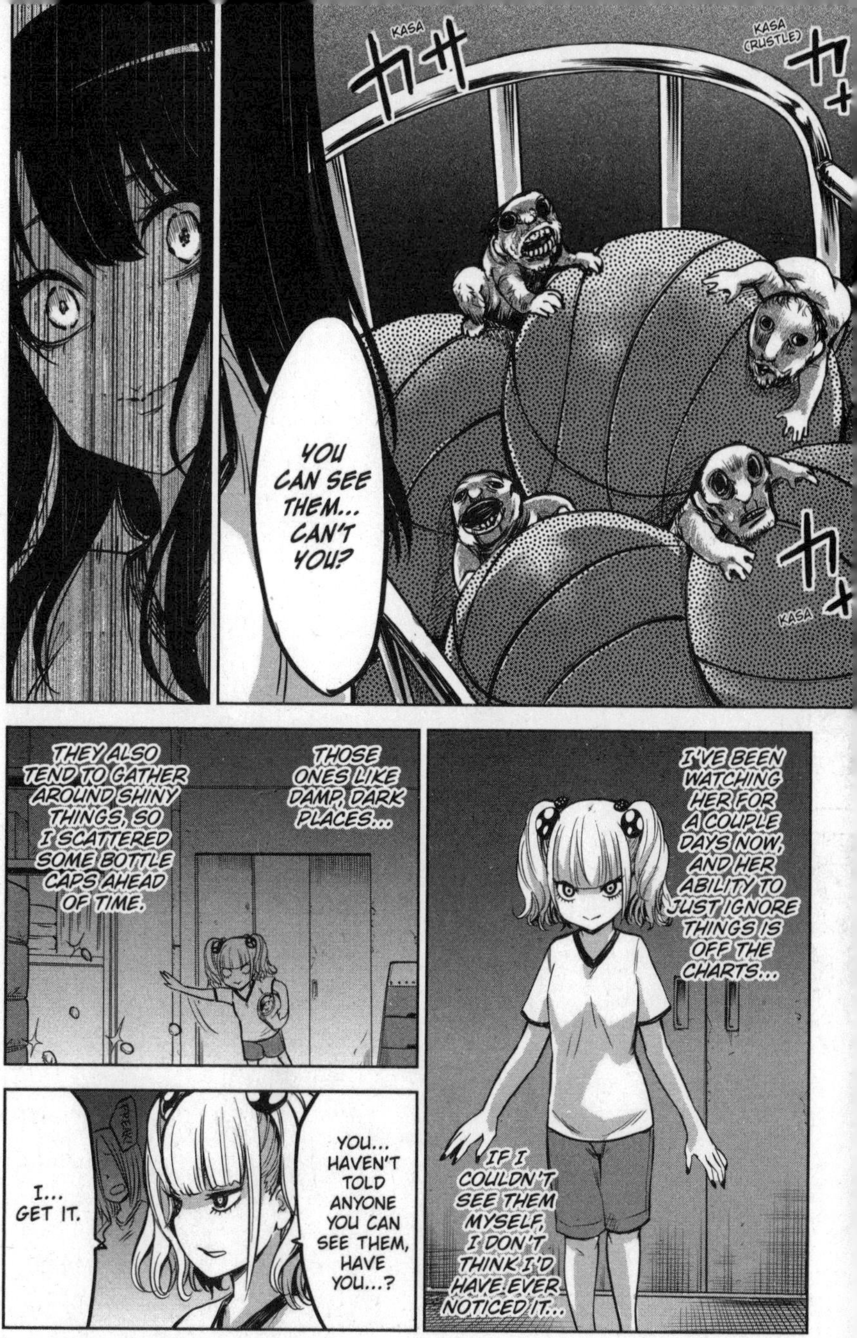
KASA (RUSTLE)
KASA
KASA
YOU CAN SEE THEM... CAN'T YOU?
I'VE BEEN WATCHING HER FOR A COUPLE DAYS NOW, AND HER ABILITY TO JUST IGNORE THINGS IS OFF THE CHARTS...
IF I COULDN'T SEE THEM MYSELF, I DON'T THINK I'D HAVE EVER NOTICED IT...
THOSE ONES LIKE DAMP, DARK PLACES...
THEY ALSO TEND TO GATHER AROUND SHINY THINGS, SO I SCATTERED SOME BOTTLE CAPS AHEAD OF TIME.
YOU... HAVEN'T TOLD ANYONE YOU CAN SEE THEM, HAVE YOU...?
I... GET IT.

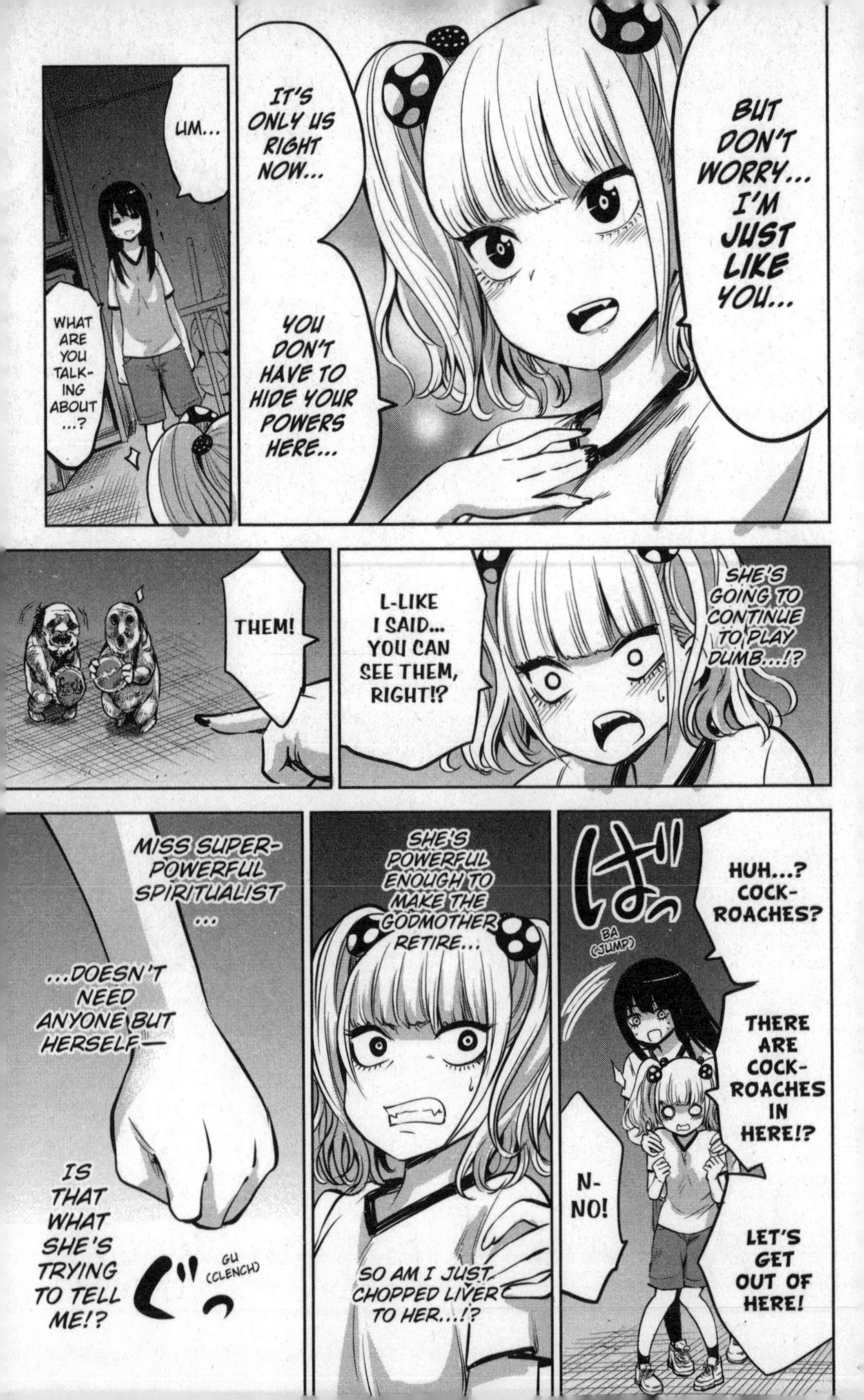
BUT DON'T WORRY... I'M JUST LIKE YOU...
IT'S ONLY US RIGHT NOW...
YOU DON'T HAVE TO HIDE YOUR POWERS HERE...
UM...
WHAT ARE YOU TALKING ABOUT...?
SHE'S GOING TO CONTINUE TO PLAY DUMB...!?
L-LIKE I SAID... YOU CAN SEE THEM, RIGHT!?
THEM!
HUH...? COCKROACHES?
ばっ
BA (JUMP)
THERE ARE COCKROACHES IN HERE!?
LET'S GET OUT OF HERE!
N-NO!
SHE'S POWERFUL ENOUGH TO MAKE THE GODMOTHER RETIRE...
SO AM I JUST CHOPPED LIVER TO HER...!?
MISS SUPER-POWERFUL SPIRITUALIST...
...DOESN'T NEED ANYONE BUT HERSELF—
IS THAT WHAT SHE'S TRYING TO TELL ME!?
ぐっ
GU (CLENCH)

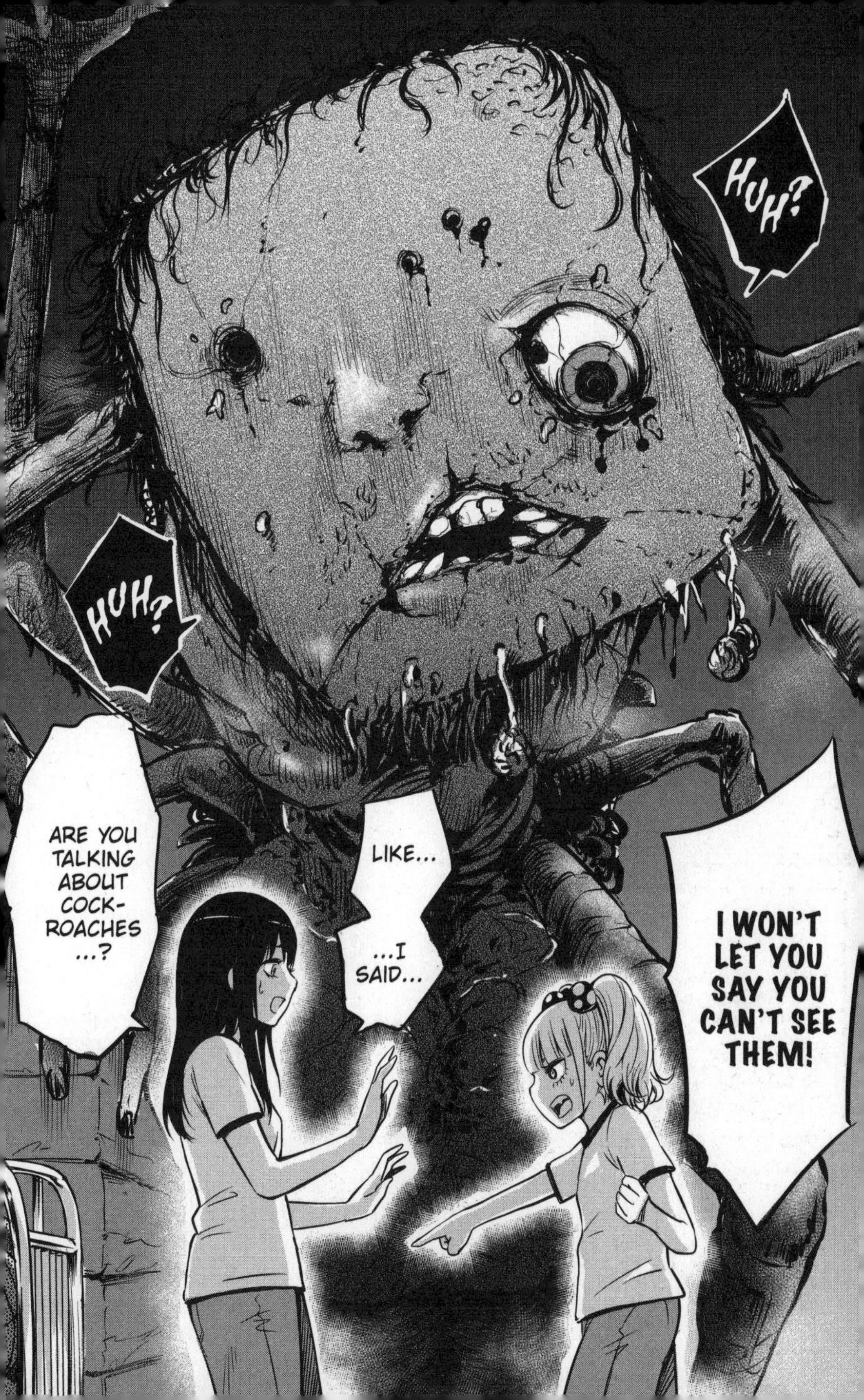
HUH?
HUH?
I WON'T LET YOU SAY YOU CAN'T SEE THEM!
LIKE...
...I SAID...
ARE YOU TALKING ABOUT COCK-ROACHES ...?

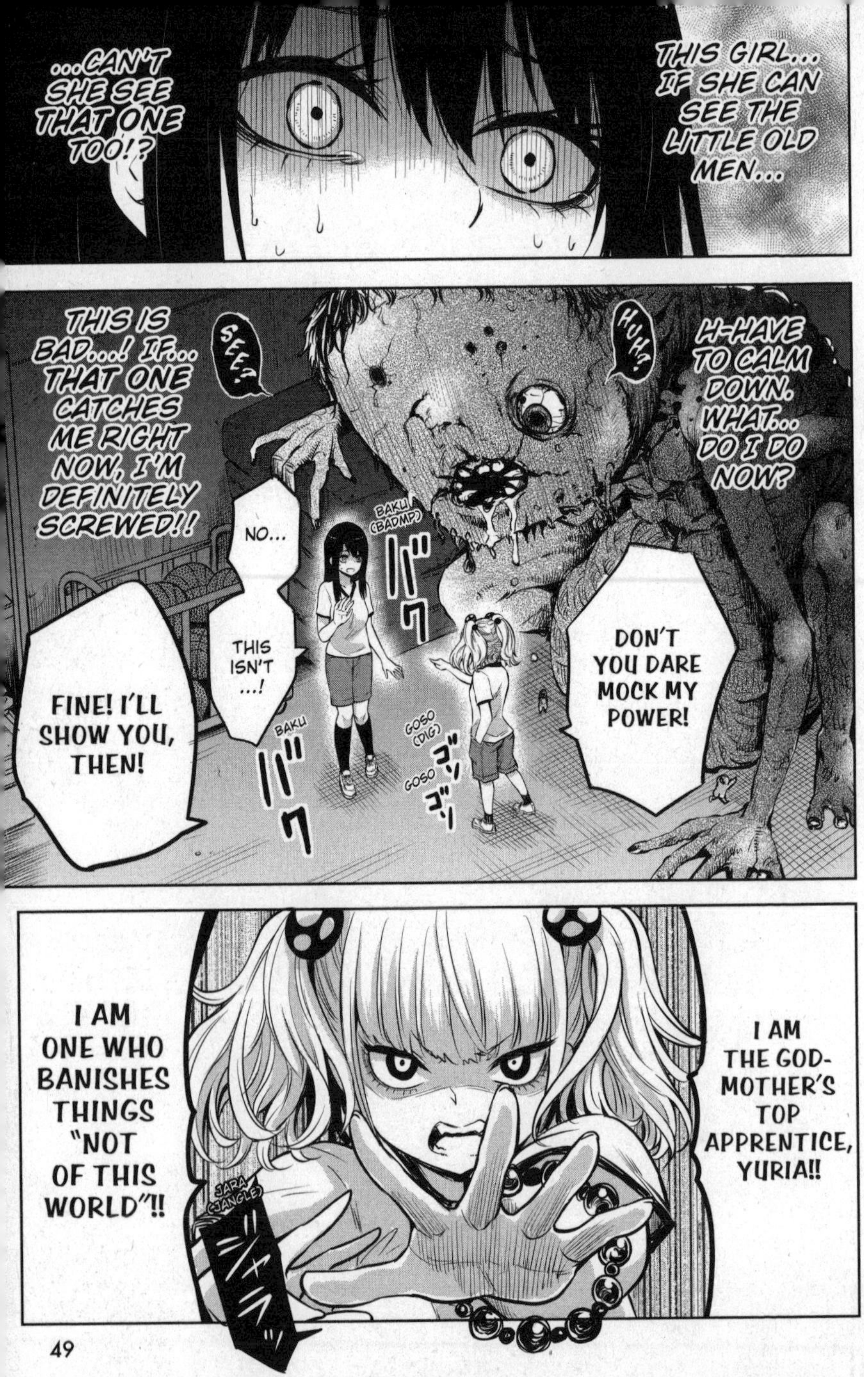

THIS GIRL... IF SHE CAN SEE THE LITTLE OLD MEN...
...CAN'T SHE SEE THAT ONE TOO!?
H-HAVE TO CALM DOWN. WHAT... DO I DO NOW?
HUH?
SEE?
THIS IS BAD...! IF... THAT ONE CATCHES ME RIGHT NOW, I'M DEFINITELY SCREWED!!
DON'T YOU DARE MOCK MY POWER!
BAKU (BADMP)
NO...
THIS ISN'T ...!
GOSO (DIG) GOSO
BAKU
FINE! I'LL SHOW YOU, THEN!
I AM THE GOD-MOTHER'S TOP APPRENTICE, YURIA!!
I AM ONE WHO BANISHES THINGS "NOT OF THIS WORLD"!!
JARA (JANGLE)

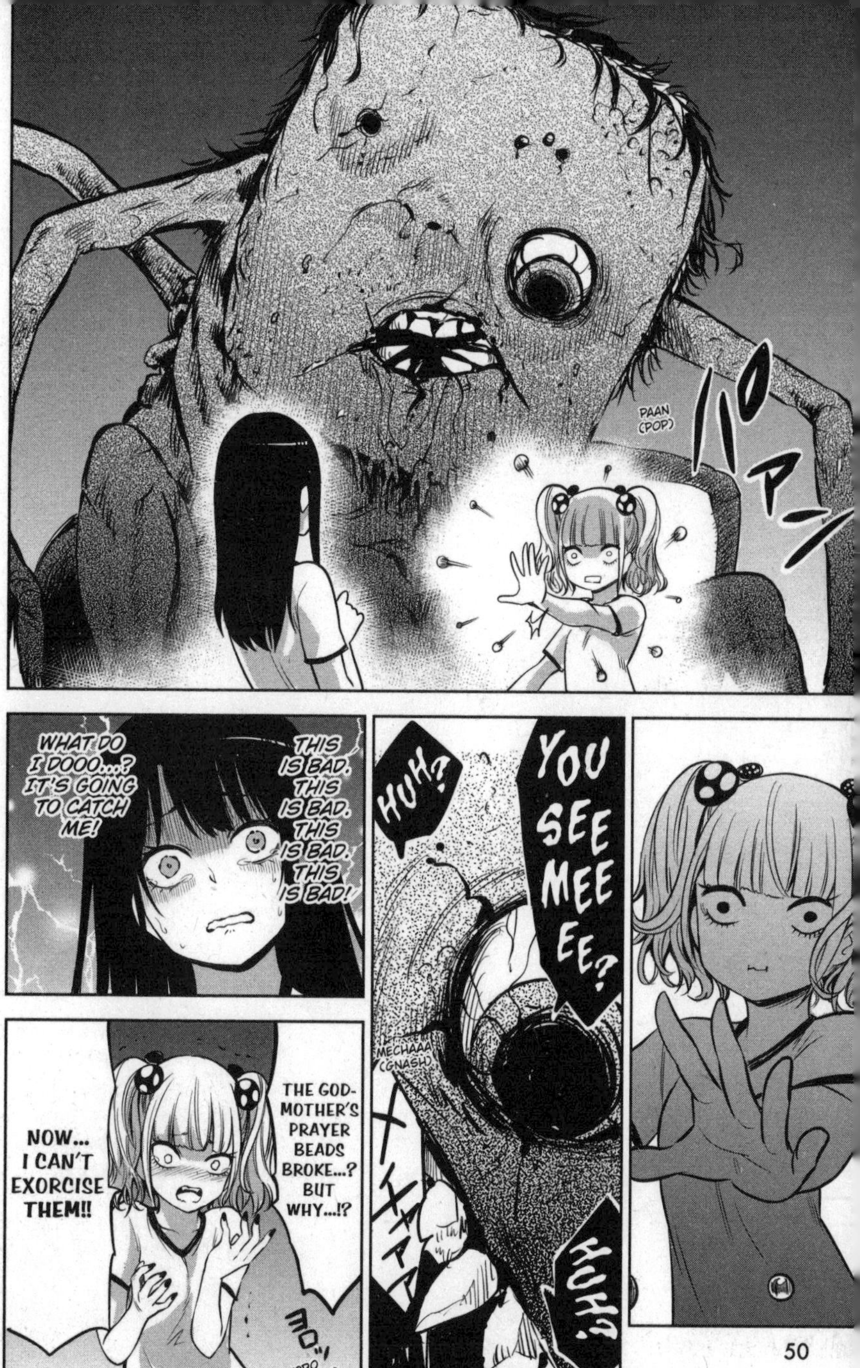
PAAN (POP)
YOU SEE MEEEE?
HUH?
MECHAAA (GNASH)
HUH?
THIS IS BAD. THIS IS BAD. THIS IS BAD. THIS IS BAD!
WHAT DO I DOOO...? IT'S GOING TO CATCH ME!
THE GOD-MOTHER'S PRAYER BEADS BROKE...? BUT WHY...!?
NOW... I CAN'T EXORCISE THEM!!
YORO (STAGGER)

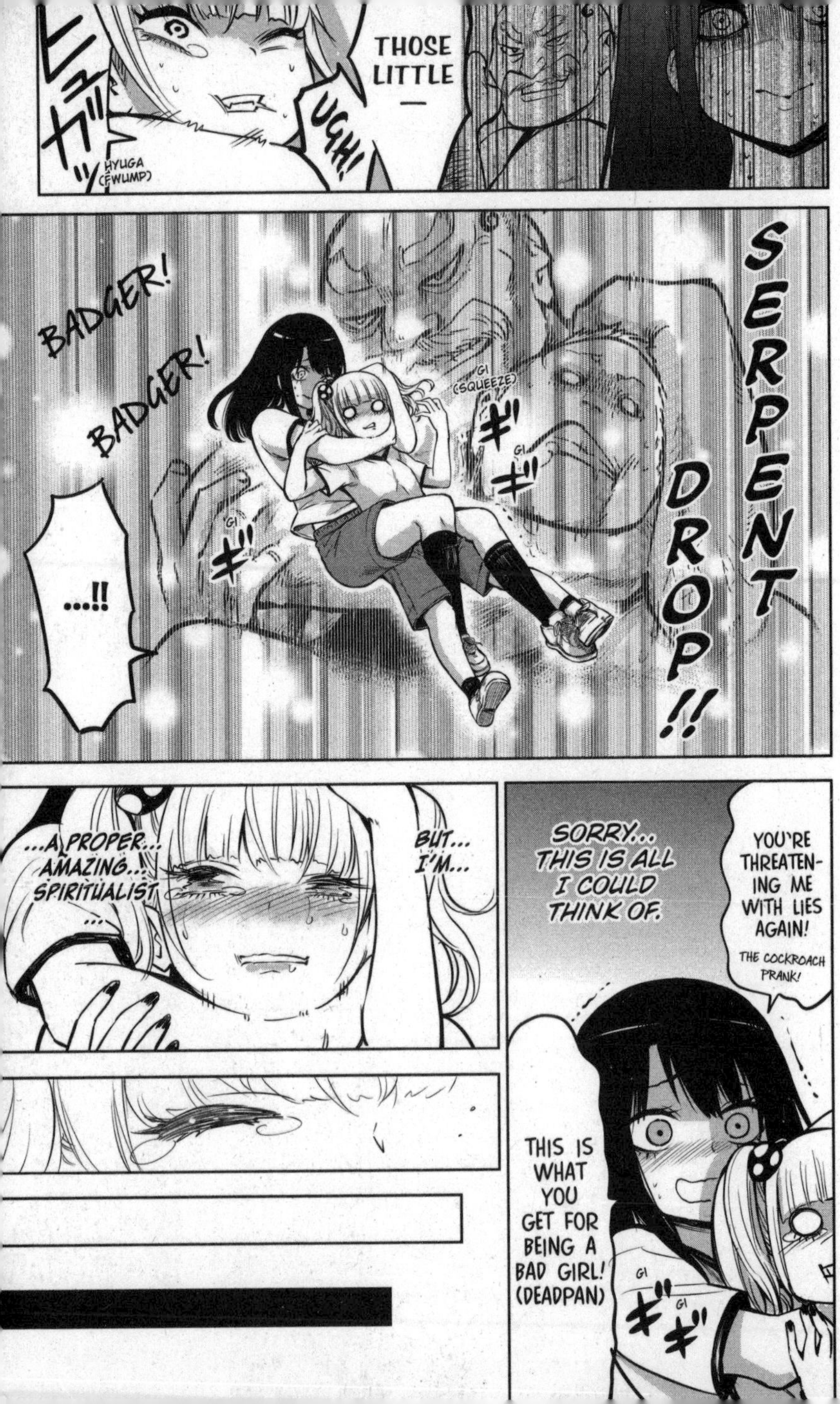
THOSE LITTLE —
UGH!
HYUGA (FWUMP)
SERPENT DROP!!
BADGER! BADGER!
GI (SQUEEZE)
GI
GI
...!!
YOU'RE THREATENING ME WITH LIES AGAIN!
THE COCKROACH PRANK!
SORRY... THIS IS ALL I COULD THINK OF.
THIS IS WHAT YOU GET FOR BEING A BAD GIRL! (DEADPAN)
GI
GI
BUT... I'M...
...A PROPER... AMAZING...! SPIRITUALIST...

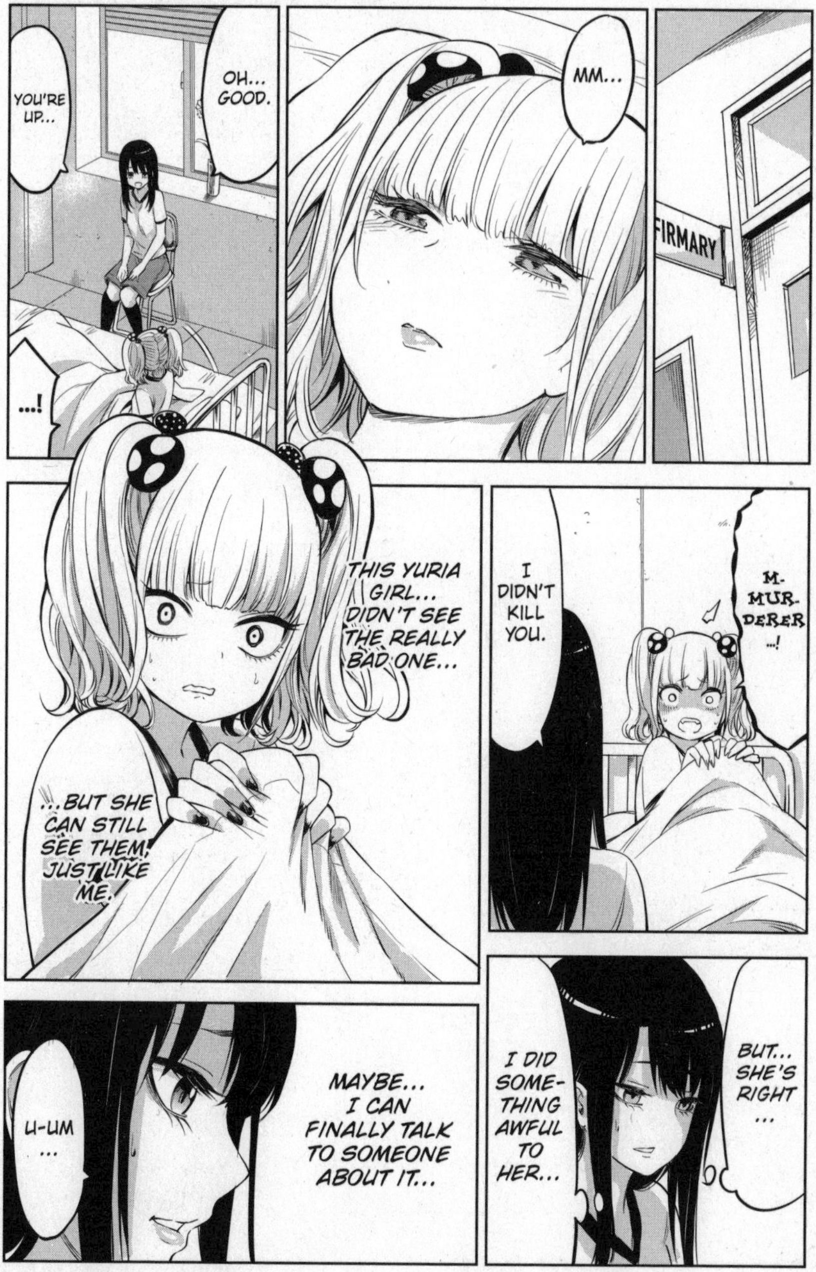
FIRMARY
MM...
OH... GOOD.
YOU'RE UP...
...!
M-MUR-DERER ...!
I DIDN'T KILL YOU.
THIS YURIA GIRL... DIDN'T SEE THE REALLY BAD ONE...
...BUT SHE CAN STILL SEE THEM, JUST LIKE ME.
BUT... SHE'S RIGHT ...
I DID SOME-THING AWFUL TO HER...
MAYBE... I CAN FINALLY TALK TO SOMEONE ABOUT IT...
U-UM ...

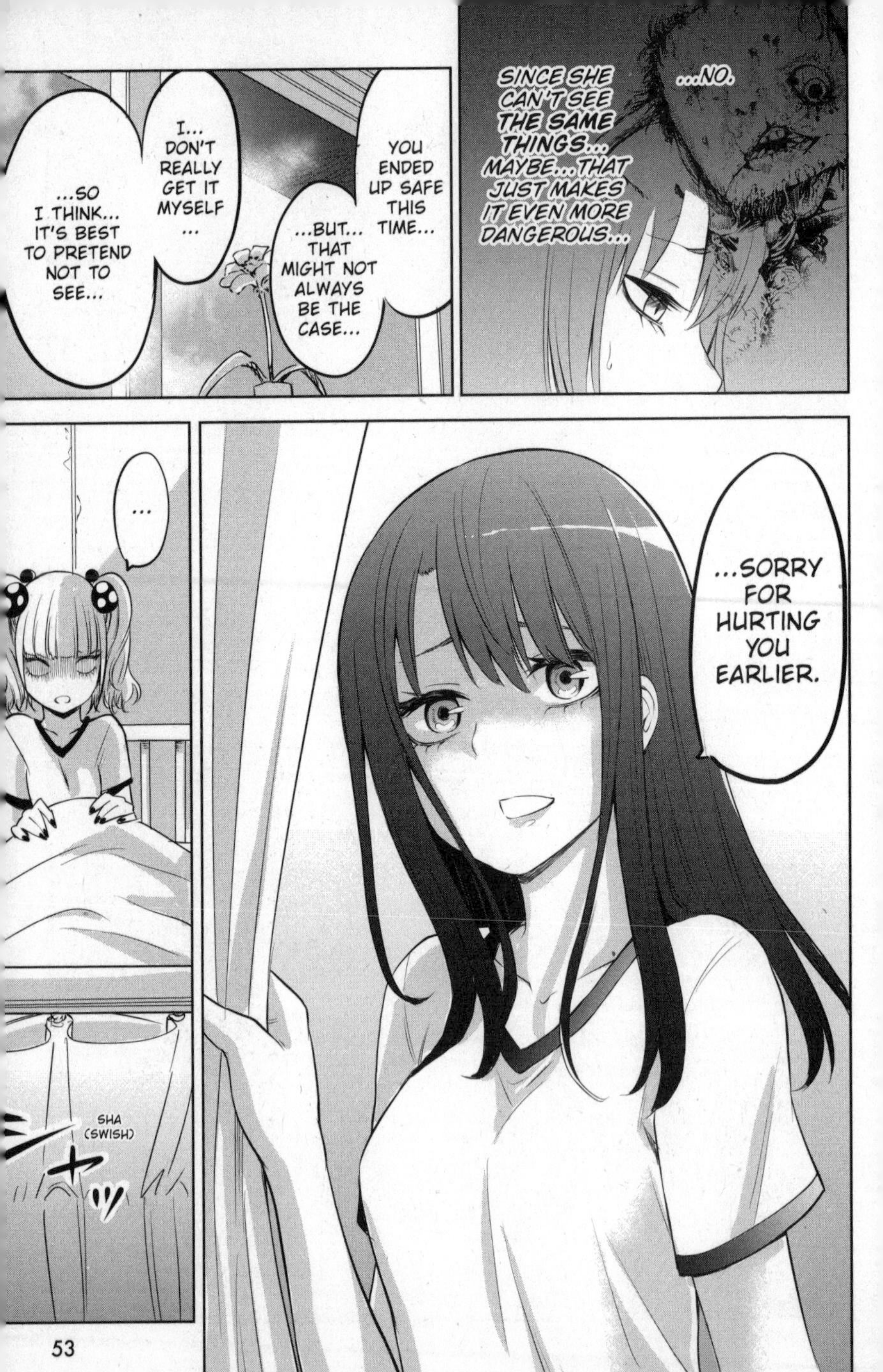

...NO.
SINCE SHE CAN'T SEE THE SAME THINGS... MAYBE... THAT JUST MAKES IT EVEN MORE DANGEROUS...
YOU ENDED UP SAFE THIS TIME...
...BUT... THAT MIGHT NOT ALWAYS BE THE CASE...
I... DON'T REALLY GET IT MYSELF...
...SO I THINK... IT'S BEST TO PRETEND NOT TO SEE...
...SORRY FOR HURTING YOU EARLIER.
...
SHA (SWISH)

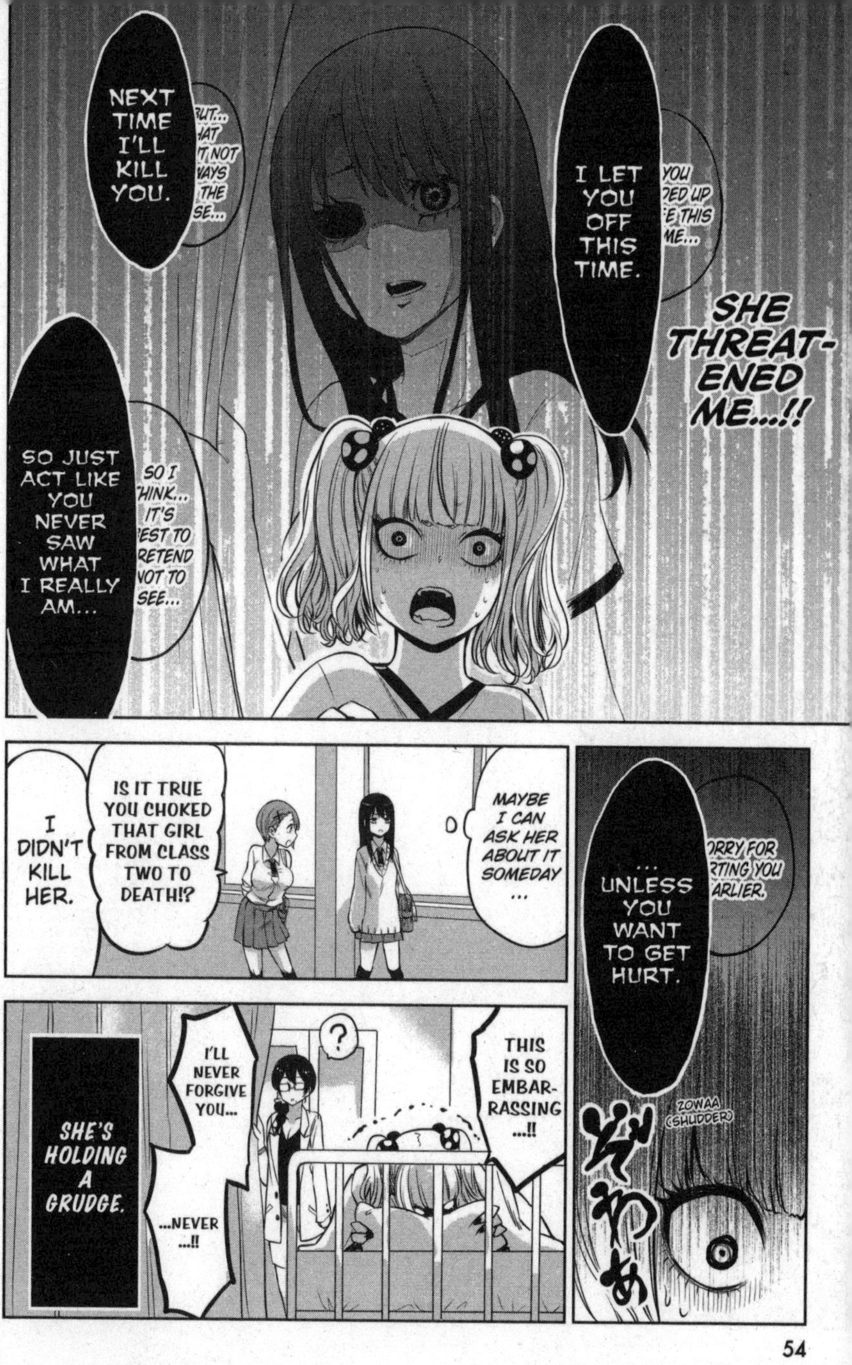
I LET YOU OFF THIS TIME.
YOU ...ED UP ...E THIS ...ME...
SHE THREAT-ENED ME...!!
NEXT TIME I'LL KILL YOU.
BUT... THAT ...T NOT ...WAYS THE ...SE...
SO JUST ACT LIKE YOU NEVER SAW WHAT I REALLY AM...
SO I THINK... IT'S ...EST TO ...RETEND NOT TO SEE...
... UNLESS YOU WANT TO GET HURT.
...ORRY FOR ...RTING YOU ...ARLIER.
ZOWAA (SHUDDER)
MAYBE I CAN ASK HER ABOUT IT SOMEDAY ...
IS IT TRUE YOU CHOKED THAT GIRL FROM CLASS TWO TO DEATH!?
I DIDN'T KILL HER.
THIS IS SO EMBAR-RASSING ...!!
?
I'LL NEVER FORGIVE YOU...
...NEVER ...!!
SHE'S HOLDING A GRUDGE.

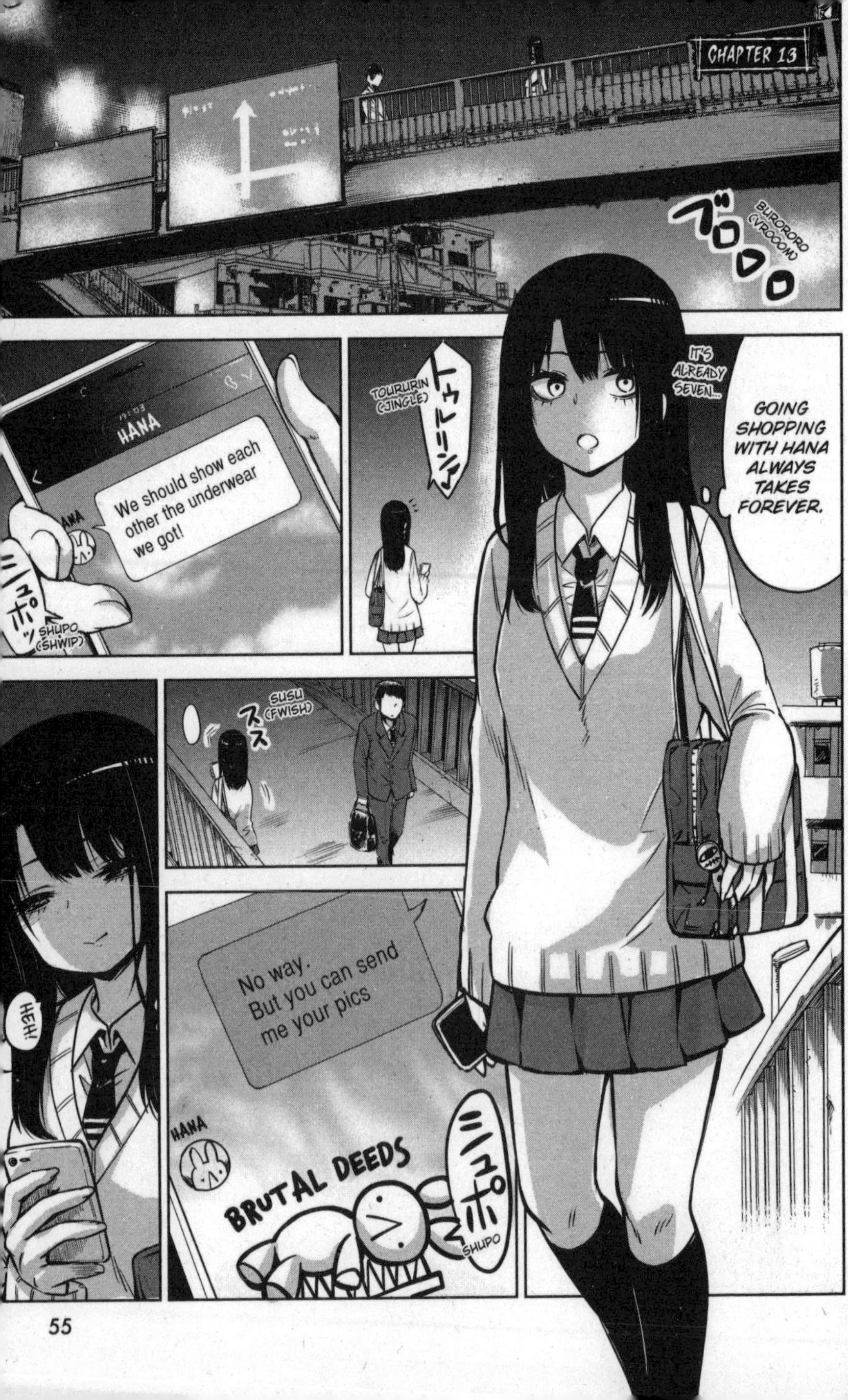
CHAPTER 13
BURORORO (VROOOM)
IT'S ALREADY SEVEN...
GOING SHOPPING WITH HANA ALWAYS TAKES FOREVER.
TOURURIN (JINGLE)
HANA
We should show each other the underwear we got!
HANA
SHUPO (SHWIP)
SUSU (FWISH)
No way. But you can send me your pics
HANA
BRUTAL DEEDS
SHUPO
HEH!

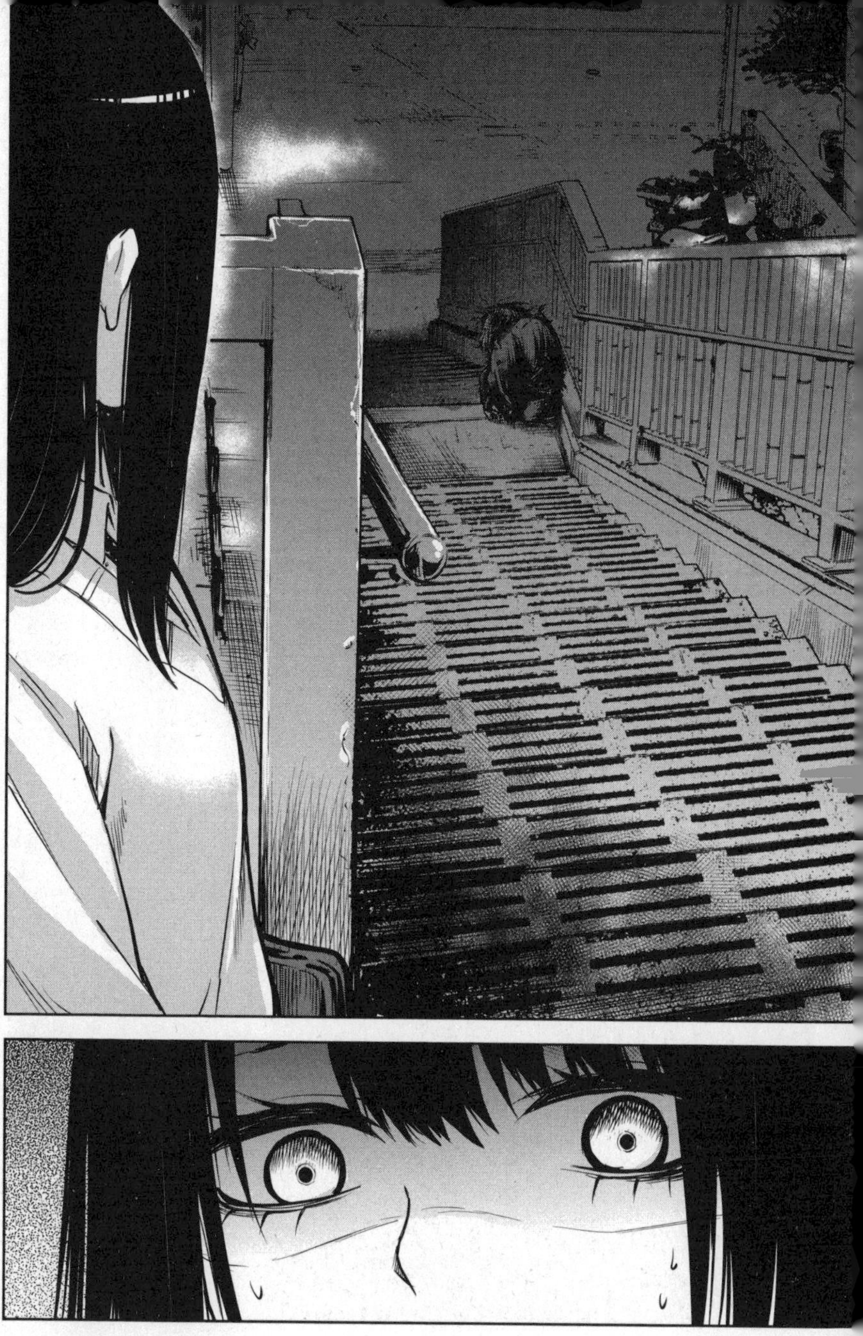

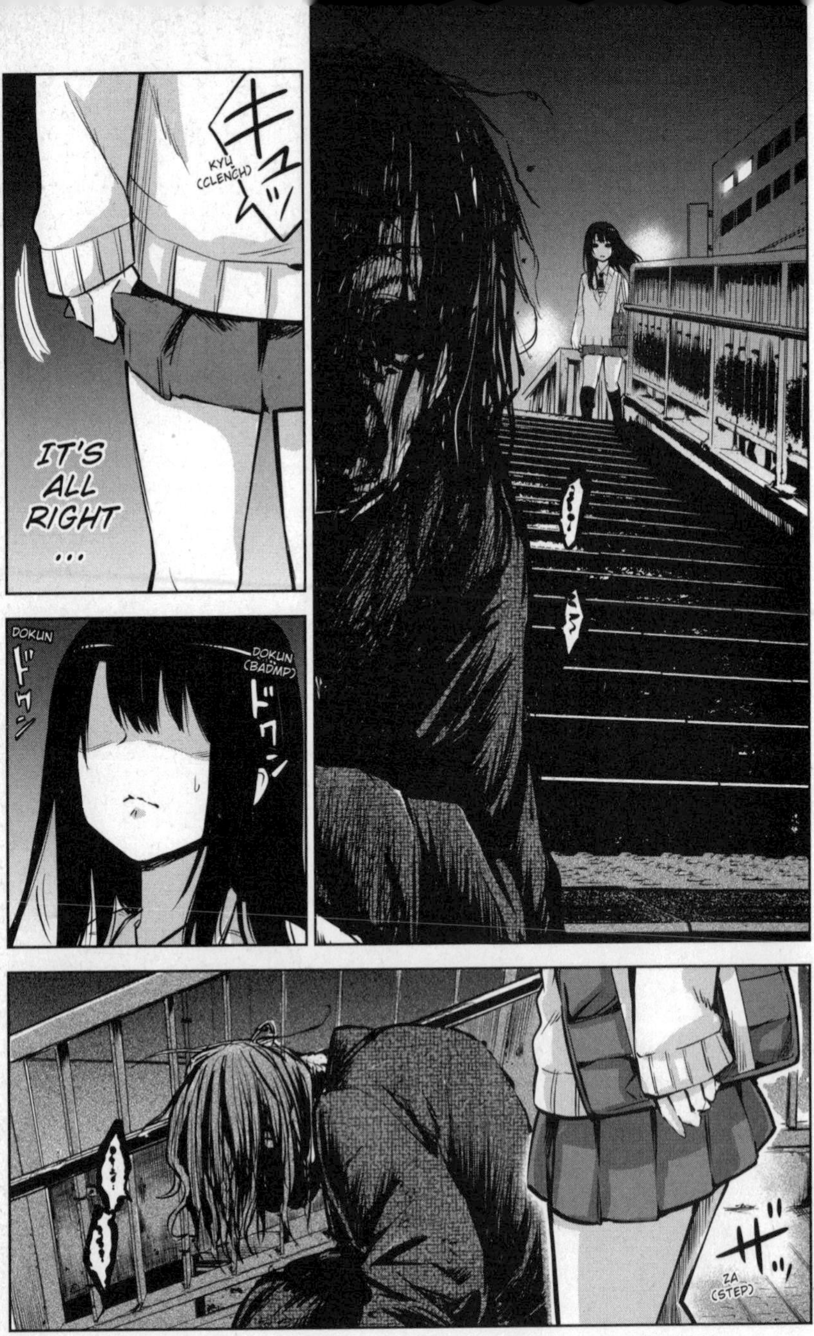
キュッ
KYU (CLENCH)
IT'S ALL RIGHT ...
ドクン
DOKUN
ドクン
DOKUN (BADMP)
ザッ
ZA (STEP)

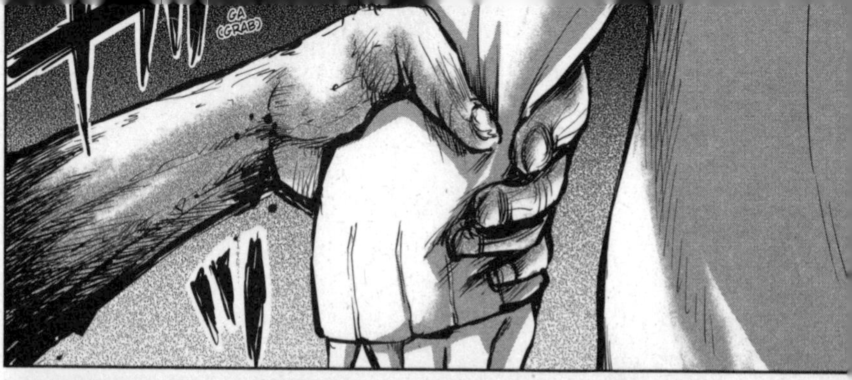
GA
(GRAB)
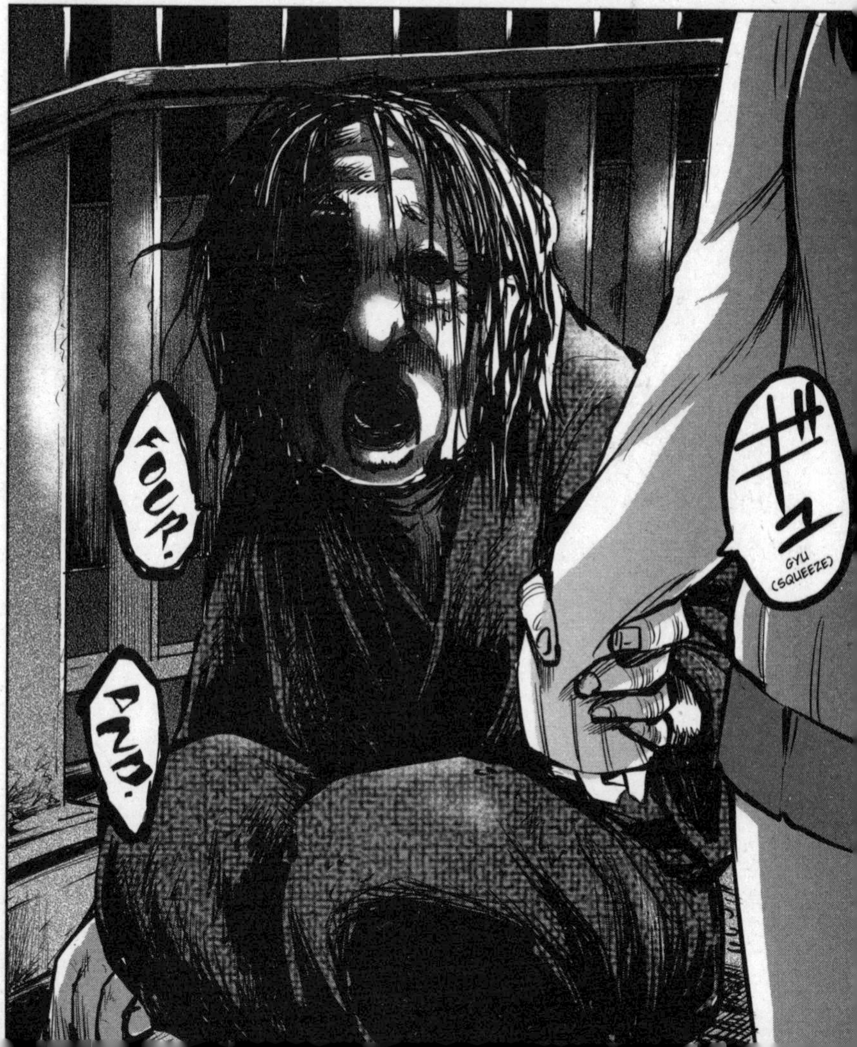
GYU
(SQUEEZE)
FOUR.
AND.

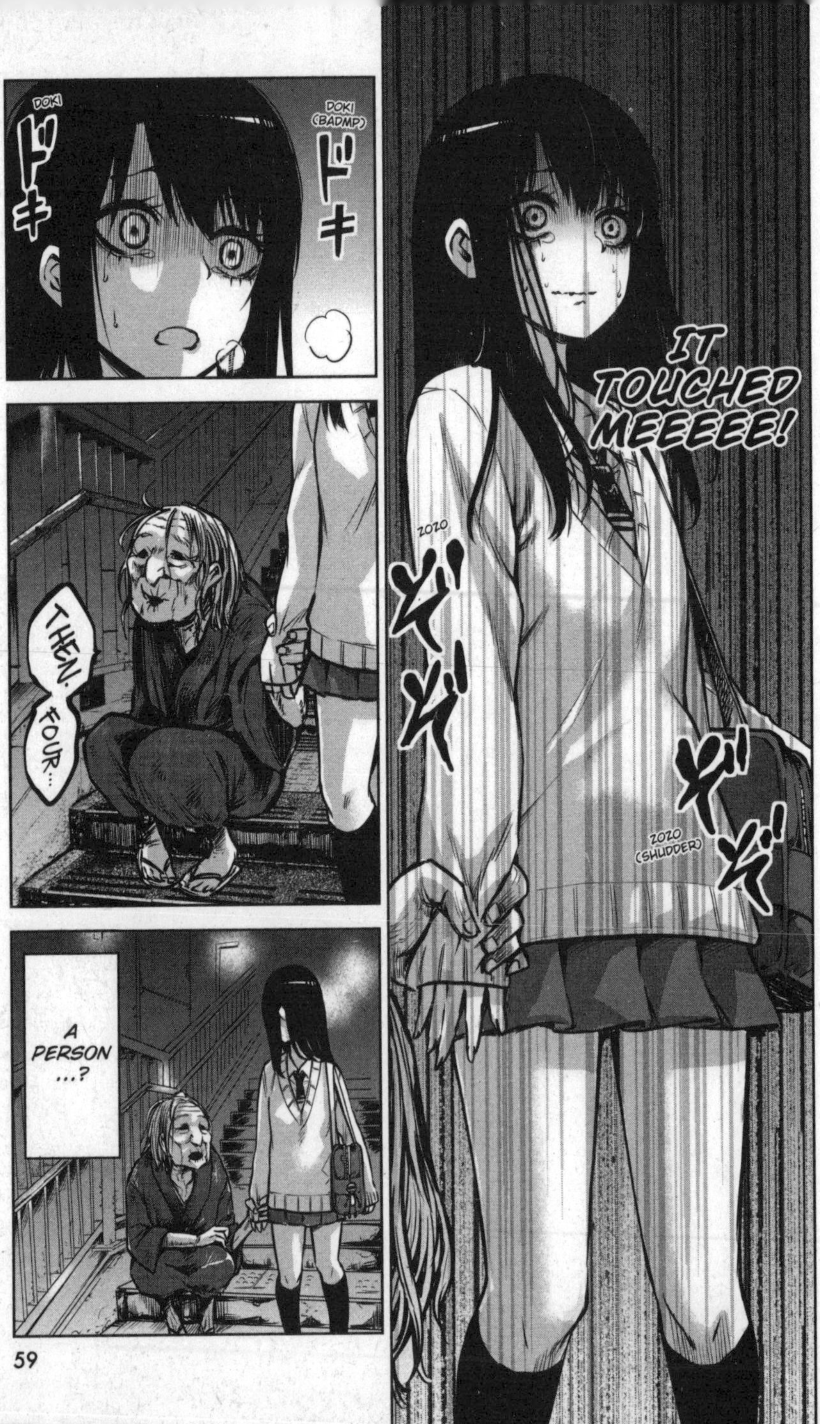
IT TOUCHED MEEEEEE!
ZOZO
ZOZO (SHUDDER)
DOKI (BADMP)
DOKI
THEN. FOUR...
A PERSON ...?

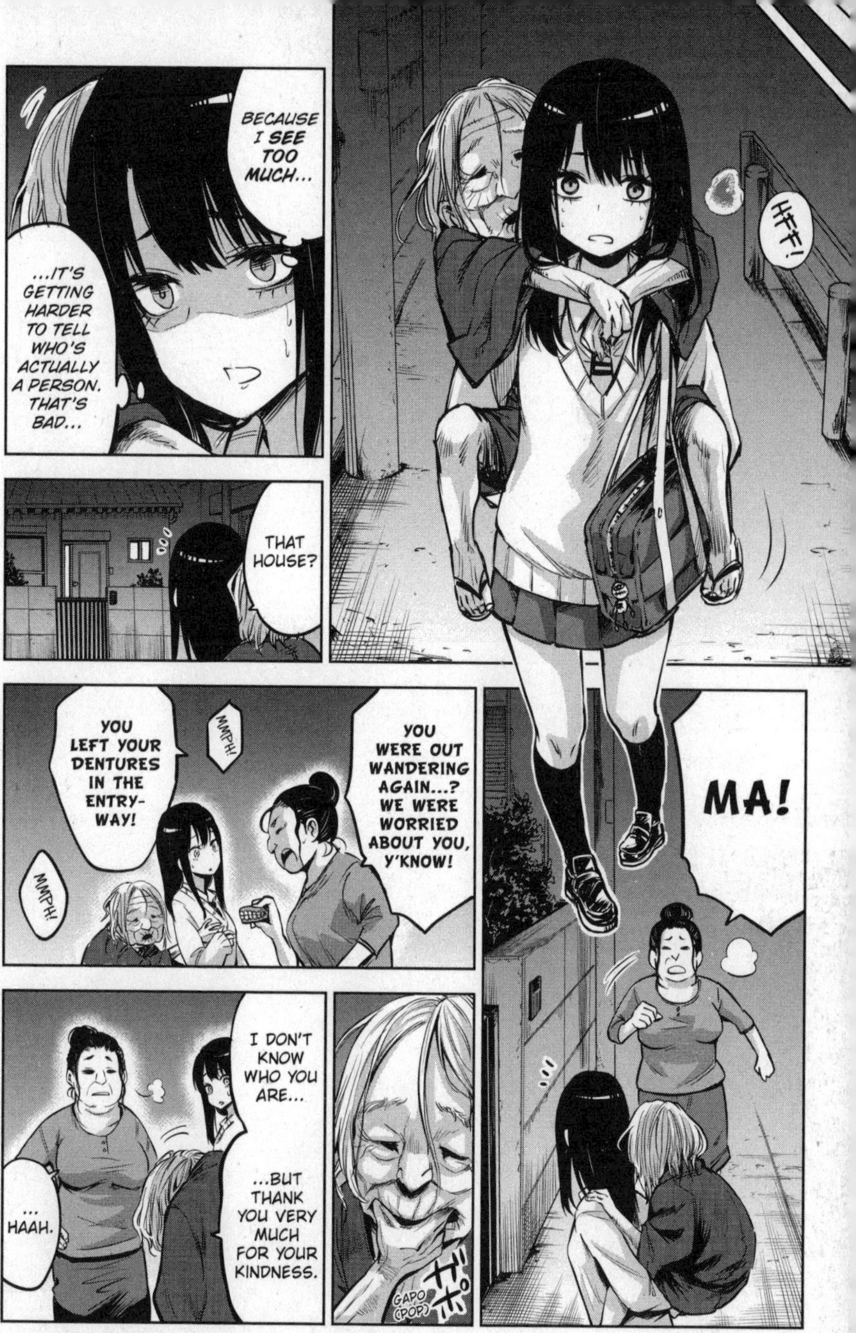
HFF!
BECAUSE I SEE TOO MUCH...
...IT'S GETTING HARDER TO TELL WHO'S ACTUALLY A PERSON. THAT'S BAD...
THAT HOUSE?
MA!
YOU WERE OUT WANDERING AGAIN...? WE WERE WORRIED ABOUT YOU, Y'KNOW!
MMPH!
YOU LEFT YOUR DENTURES IN THE ENTRY-WAY!
MMPH!
GAPO (POP)
I DON'T KNOW WHO YOU ARE...
...BUT THANK YOU VERY MUCH FOR YOUR KINDNESS.
... HAAH.

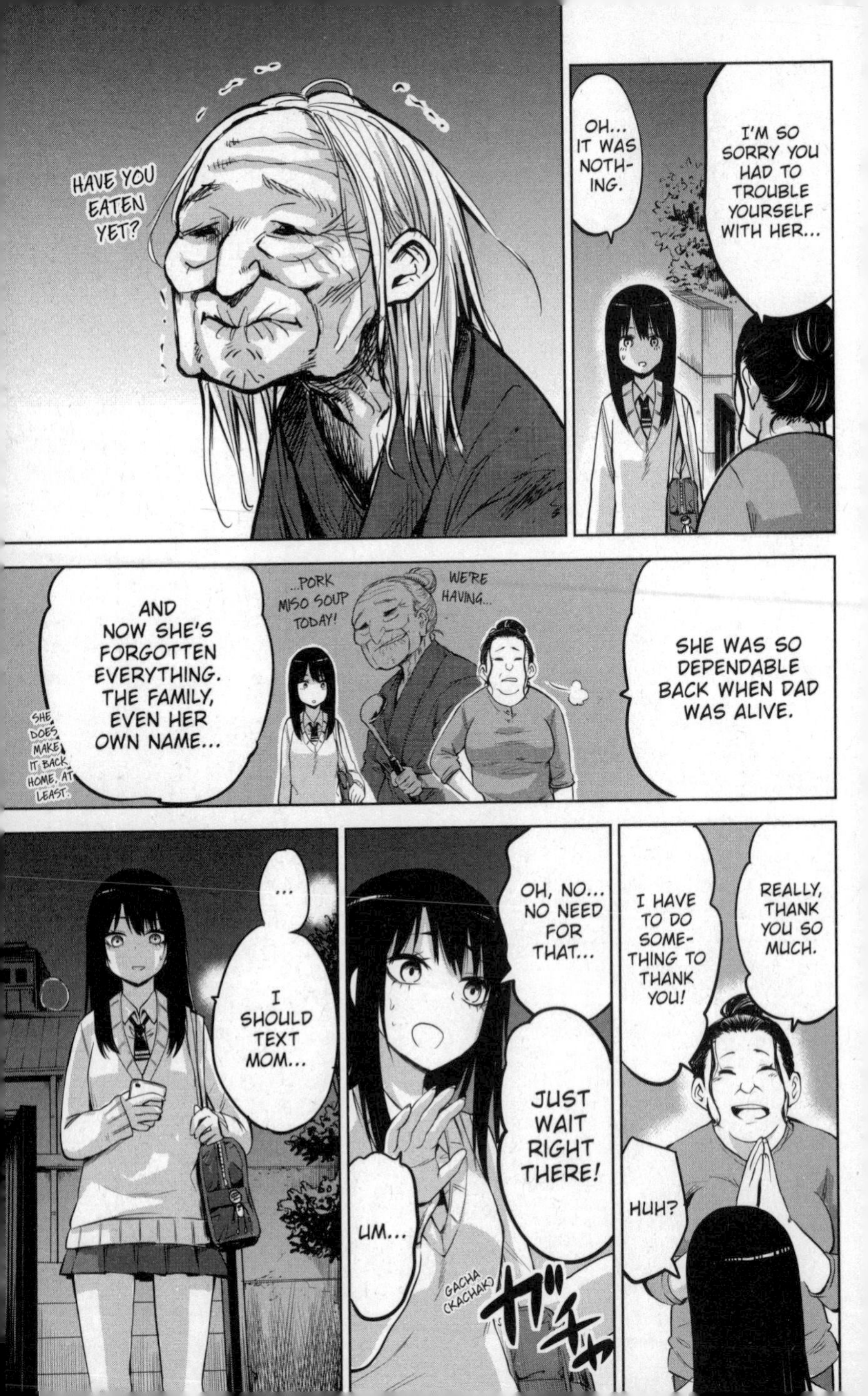
I'M SO SORRY YOU HAD TO TROUBLE YOURSELF WITH HER...
OH... IT WAS NOTHING.
HAVE YOU EATEN YET?
SHE WAS SO DEPENDABLE BACK WHEN DAD WAS ALIVE.
WE'RE HAVING...
...PORK MISO SOUP TODAY!
AND NOW SHE'S FORGOTTEN EVERYTHING. THE FAMILY, EVEN HER OWN NAME...
SHE DOES MAKE IT BACK HOME, AT LEAST.
REALLY, THANK YOU SO MUCH.
I HAVE TO DO SOMETHING TO THANK YOU!
HUH?
OH, NO... NO NEED FOR THAT...
JUST WAIT RIGHT THERE!
UM...
GACHA (KACHAK)
...
I SHOULD TEXT MOM...

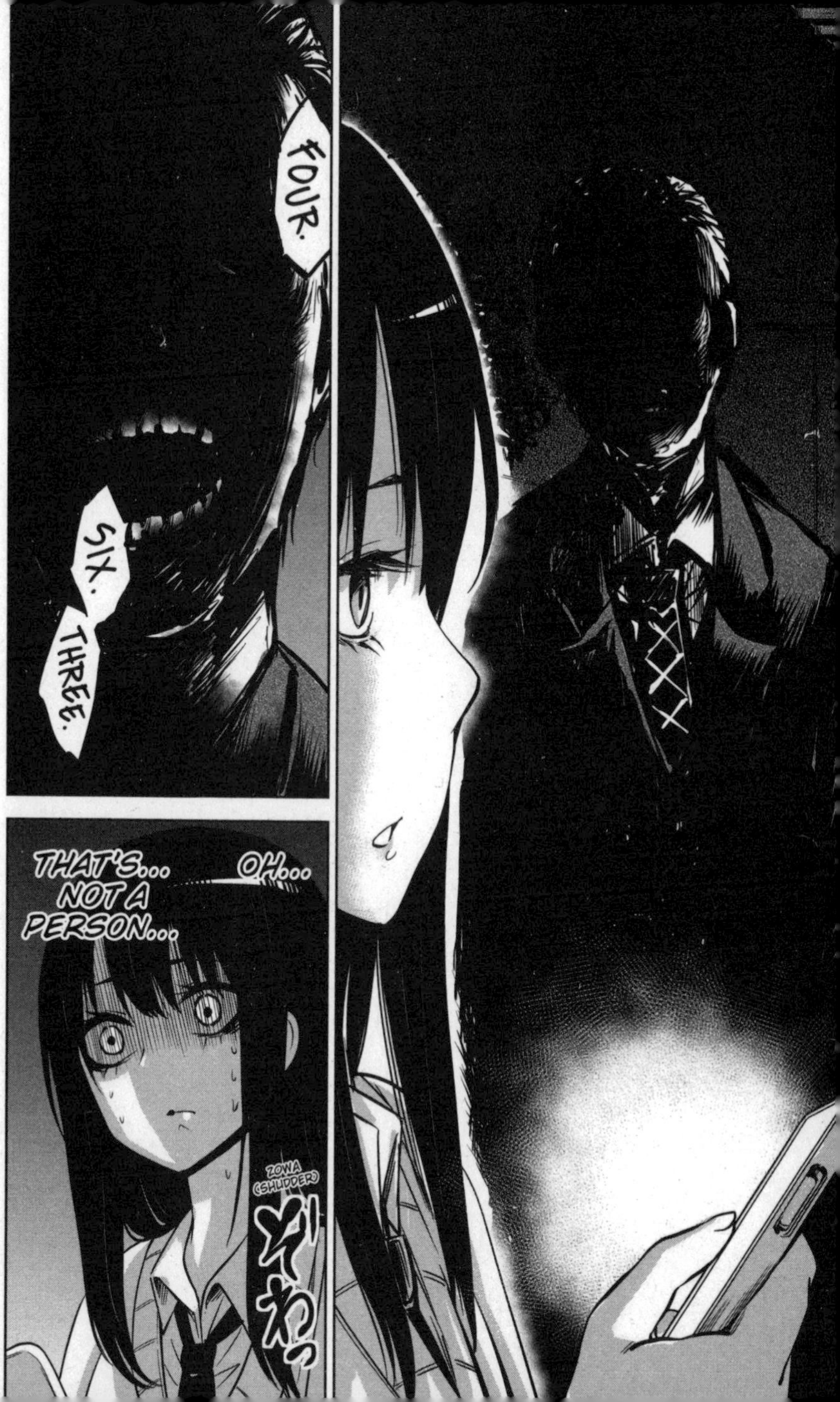
FOUR.
SIX.
THREE.
OH...
THAT'S... NOT A PERSON...
ZOWA (SHUDDER)

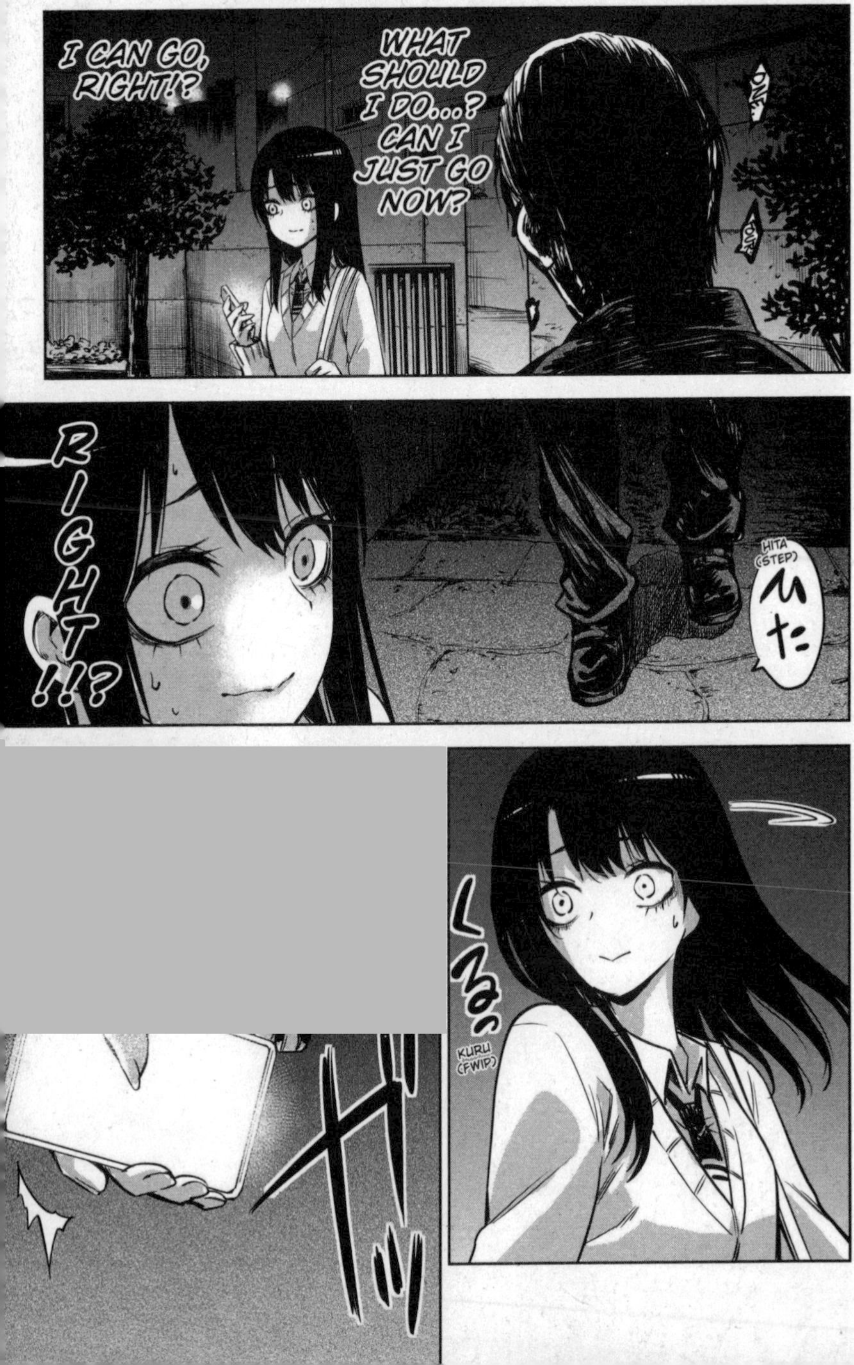
WHAT SHOULD I DO...? CAN I JUST GO NOW?
I CAN GO, RIGHT!?
HITA (STEP)
ひた
RIGHT!!?
KURU (FWIP)

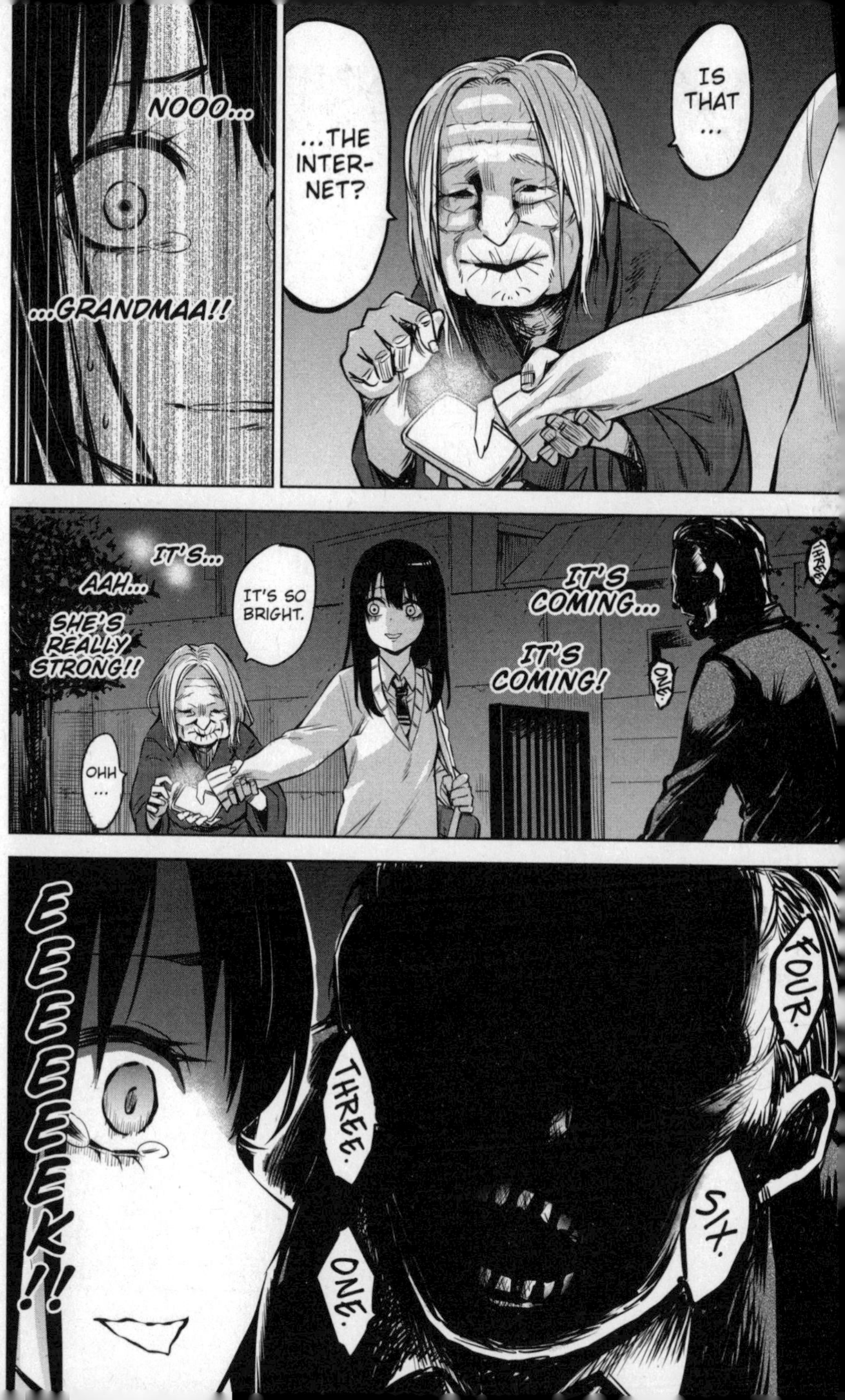
IS THAT ...
...THE INTERNET?
NOOO...
...GRANDMAA!!
THREE.
IT'S COMING...
IT'S COMING!
ONE.
IT'S SO BRIGHT.
IT'S...
AAH...
SHE'S REALLY STRONG!!
OHH ...
FOUR.
SIX.
THREE.
ONE.
EEEEEEEK!!

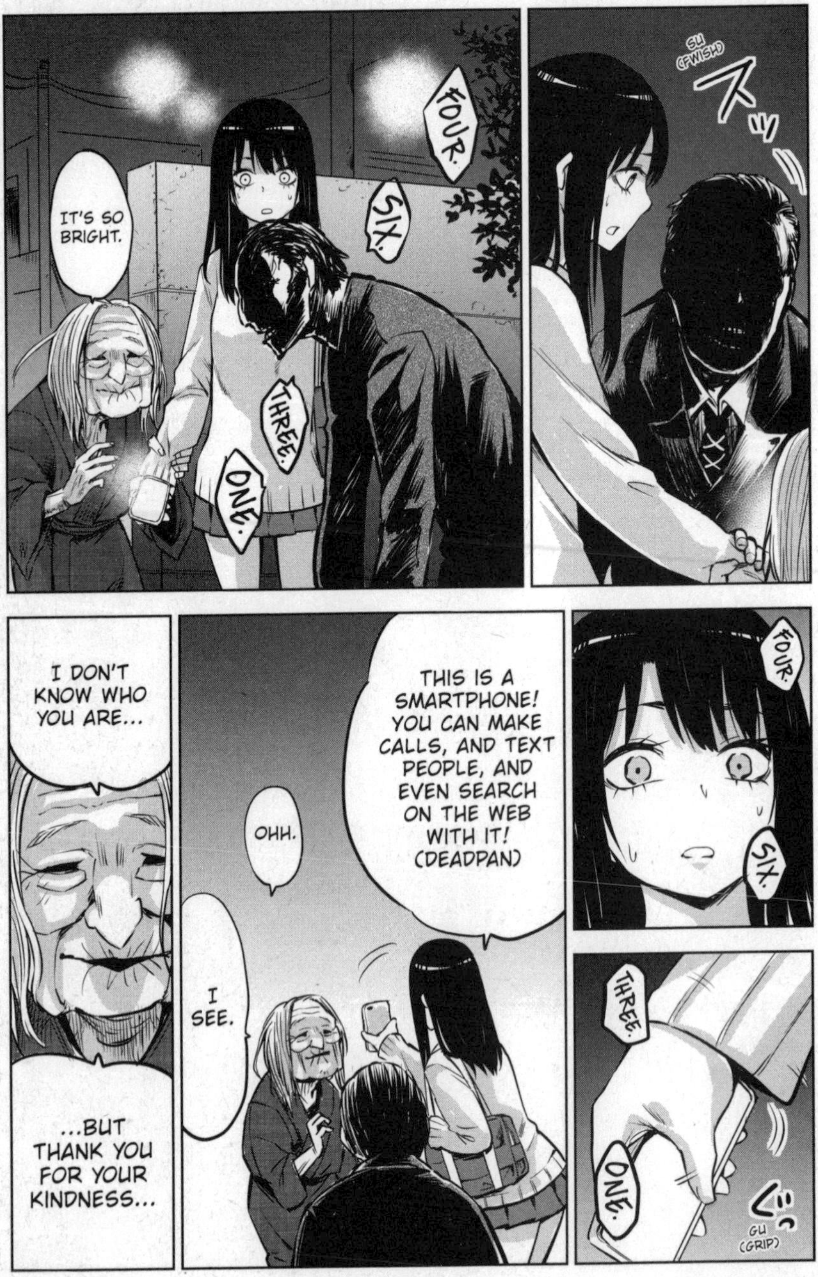
SU (FWISH)
FOUR.
SIX.
IT'S SO BRIGHT.
THREE.
ONE.
FOUR.
SIX.
THREE.
ONE.
GU (GRIP)
THIS IS A SMARTPHONE! YOU CAN MAKE CALLS, AND TEXT PEOPLE, AND EVEN SEARCH ON THE WEB WITH IT! (DEADPAN)
OHH.
I SEE.
I DON'T KNOW WHO YOU ARE...
...BUT THANK YOU FOR YOUR KINDNESS...

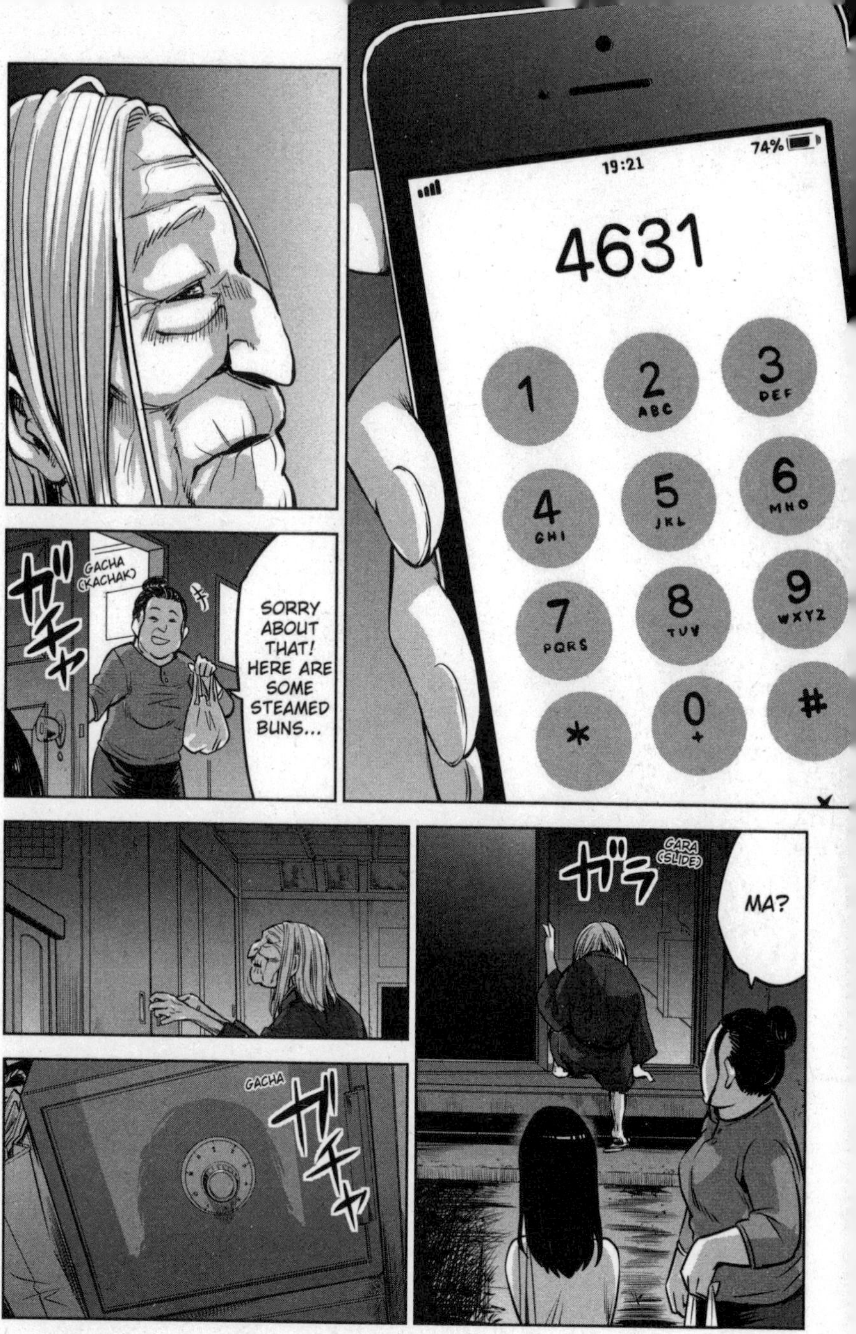
74%
19:21
4631
1
2 ABC
3 DEF
4 GHI
5 JKL
6 MNO
7 PQRS
8 TUV
9 WXYZ
*
0 +
#
GACHA (KACHAK)
SORRY ABOUT THAT! HERE ARE SOME STEAMED BUNS...
GARA (SLIDE)
MA?
GACHA

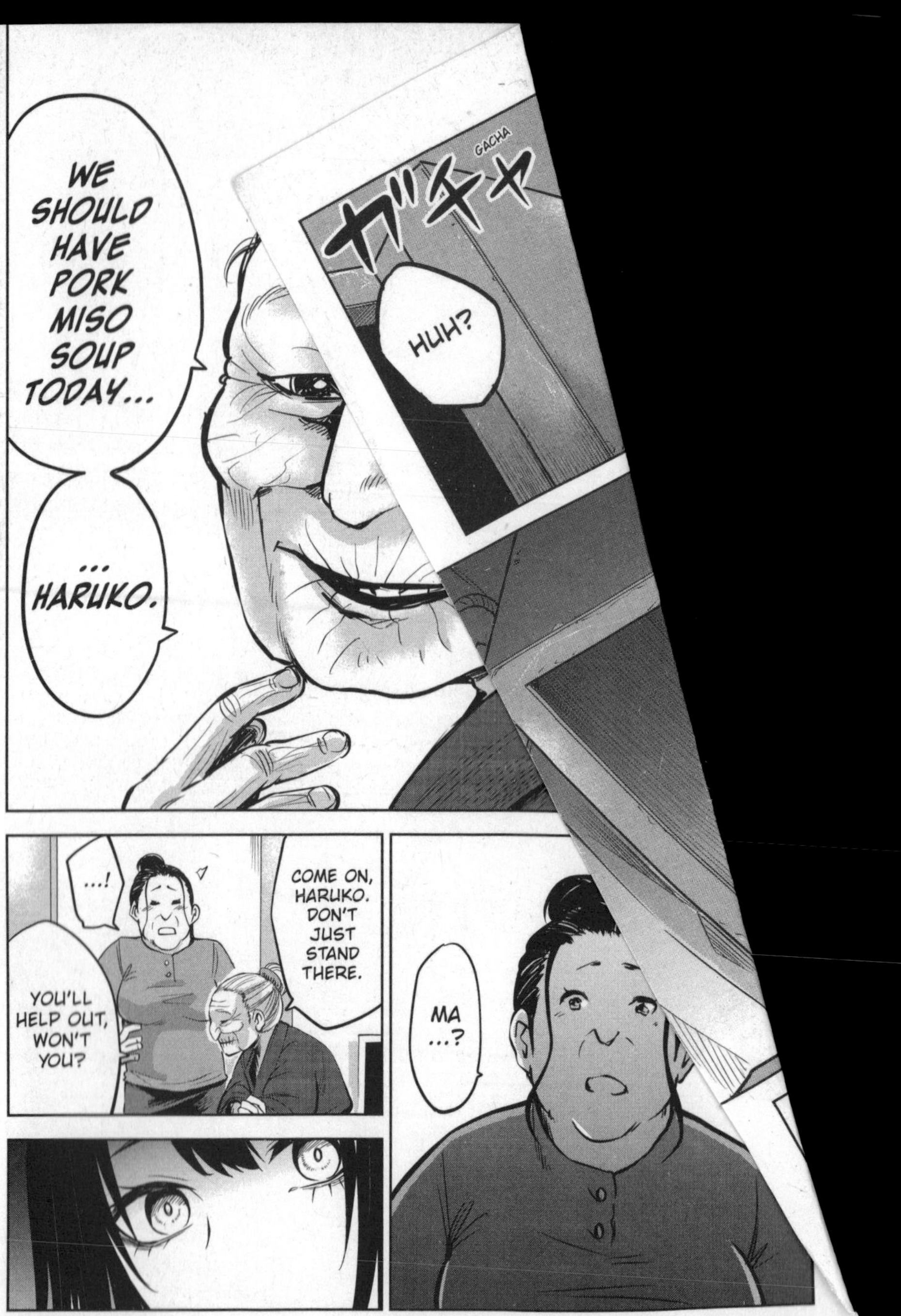
ガチャ
GACHA
HUH?
WE SHOULD HAVE PORK MISO SOUP TODAY...
...HARUKO.
MA ...?
COME ON, HARUKO. DON'T JUST STAND THERE.
...!
YOU'LL HELP OUT, WON'T YOU?

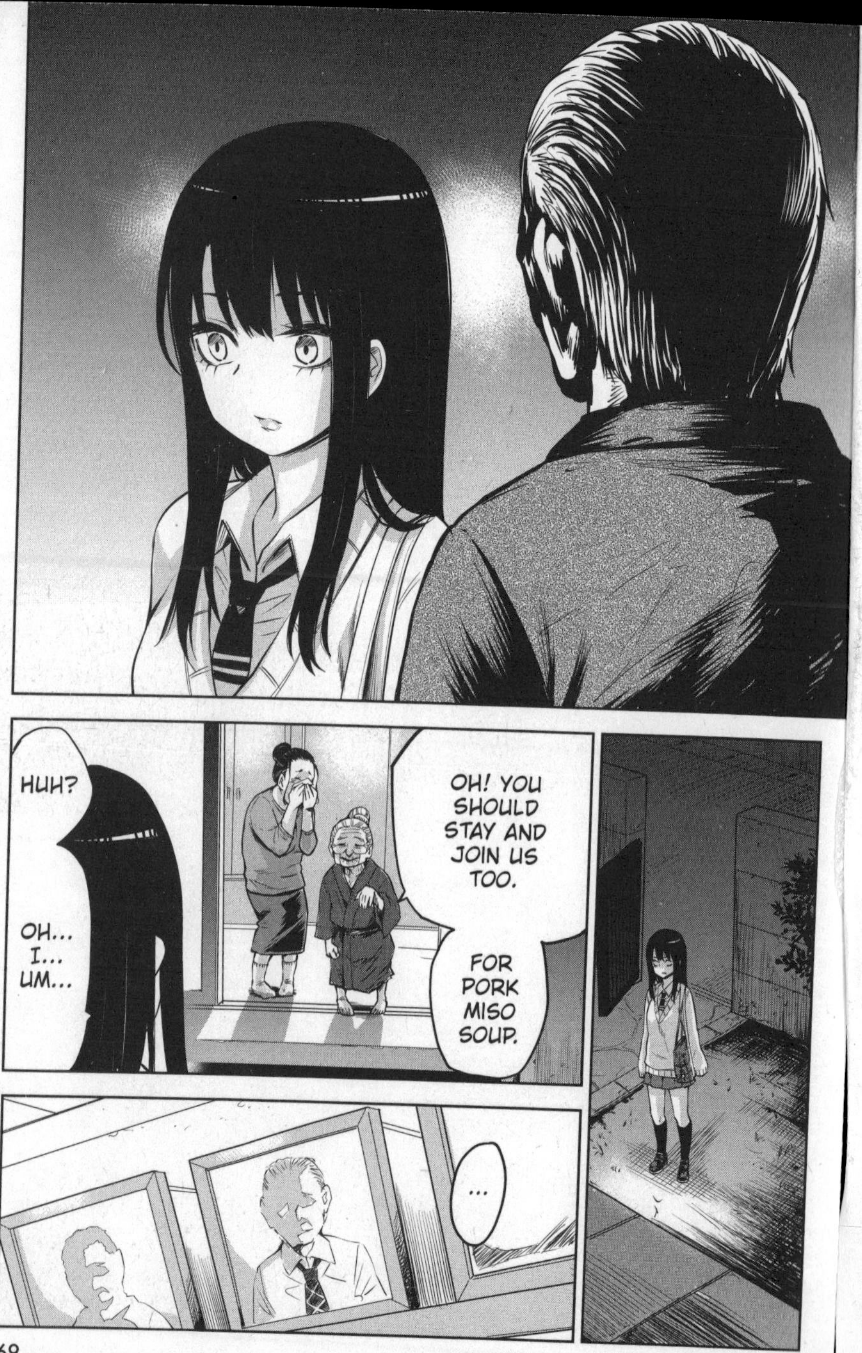
OH! YOU SHOULD STAY AND JOIN US TOO.
FOR PORK MISO SOUP.
HUH?
OH... I... UM...
...

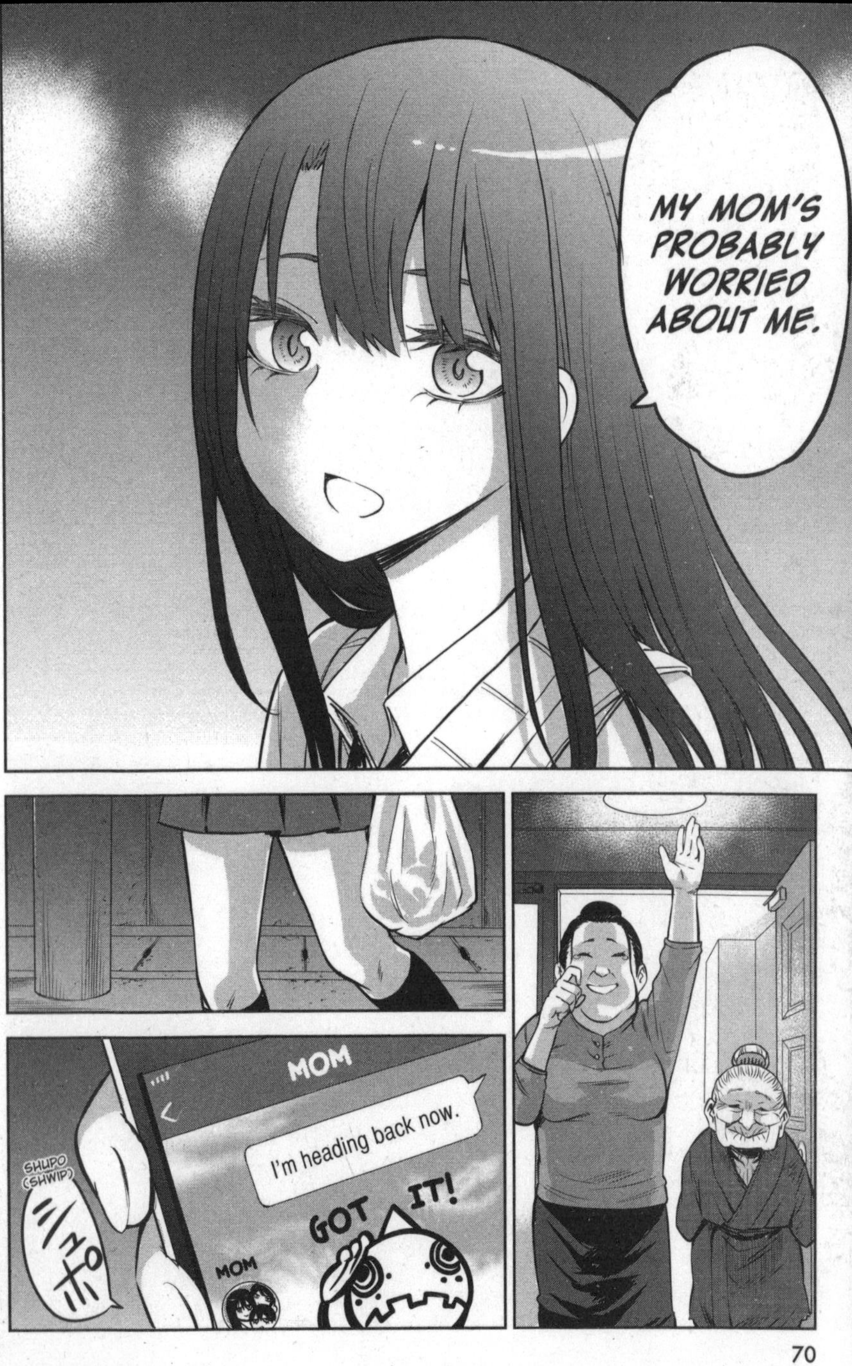
MY MOM'S PROBABLY WORRIED ABOUT ME.
MOM
I'm heading back now.
SHUPO (SHWIP)
シュポ
GOT IT!
MOM

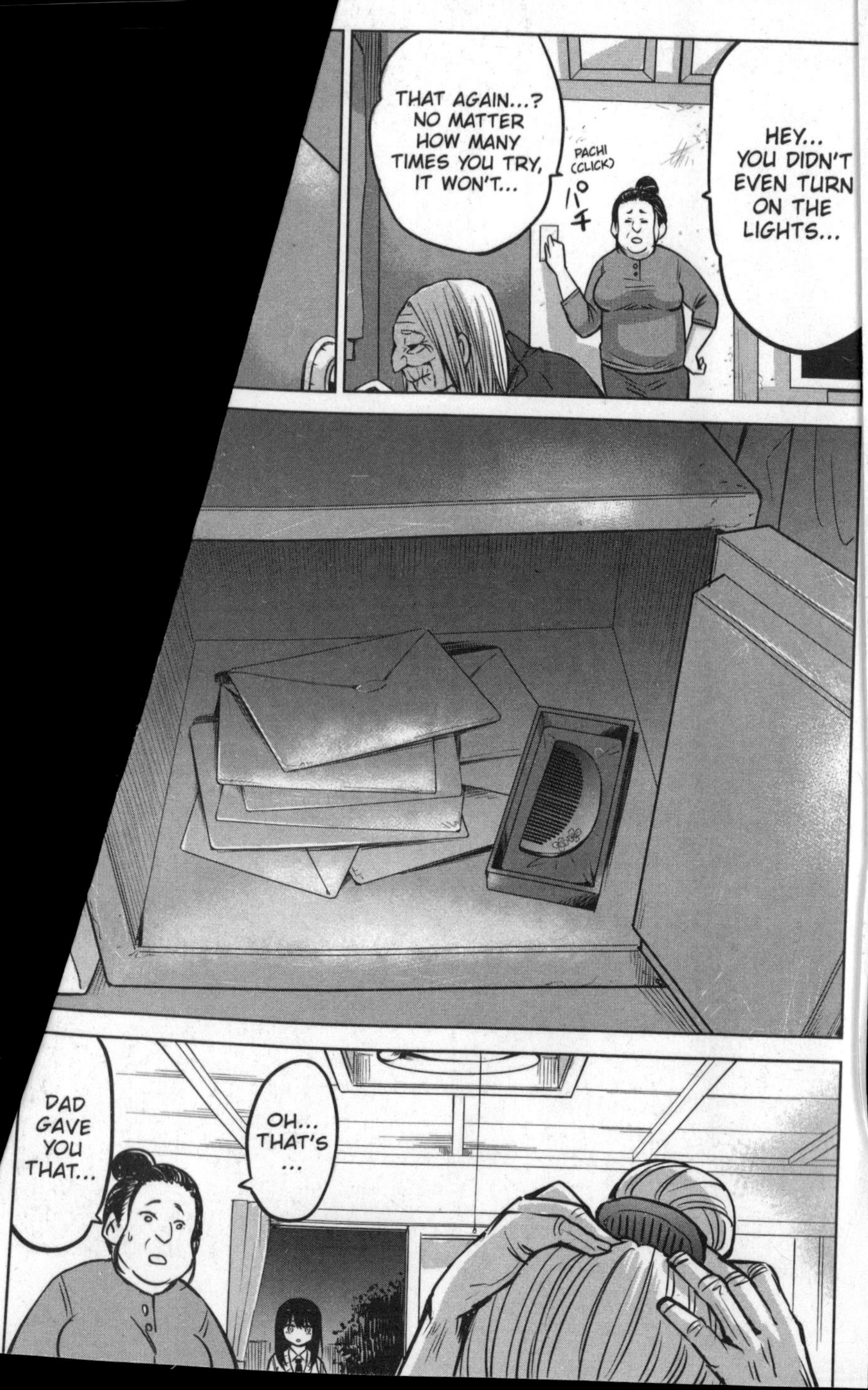
HEY... YOU DIDN'T EVEN TURN ON THE LIGHTS...
PACHI (CLICK)
パチ
THAT AGAIN...? NO MATTER HOW MANY TIMES YOU TRY, IT WON'T...
OH... THAT'S ...
DAD GAVE YOU THAT...

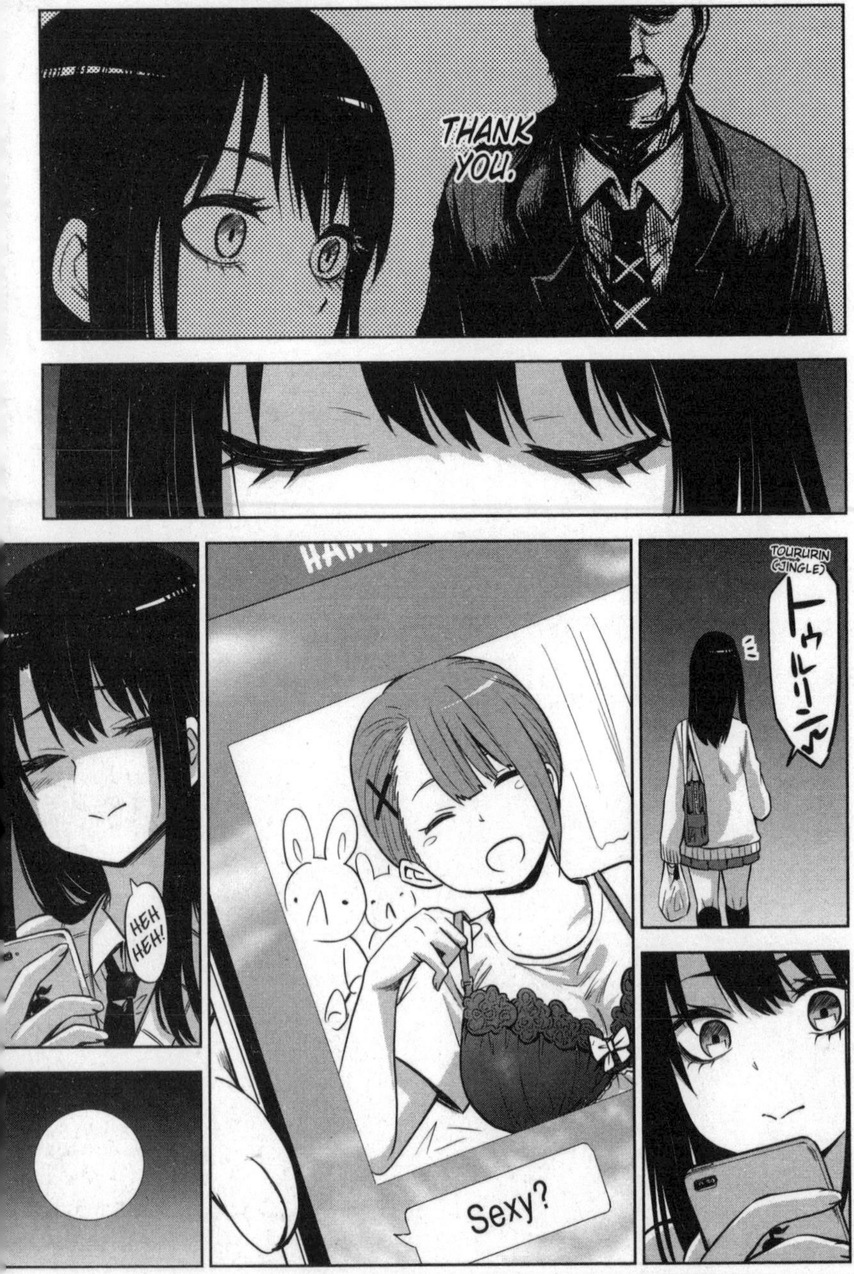
THANK YOU.
TOURURIN (JINGLE)
トゥルリーン♪
Sexy?
HEH HEH!

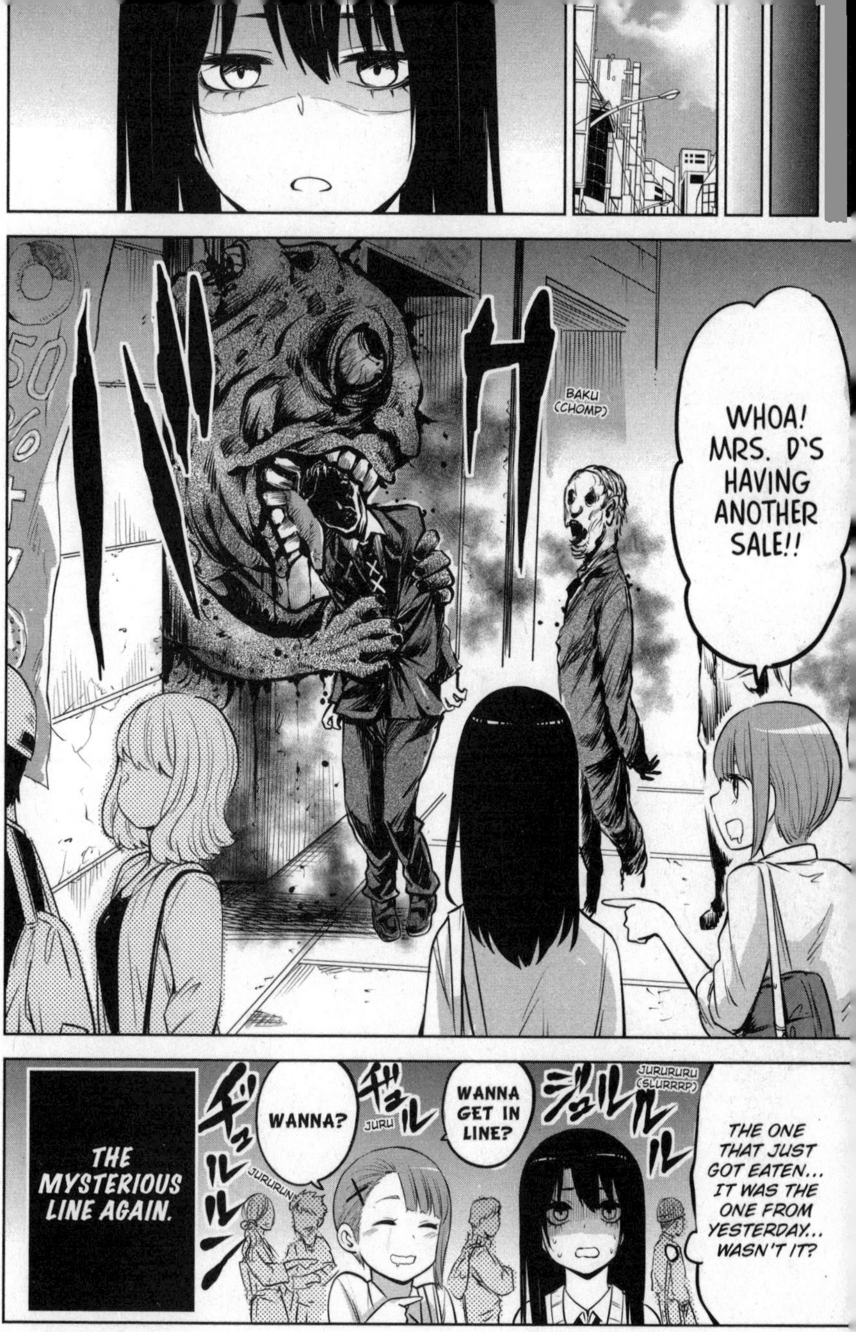
WHOA! MRS. D'S HAVING ANOTHER SALE!!
BAKU (CHOMP)
THE ONE THAT JUST GOT EATEN... IT WAS THE ONE FROM YESTERDAY... WASN'T IT?
JURURURU (SLURRRP)
WANNA GET IN LINE?
JURU
WANNA?
JURURUN
THE MYSTERIOUS LINE AGAIN.

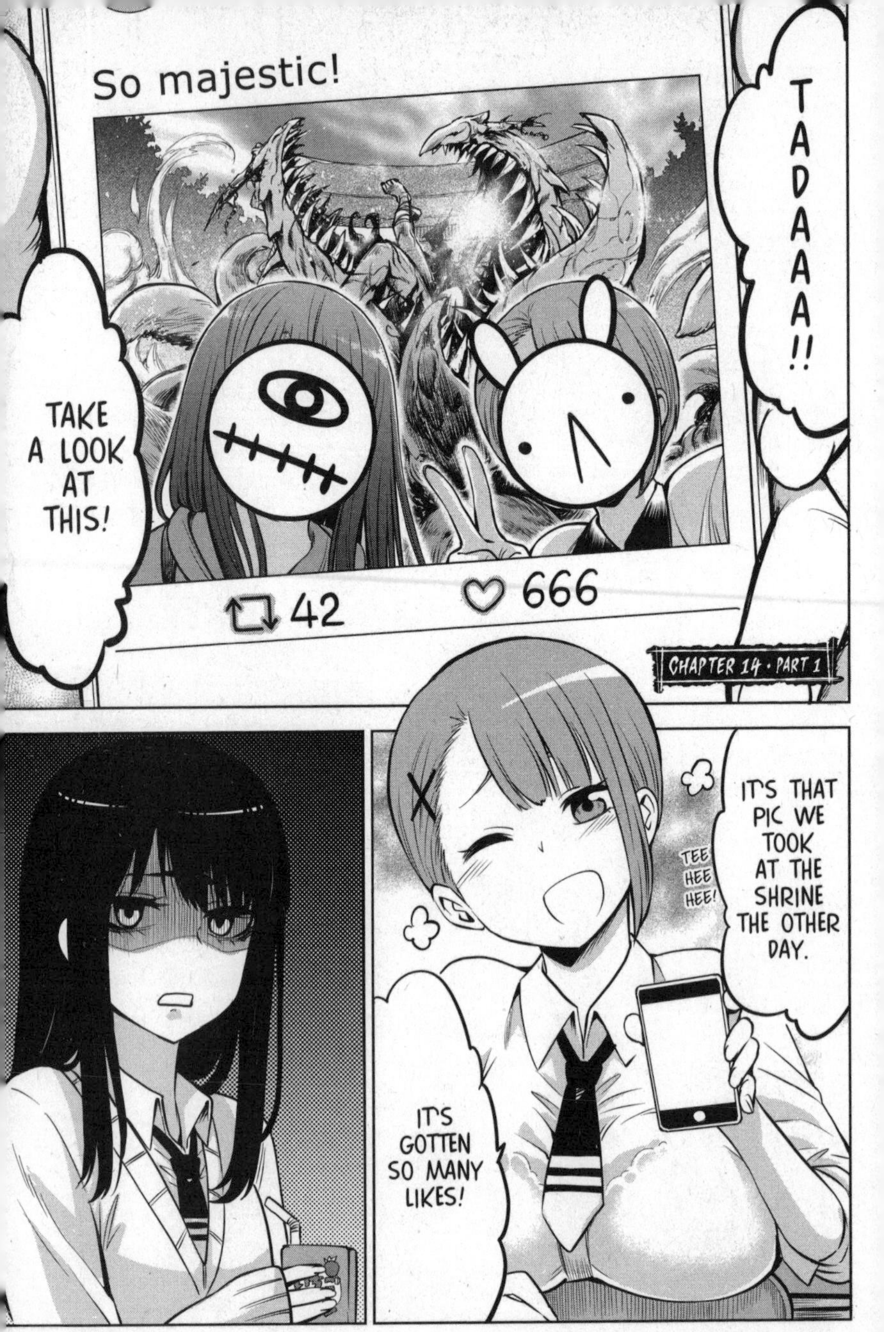
TADAAAA!!
So majestic!
TAKE A LOOK AT THIS!
666
42
CHAPTER 14 • PART 1
IT'S THAT PIC WE TOOK AT THE SHRINE THE OTHER DAY.
TEE HEE HEE!
IT'S GOTTEN SO MANY LIKES!

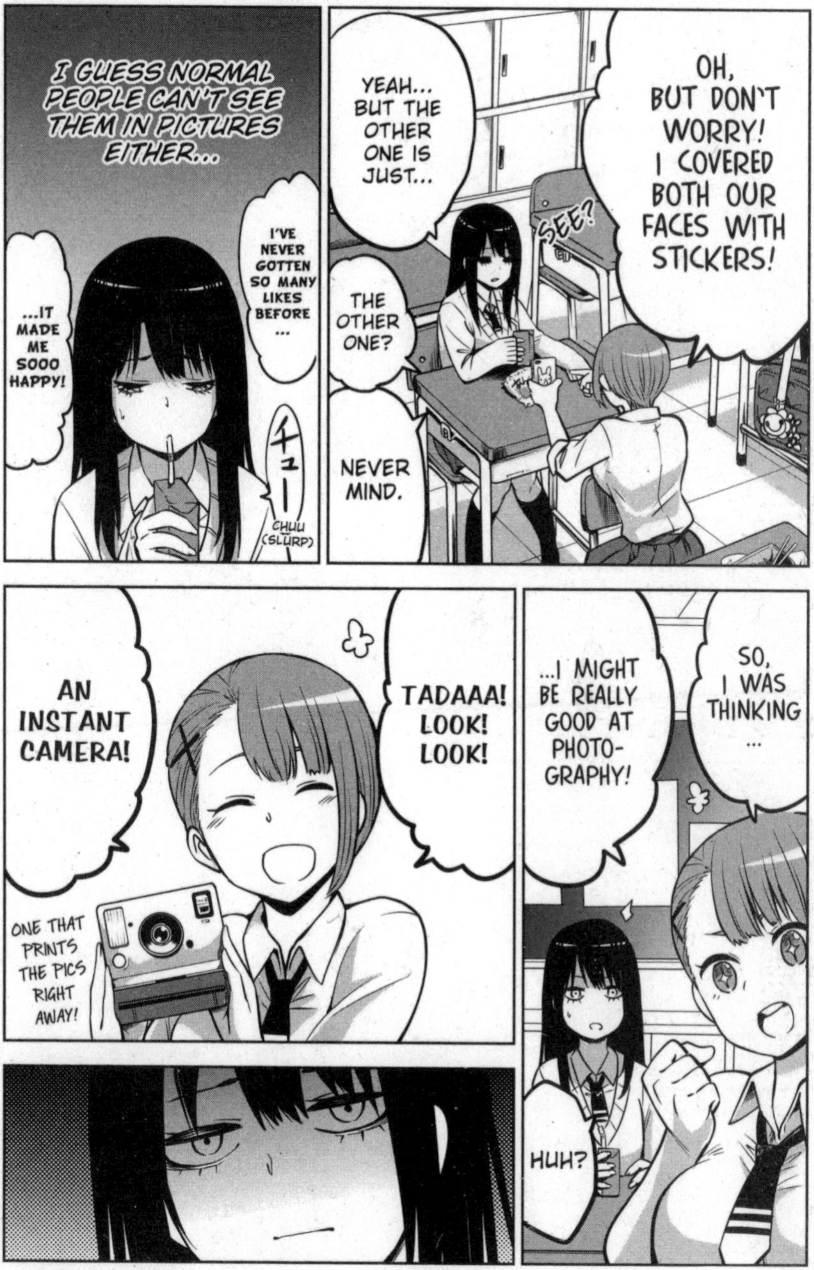
OH, BUT DON'T WORRY! I COVERED BOTH OUR FACES WITH STICKERS!
SEE?
YEAH... BUT THE OTHER ONE IS JUST...
THE OTHER ONE?
NEVER MIND.
I GUESS NORMAL PEOPLE CAN'T SEE THEM IN PICTURES EITHER...
I'VE NEVER GOTTEN SO MANY LIKES BEFORE...
...IT MADE ME SOOO HAPPY!
チュー
CHUU (SLURP)
SO, I WAS THINKING...
...I MIGHT BE REALLY GOOD AT PHOTO-GRAPHY!
HUH?
TADAAA! LOOK! LOOK!
AN INSTANT CAMERA!
ONE THAT PRINTS THE PICS RIGHT AWAY!

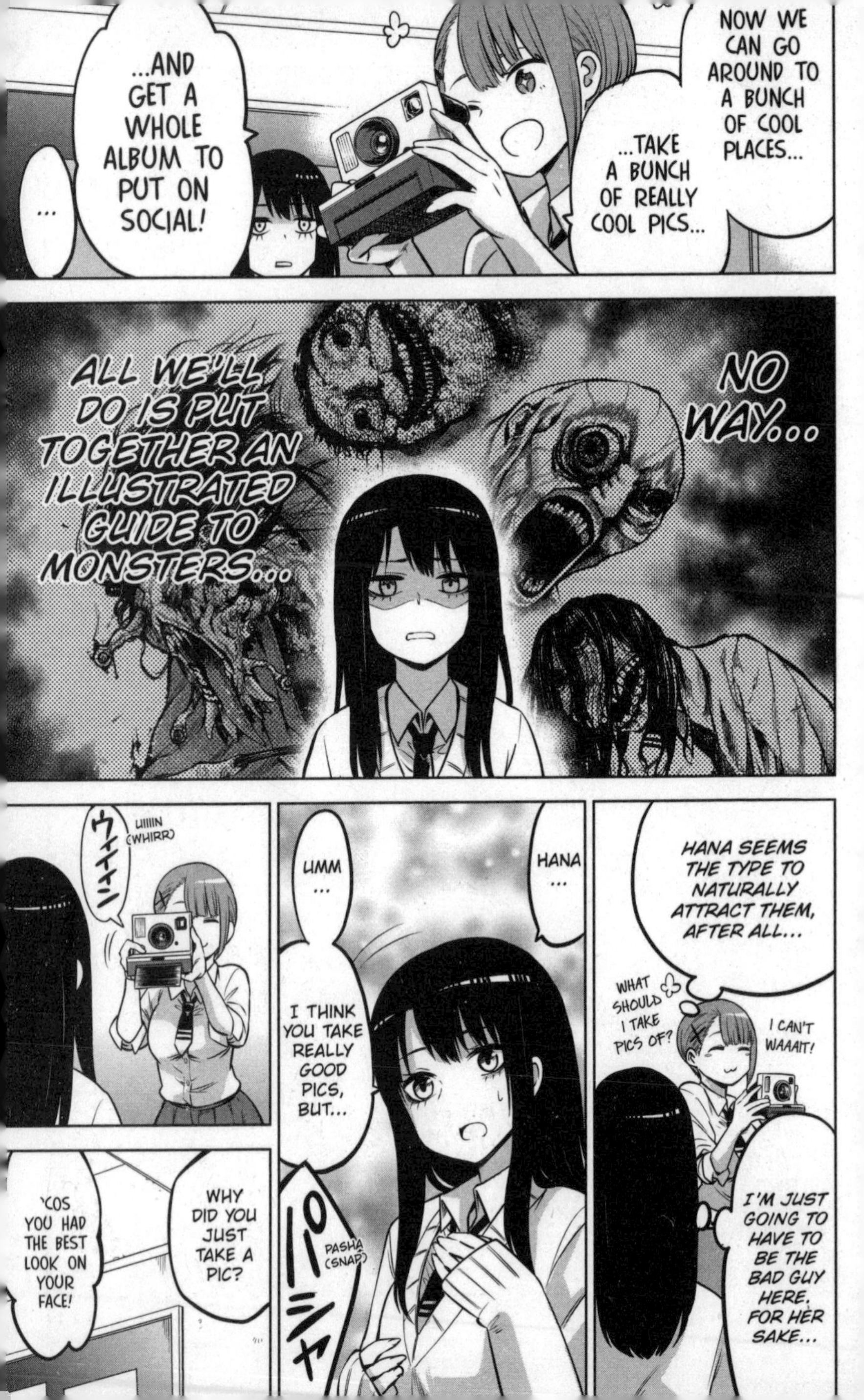
NOW WE CAN GO AROUND TO A BUNCH OF COOL PLACES...
...TAKE A BUNCH OF REALLY COOL PICS...
...AND GET A WHOLE ALBUM TO PUT ON SOCIAL!
...
NO WAY...
ALL WE'LL DO IS PUT TOGETHER AN ILLUSTRATED GUIDE TO MONSTERS...
HANA SEEMS THE TYPE TO NATURALLY ATTRACT THEM, AFTER ALL...
I CAN'T WAAAIT!
WHAT SHOULD I TAKE PICS OF?
I'M JUST GOING TO HAVE TO BE THE BAD GUY HERE, FOR HER SAKE...
HANA ...
UMM ...
I THINK YOU TAKE REALLY GOOD PICS, BUT...
パシャ
PASHA (SNAP)
ウィイン
UIIIIN (WHIRR)
WHY DID YOU JUST TAKE A PIC?
'COS YOU HAD THE BEST LOOK ON YOUR FACE!

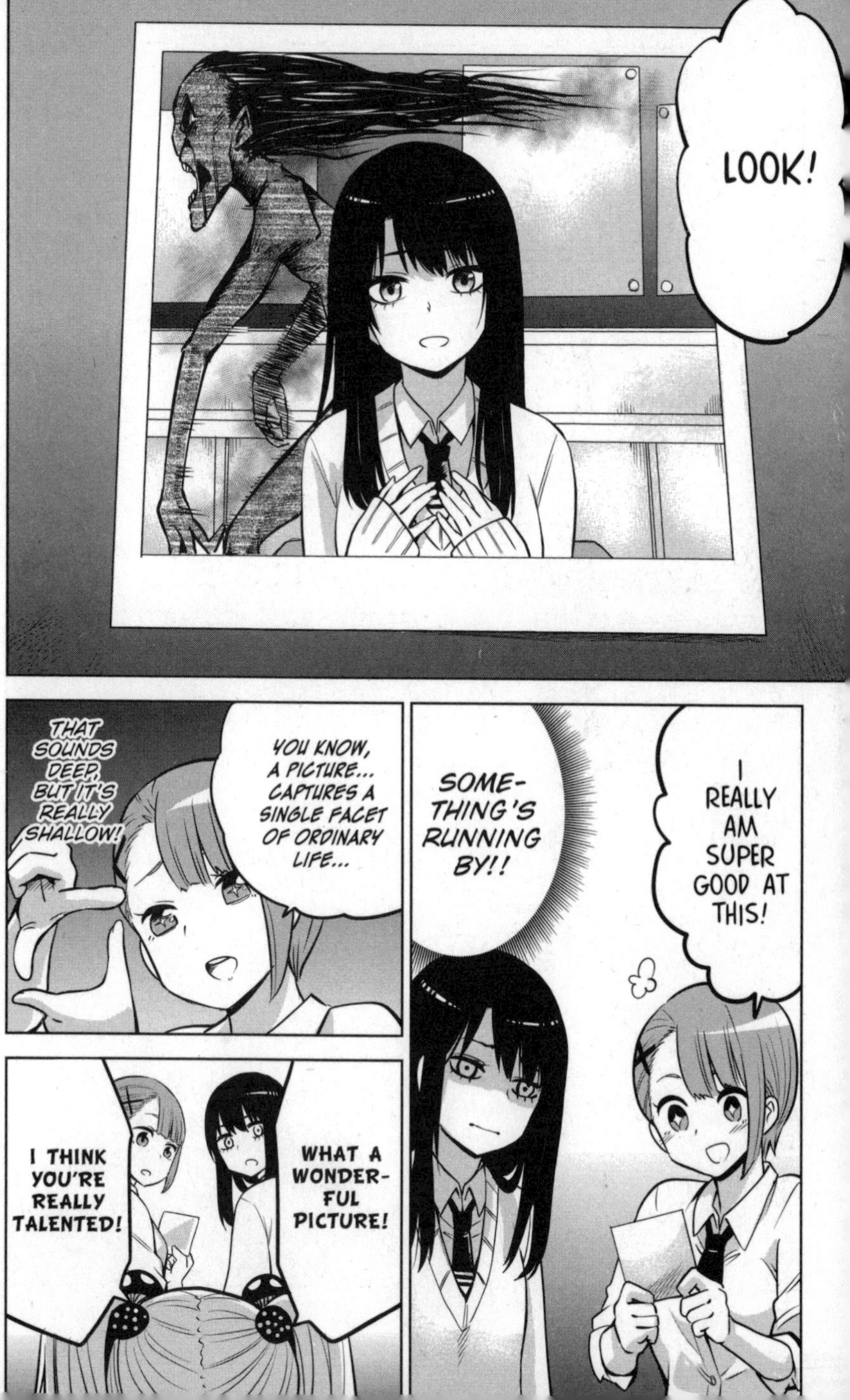
LOOK!
I REALLY AM SUPER GOOD AT THIS!
SOME-THING'S RUNNING BY!!
YOU KNOW, A PICTURE... CAPTURES A SINGLE FACET OF ORDINARY LIFE...
THAT SOUNDS DEEP, BUT IT'S REALLY SHALLOW!
WHAT A WONDER-FUL PICTURE!
I THINK YOU'RE REALLY TALENTED!

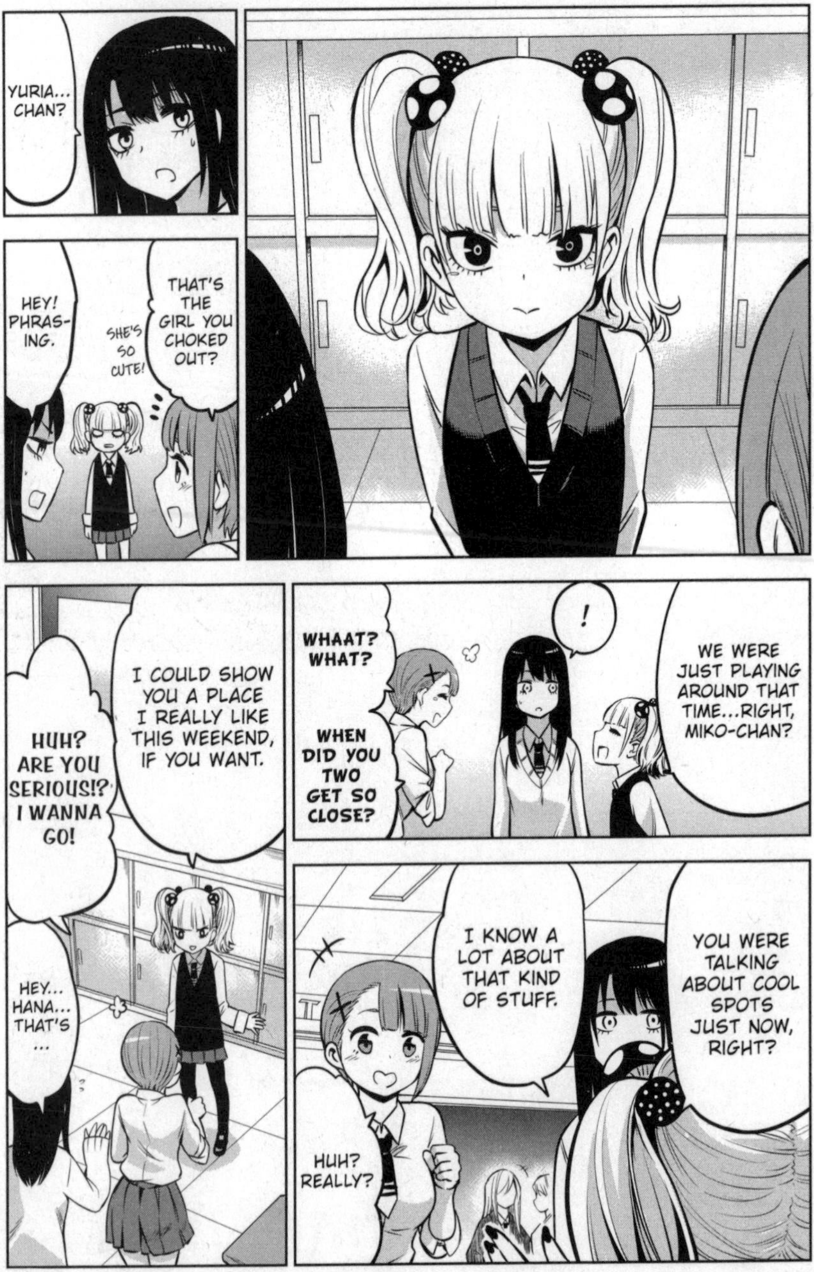
YURIA... CHAN?
THAT'S THE GIRL YOU CHOKED OUT?
SHE'S SO CUTE!
HEY! PHRASING.
WE WERE JUST PLAYING AROUND THAT TIME...RIGHT, MIKO-CHAN?
!
WHAAT? WHAT?
WHEN DID YOU TWO GET SO CLOSE?
YOU WERE TALKING ABOUT COOL SPOTS JUST NOW, RIGHT?
I KNOW A LOT ABOUT THAT KIND OF STUFF.
HUH? REALLY?
I COULD SHOW YOU A PLACE I REALLY LIKE THIS WEEKEND, IF YOU WANT.
HUH? ARE YOU SERIOUS!? I WANNA GO!
HEY... HANA... THAT'S ...

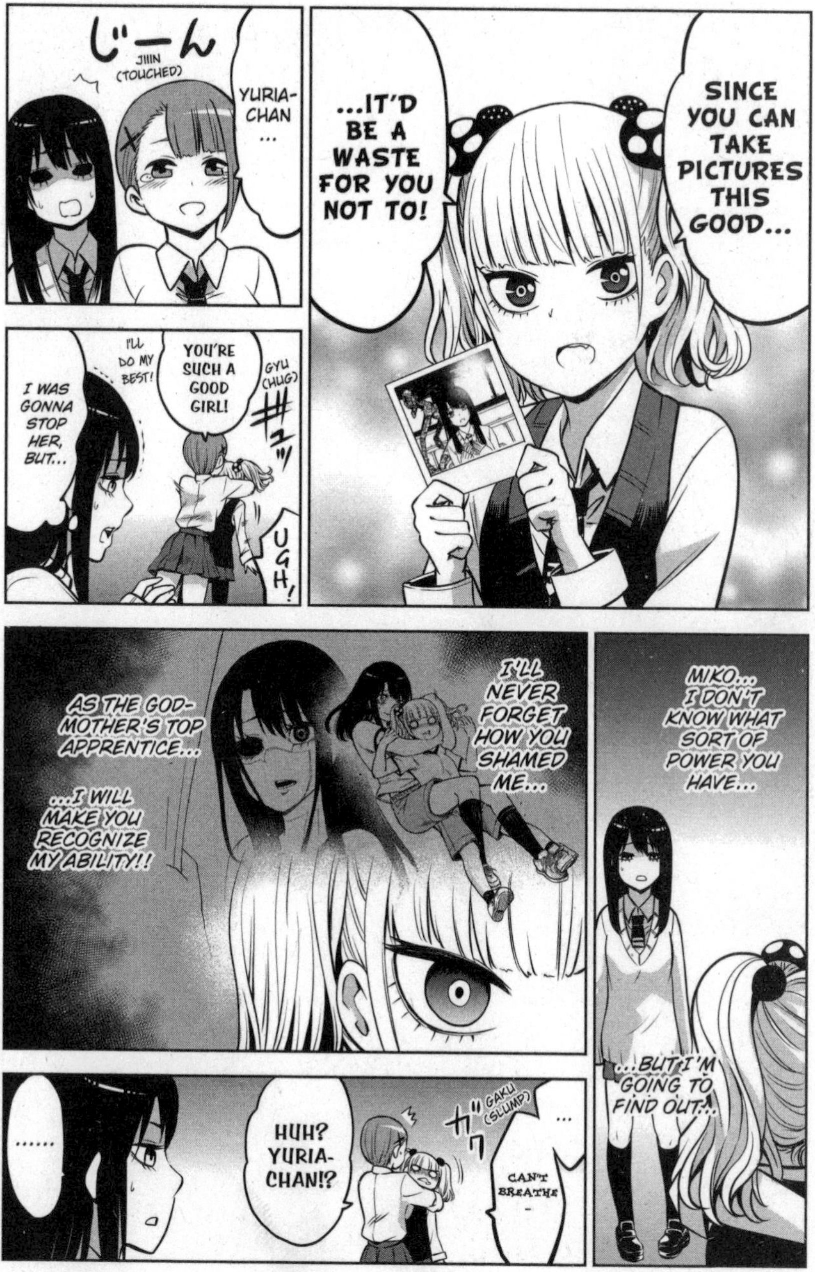
SINCE YOU CAN TAKE PICTURES THIS GOOD...
...IT'D BE A WASTE FOR YOU NOT TO!
じーん
JIIIN (TOUCHED)
YURIA-CHAN ...
GYU (HUG)
YOU'RE SUCH A GOOD GIRL!
I'LL DO MY BEST!
UGH!
I WAS GONNA STOP HER, BUT...
MIKO... I DON'T KNOW WHAT SORT OF POWER YOU HAVE...
...BUT I'M GOING TO FIND OUT...
I'LL NEVER FORGET HOW YOU SHAMED ME...
AS THE GOD-MOTHER'S TOP APPRENTICE...
...I WILL MAKE YOU RECOGNIZE MY ABILITY!!
...
CAN'T BREATHE ...
GAKU (SLUMP)
HUH? YURIA-CHAN!?
......

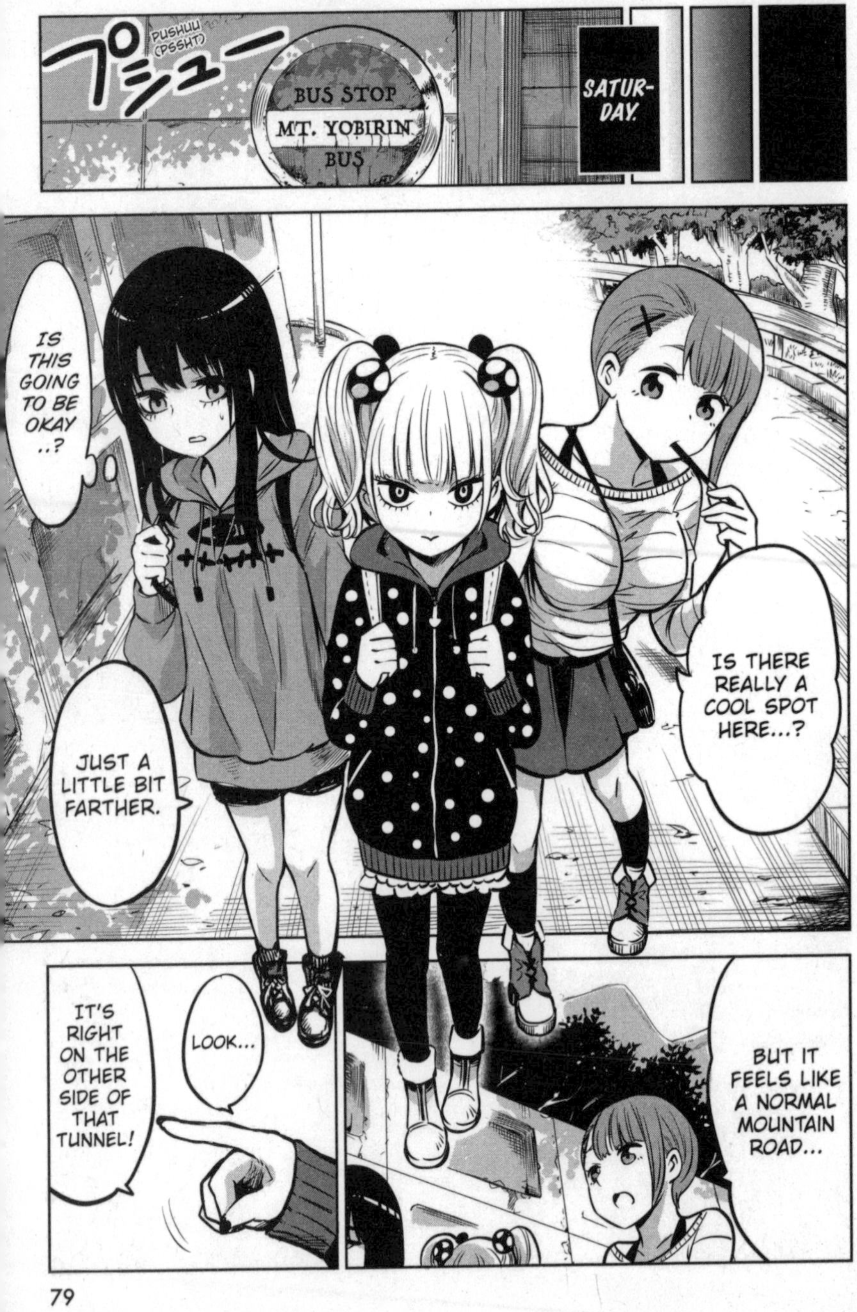
SATUR-DAY.
BUS STOP
MT. YOBIRIN
BUS
プシュー
PUSHUU (PSSHT)
IS THIS GOING TO BE OKAY ..?
IS THERE REALLY A COOL SPOT HERE...?
JUST A LITTLE BIT FARTHER.
BUT IT FEELS LIKE A NORMAL MOUNTAIN ROAD...
LOOK...
IT'S RIGHT ON THE OTHER SIDE OF THAT TUNNEL!

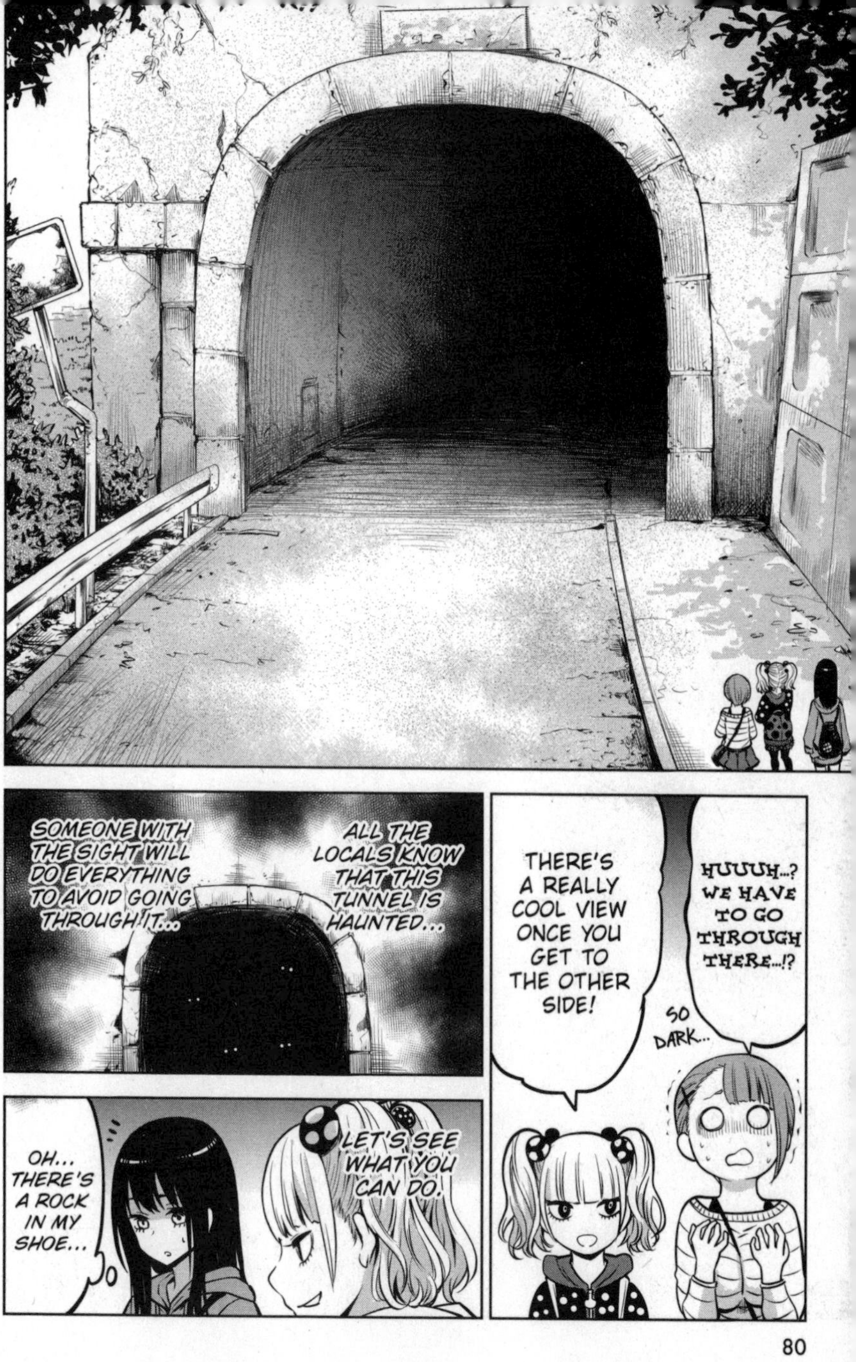
HUUUH...? WE HAVE TO GO THROUGH THERE...!?
SO DARK...
THERE'S A REALLY COOL VIEW ONCE YOU GET TO THE OTHER SIDE!
ALL THE LOCALS KNOW THAT THIS TUNNEL IS HAUNTED...
SOMEONE WITH THE SIGHT WILL DO EVERYTHING TO AVOID GOING THROUGH IT...
LET'S SEE WHAT YOU CAN DO.
OH... THERE'S A ROCK IN MY SHOE...

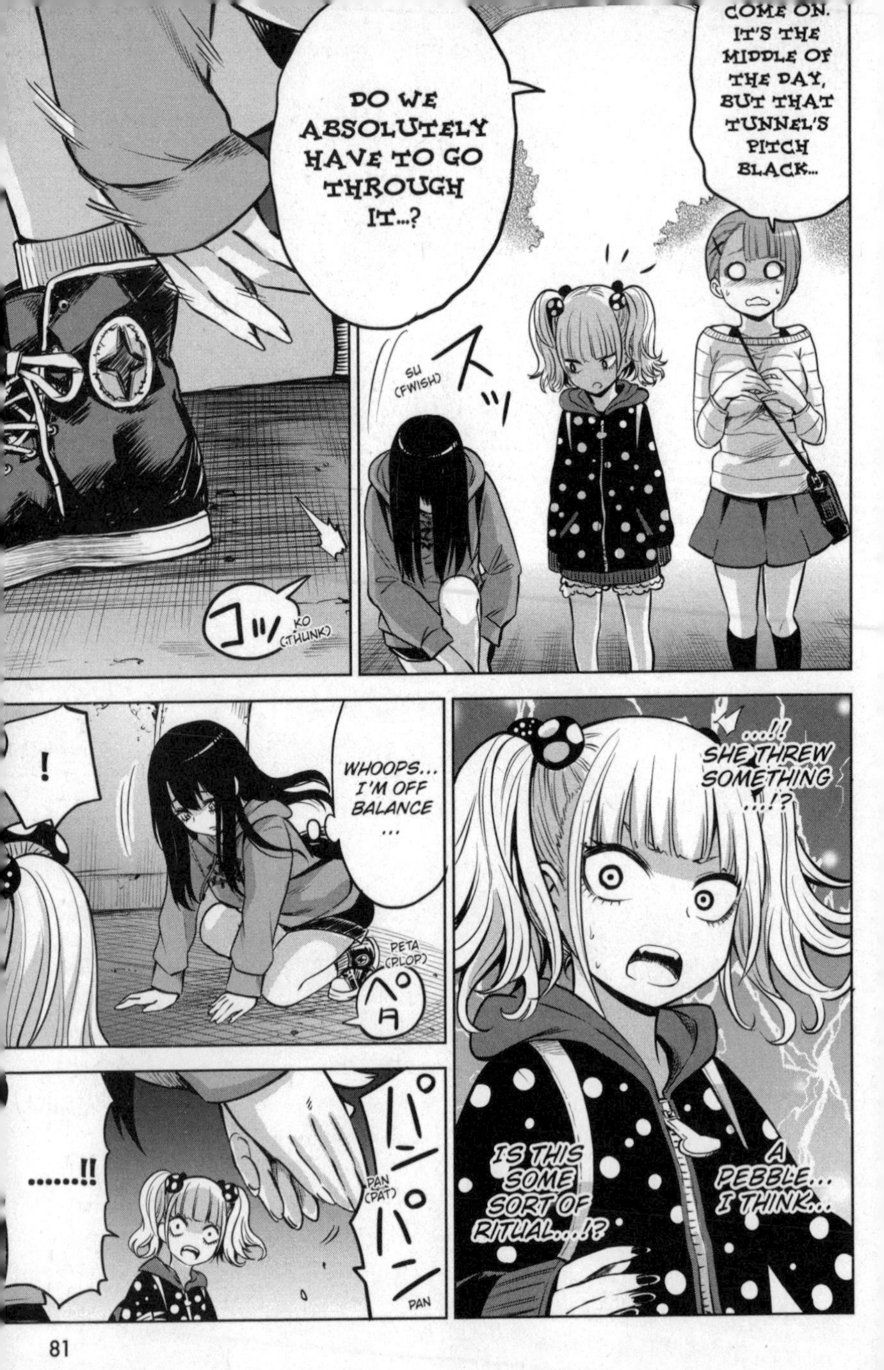
COME ON. IT'S THE MIDDLE OF THE DAY, BUT THAT TUNNEL'S PITCH BLACK...
DO WE ABSOLUTELY HAVE TO GO THROUGH IT...?
SU (FWISH)
KO (THUNK)
...!! SHE THREW SOMETHING ...!?
A PEBBLE... I THINK...
IS THIS SOME SORT OF RITUAL...!?
!
WHOOPS... I'M OFF BALANCE ...
PETA (PLOP)
PAN (PAT)
PAN
.......!!

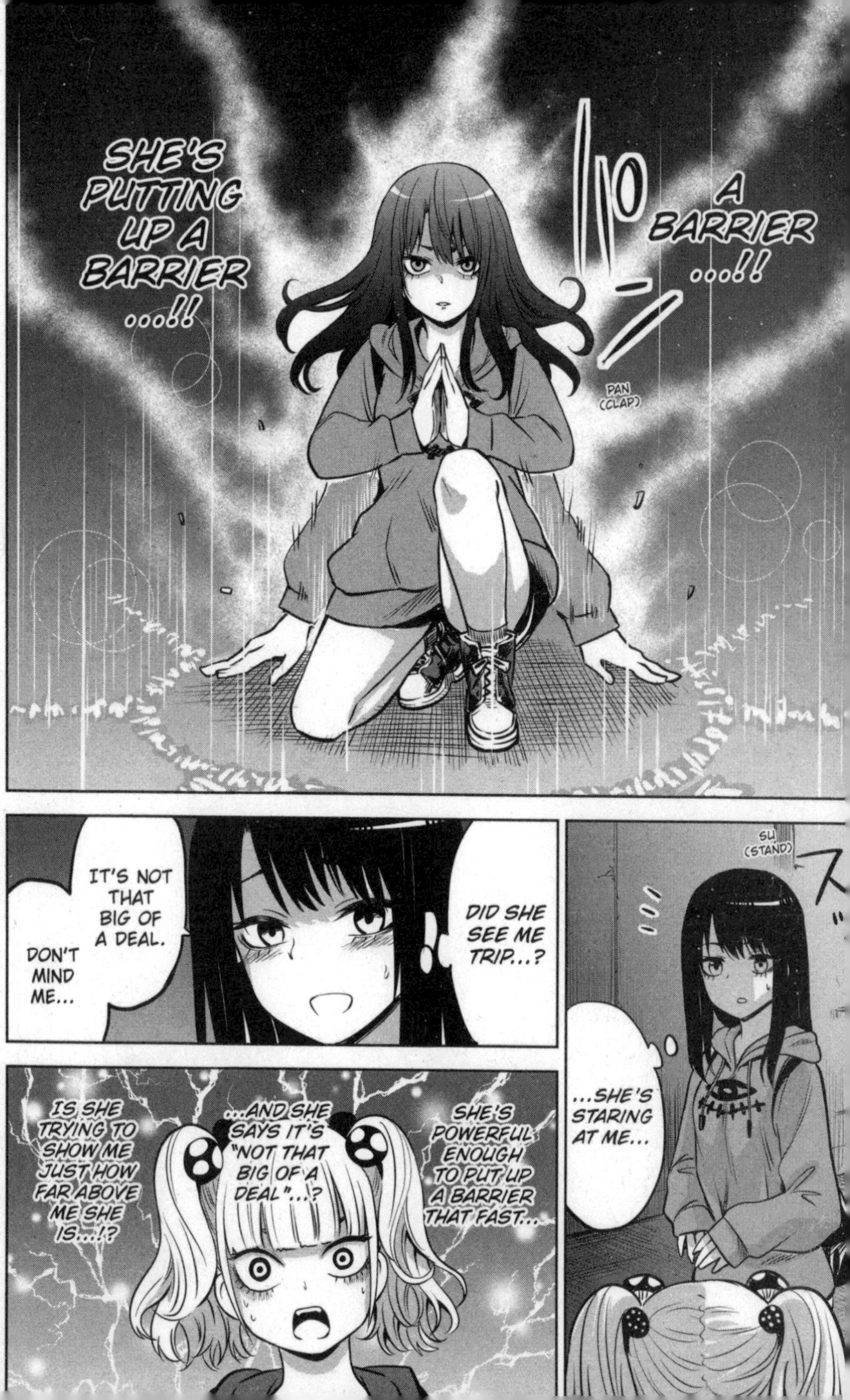
A BARRIER ...!!
PAN (CLAP)
SHE'S PUTTING UP A BARRIER ...!!
SU (STAND)
DID SHE SEE ME TRIP...?
IT'S NOT THAT BIG OF A DEAL.
DON'T MIND ME...
...SHE'S STARING AT ME...
SHE'S POWERFUL ENOUGH TO PUT UP A BARRIER THAT FAST...
...AND SHE SAYS IT'S "NOT THAT BIG OF A DEAL"...?
IS SHE TRYING TO SHOW ME JUST HOW FAR ABOVE ME SHE IS...!?

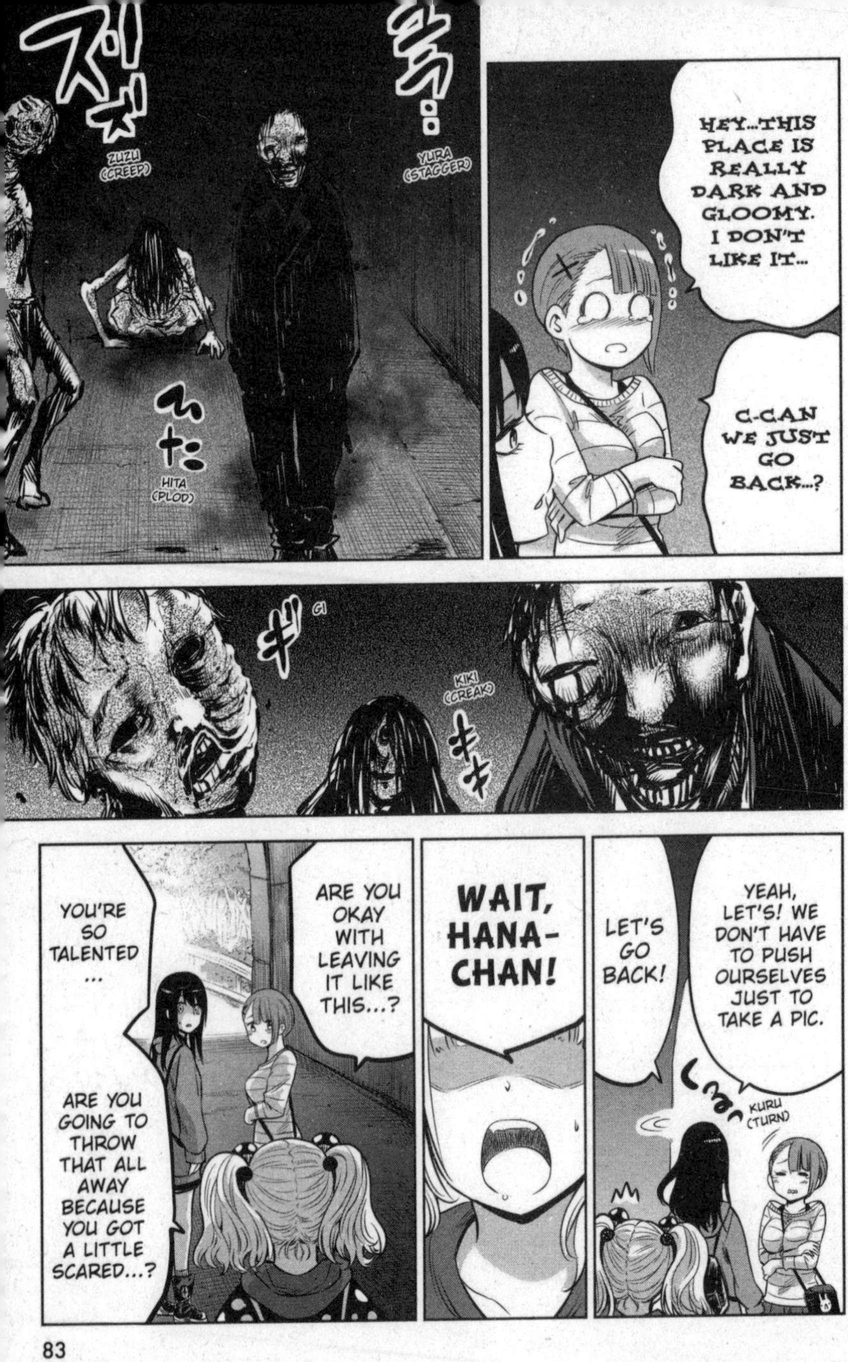
HEY...THIS PLACE IS REALLY DARK AND GLOOMY. I DON'T LIKE IT...
C-CAN WE JUST GO BACK...?
YURA (STAGGER)
ZUZU (CREEP)
HITA (PLOD)
GI
KIKI (CREAK)
YEAH, LET'S! WE DON'T HAVE TO PUSH OURSELVES JUST TO TAKE A PIC.
LET'S GO BACK!
KURU (TURN)
WAIT, HANA-CHAN!
ARE YOU OKAY WITH LEAVING IT LIKE THIS...?
YOU'RE SO TALENTED...
ARE YOU GOING TO THROW THAT ALL AWAY BECAUSE YOU GOT A LITTLE SCARED...?

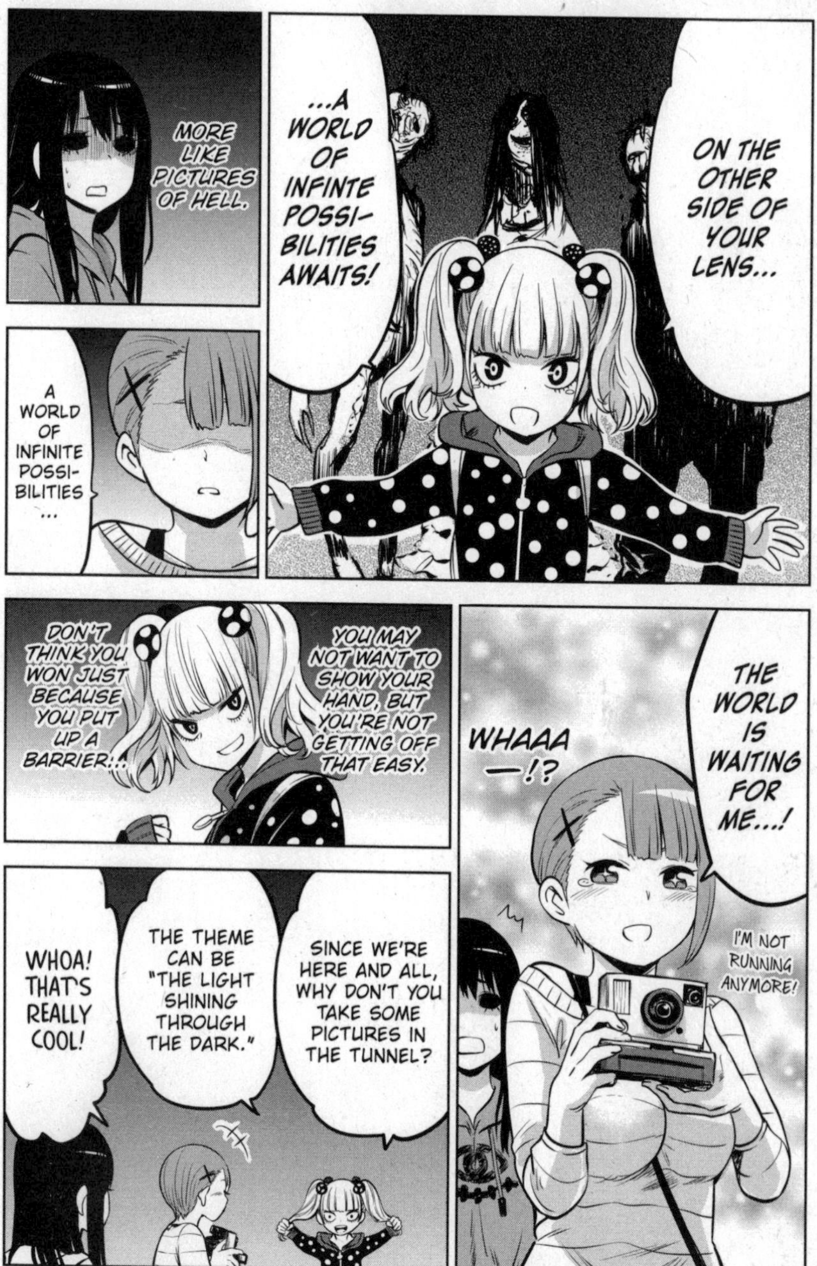
ON THE OTHER SIDE OF YOUR LENS...
...A WORLD OF INFINTE POSSIBILITIES AWAITS!
MORE LIKE PICTURES OF HELL.
A WORLD OF INFINITE POSSIBILITIES...
THE WORLD IS WAITING FOR ME...!
WHAAA—!?
I'M NOT RUNNING ANYMORE!
YOU MAY NOT WANT TO SHOW YOUR HAND, BUT YOU'RE NOT GETTING OFF THAT EASY.
DON'T THINK YOU WON JUST BECAUSE YOU PUT UP A BARRIER...
SINCE WE'RE HERE AND ALL, WHY DON'T YOU TAKE SOME PICTURES IN THE TUNNEL?
THE THEME CAN BE "THE LIGHT SHINING THROUGH THE DARK."
WHOA! THAT'S REALLY COOL!

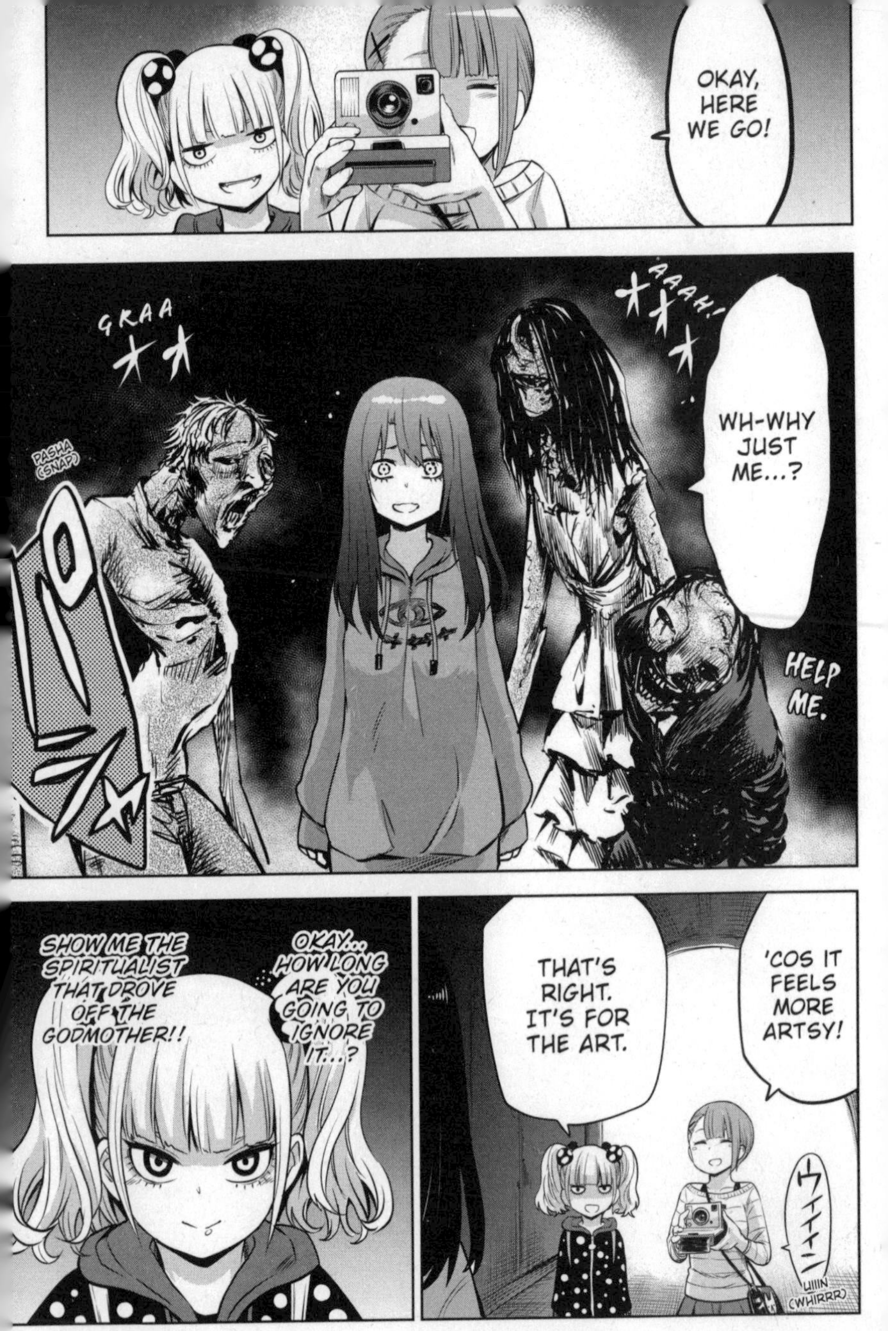
OKAY, HERE WE GO!
AAAAH!
WH-WHY JUST ME...?
HELP ME.
GRAA
PASHA (SNAP)
'COS IT FEELS MORE ARTSY!
THAT'S RIGHT. IT'S FOR THE ART.
UIIIN (WHIRRR)
OKAY... HOW LONG ARE YOU GOING TO IGNORE IT...?
SHOW ME THE SPIRITUALIST THAT DROVE OFF THE GODMOTHER!!

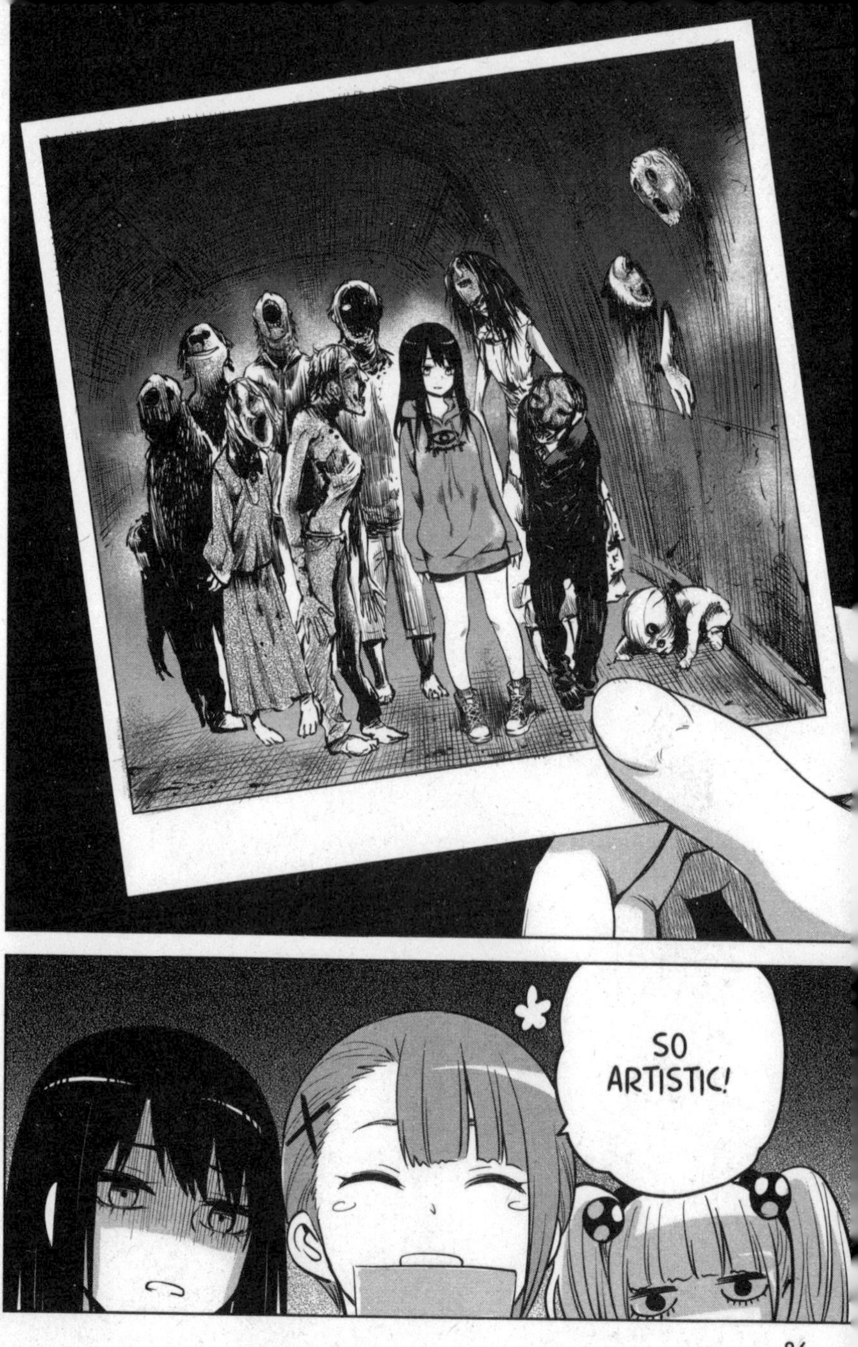
SO ARTISTIC!

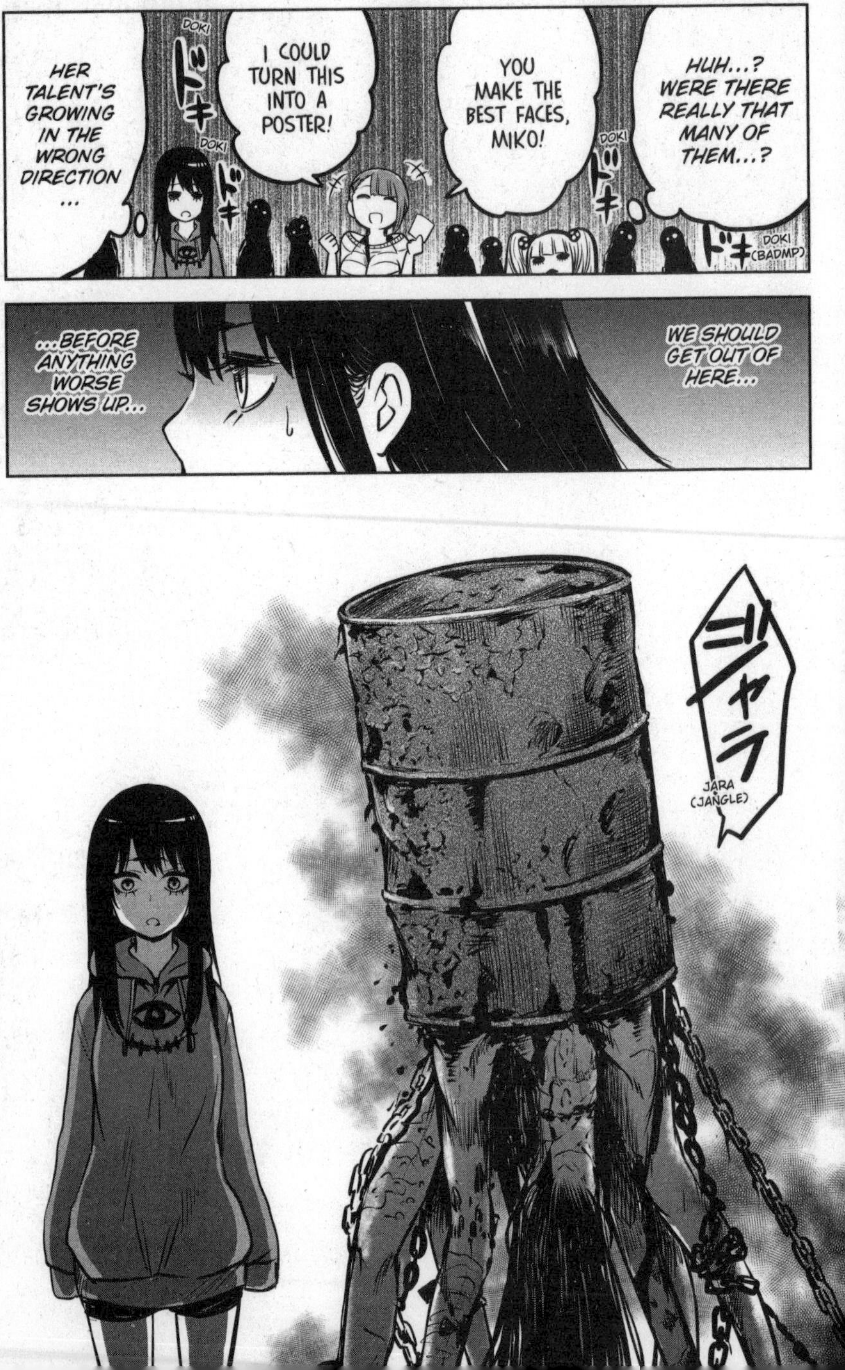
HUH...? WERE THERE REALLY THAT MANY OF THEM...?
ドキ DOKI (BADMP)
ドキ DOKI
YOU MAKE THE BEST FACES, MIKO!
I COULD TURN THIS INTO A POSTER!
ドキ DOKI
ドキ DOKI
HER TALENT'S GROWING IN THE WRONG DIRECTION ...
WE SHOULD GET OUT OF HERE...
...BEFORE ANYTHING WORSE SHOWS UP...
ジャラ JARA (JANGLE)

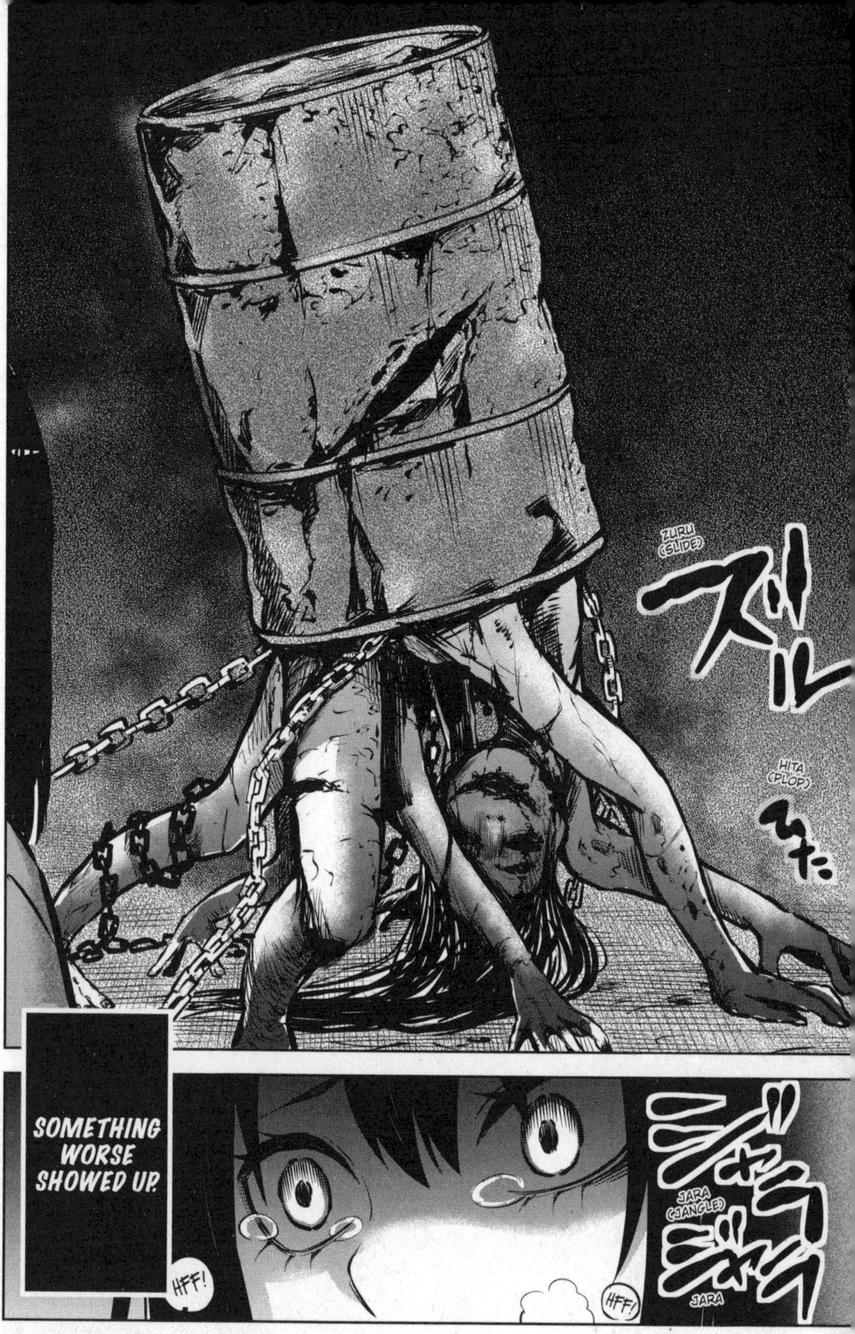
ZURU (SLIDE)
HITA (PLOP)
JARA (JANGLE)
JARA
HFF!
HFF!
SOMETHING WORSE SHOWED UP.

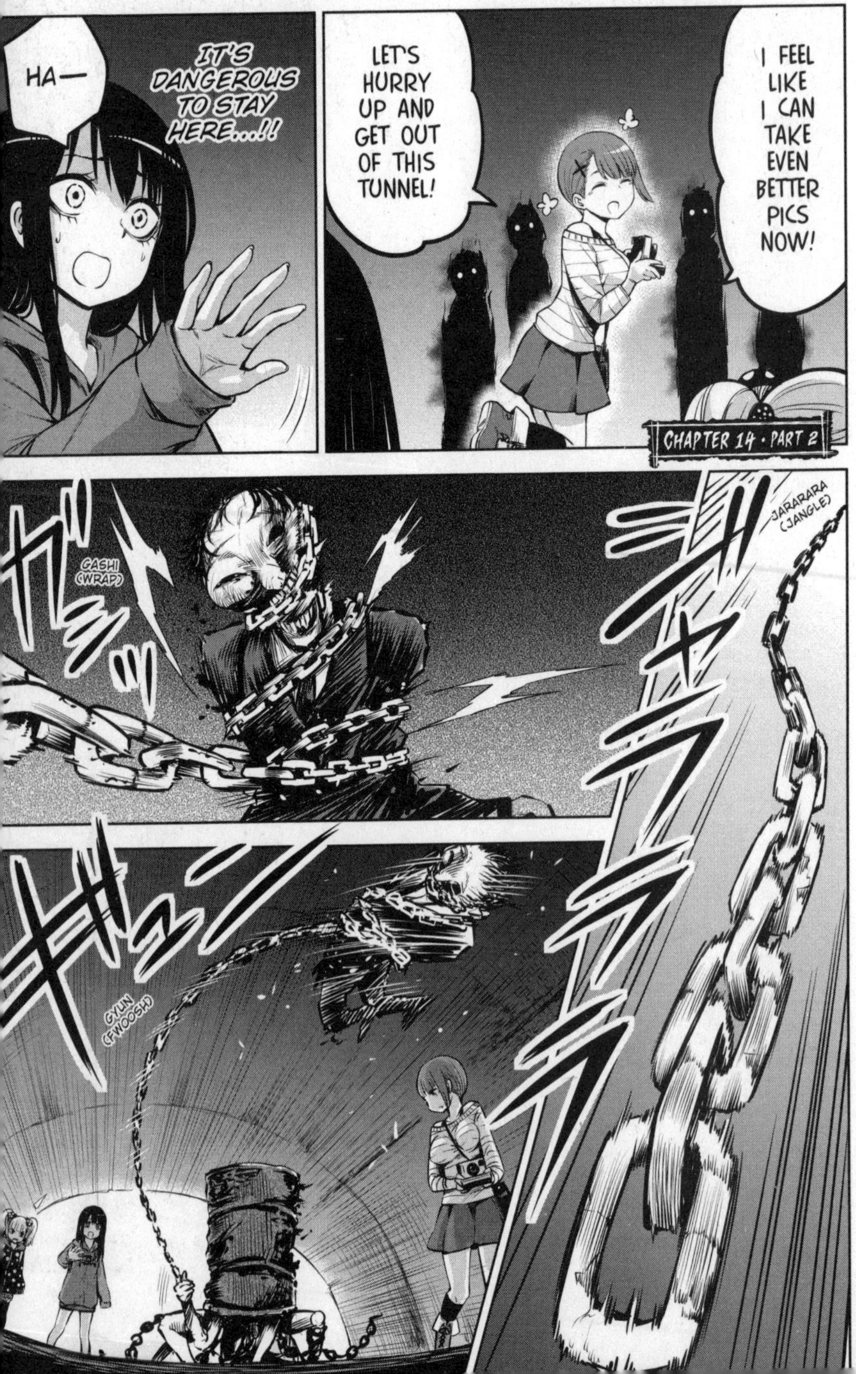
I FEEL LIKE I CAN TAKE EVEN BETTER PICS NOW!
LET'S HURRY UP AND GET OUT OF THIS TUNNEL!
CHAPTER 14 • PART 2
HA—
IT'S DANGEROUS TO STAY HERE...!!
JARARARA (JANGLE)
GASHI (WRAP)
GYUN (FWOOSH)

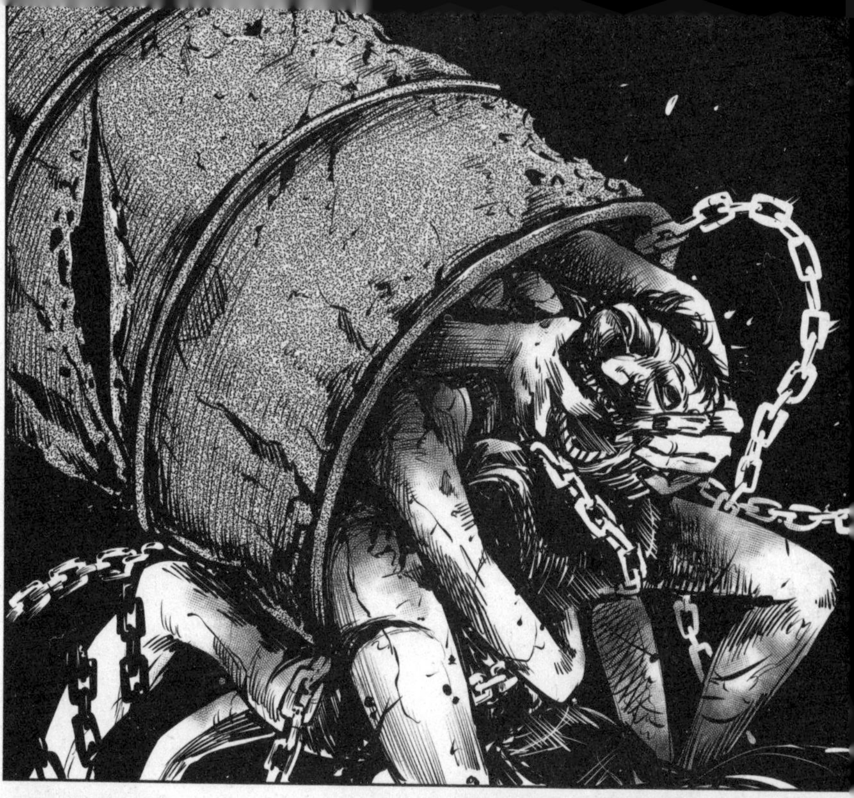

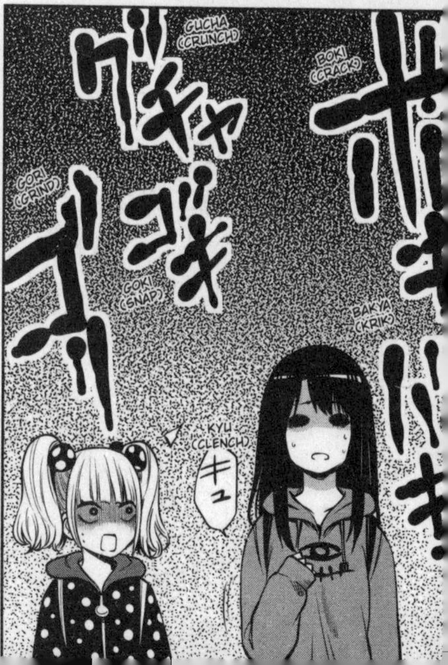

BOKI (CRACK)
BAKYA (KRIK)
GUCHA (CRUNCH)
GOKI (SNAP)
GORI (GRIND)
KYU (CLENCH)
キュ

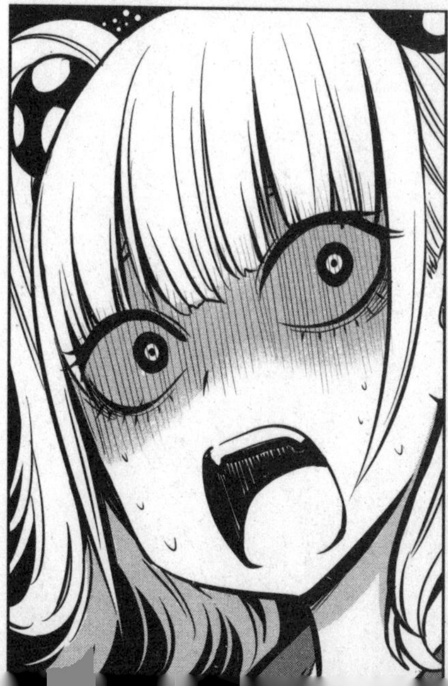

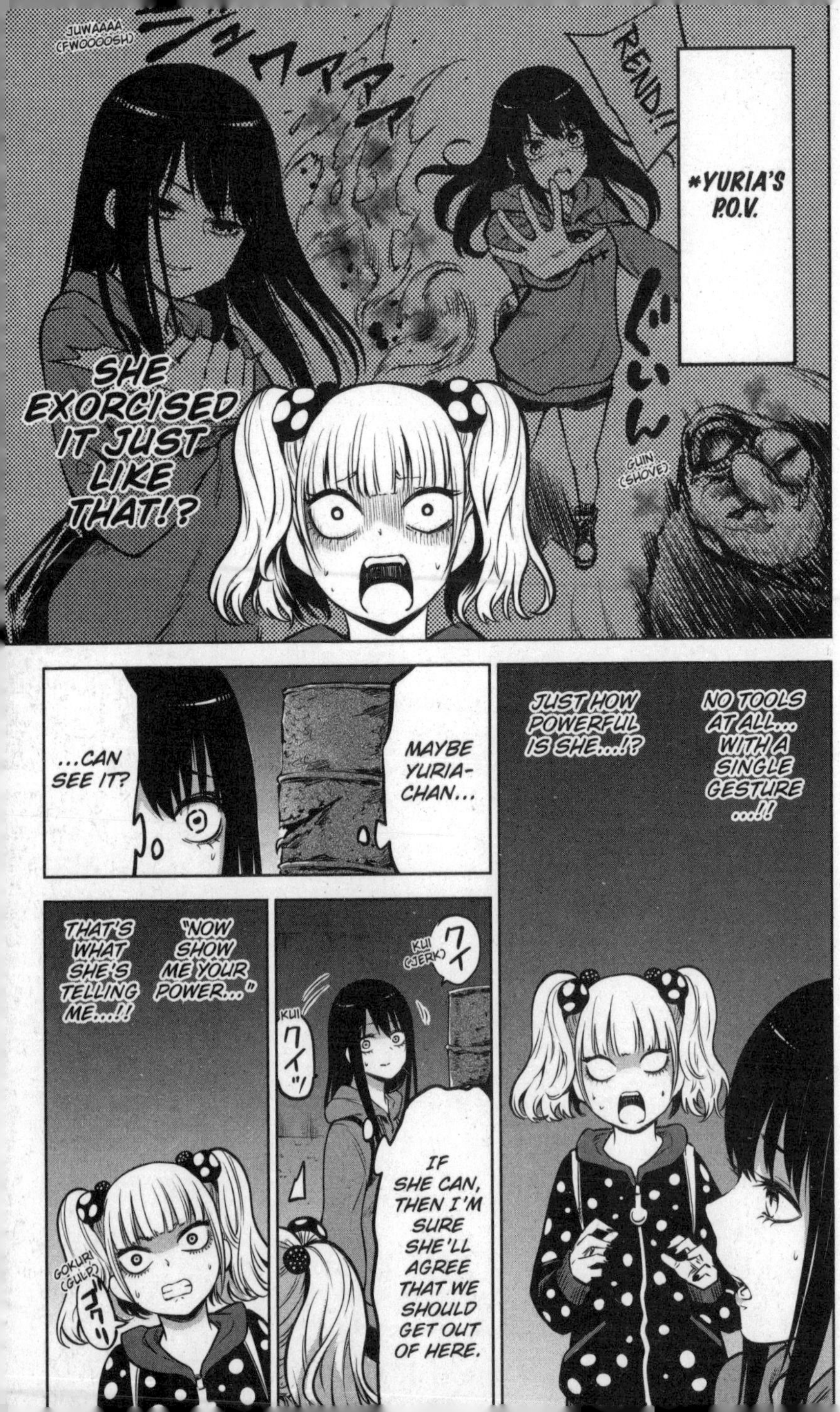

REND!!
#YURIA'S P.O.V.
JUWAAAA (FWOOOOSH)
GUIN (SHOVE)
SHE EXORCISED IT JUST LIKE THAT!?
NO TOOLS AT ALL... WITH A SINGLE GESTURE ...!!
JUST HOW POWERFUL IS SHE...!?
MAYBE YURIA-CHAN...
...CAN SEE IT?
KUI (JERK)
KUI
IF SHE CAN, THEN I'M SURE SHE'LL AGREE THAT WE SHOULD GET OUT OF HERE.
"NOW SHOW ME YOUR POWER..."
THAT'S WHAT SHE'S TELLING ME...!!
GOKURI (GULP)

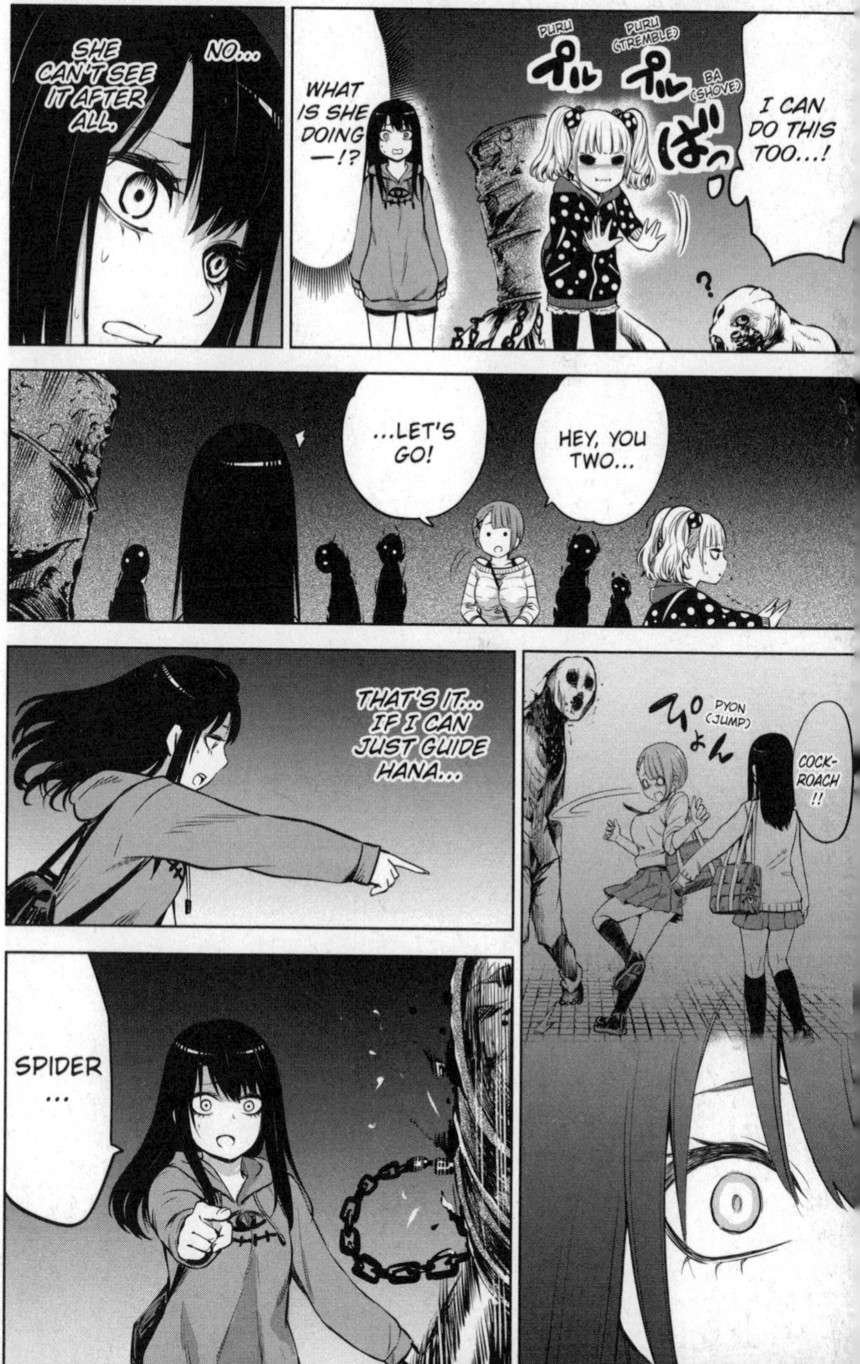
I CAN DO THIS TOO...!
PURU PURU (TREMBLE)
BA (SHOVE)
WHAT IS SHE DOING—!?
NO...
SHE CAN'T SEE IT AFTER ALL.
HEY, YOU TWO...
...LET'S GO!
COCK-ROACH!!
PYON (JUMP)
THAT'S IT... IF I CAN JUST GUIDE HANA...
SPIDER...

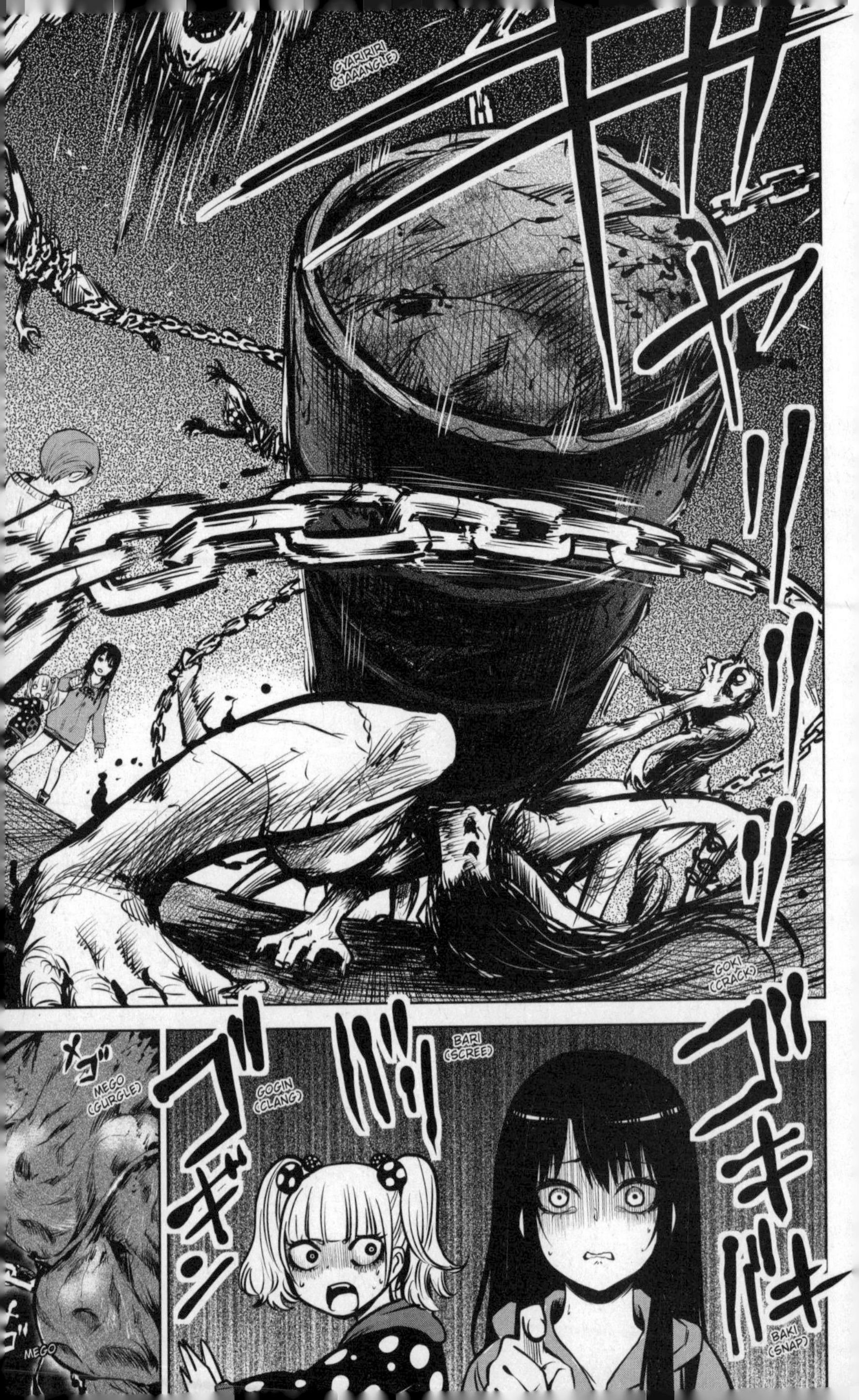
GYARIRIRI (JAAANGLE)
GOKI (CRACK)
BAKI (SNAP)
BARI (SCREE)
GOGIN (CLANG)
MEGO (GURGLE)
MEGO

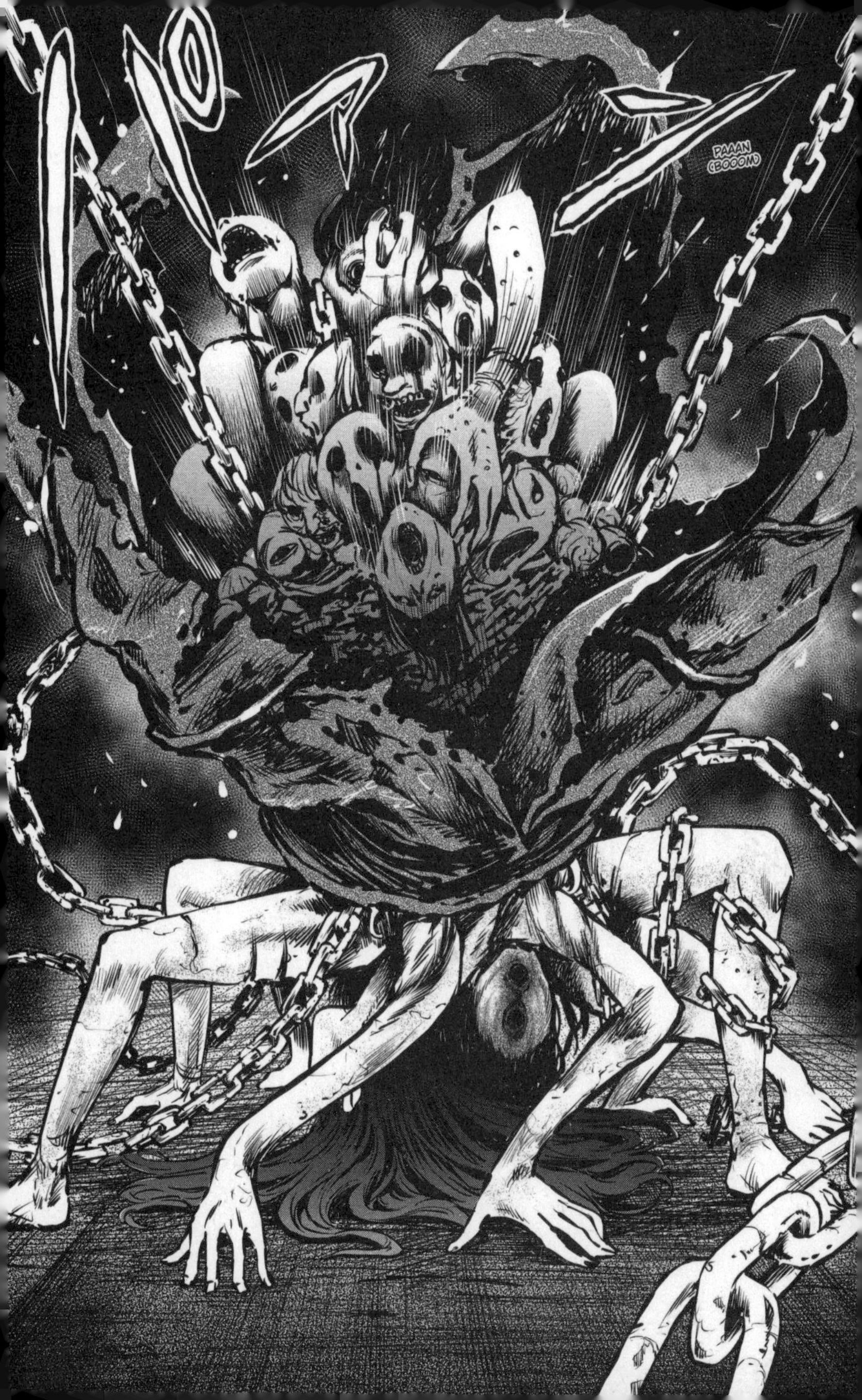
PAAAN
(BOOOM)

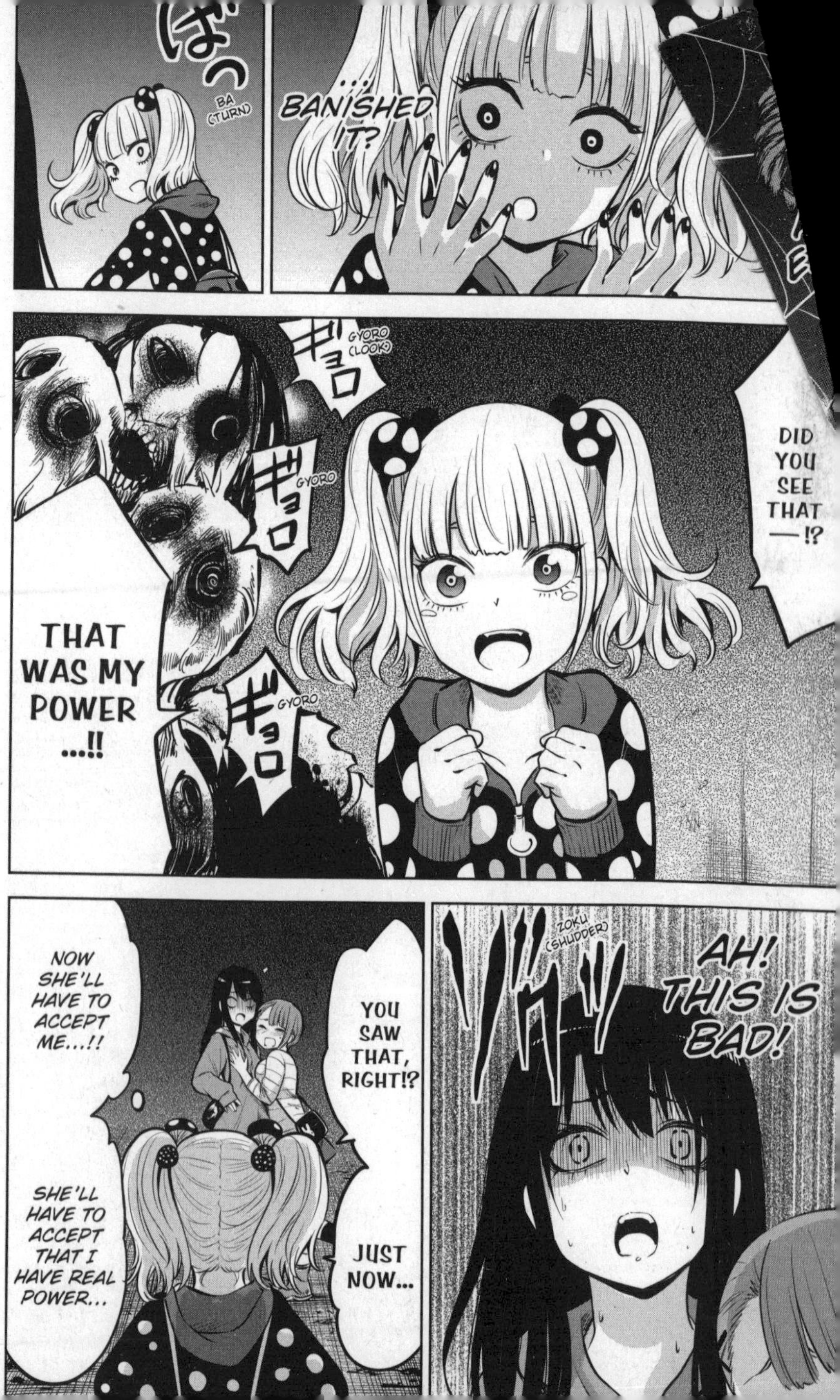
...BANISHED IT?
ぱっ
BA (TURN)
DID YOU SEE THAT—!?
ギョロ
GYORO (LOOK)
ギョロ
GYORO
ギョロ
GYORO
THAT WAS MY POWER ...!!
ZOKU (SHUDDER)
AH! THIS IS BAD!
YOU SAW THAT, RIGHT!?
NOW SHE'LL HAVE TO ACCEPT ME...!!
JUST NOW...
SHE'LL HAVE TO ACCEPT THAT I HAVE REAL POWER...

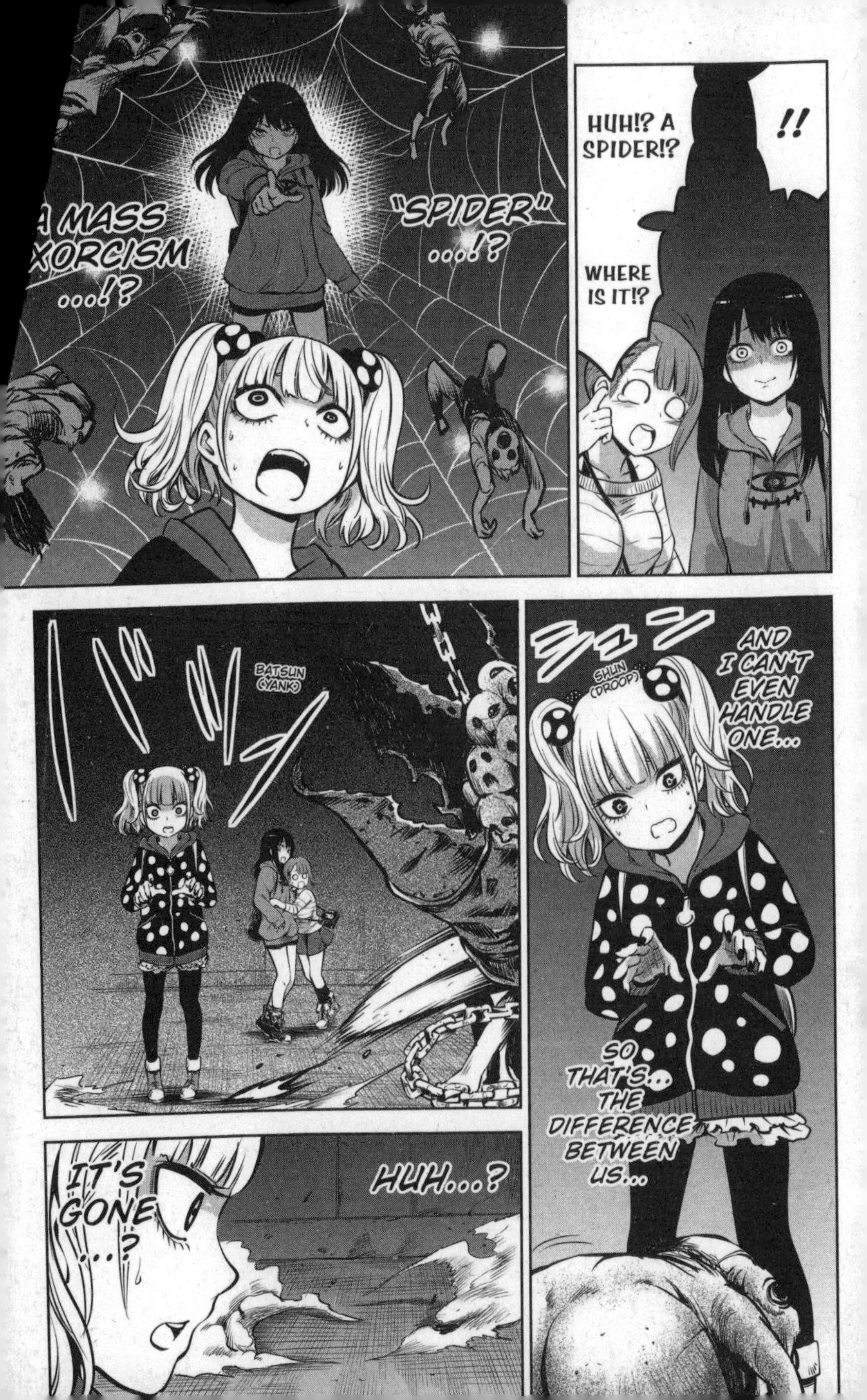

!!
HUH!? A SPIDER!?
WHERE IS IT!?
"SPIDER" ...!?
A MASS XORCISM ...!?
SHUN (DROOP)
AND I CAN'T EVEN HANDLE ONE...
SO THAT'S... THE DIFFERENCE BETWEEN US...
BATSUN (YANK)
HUH...?
IT'S GONE ...?

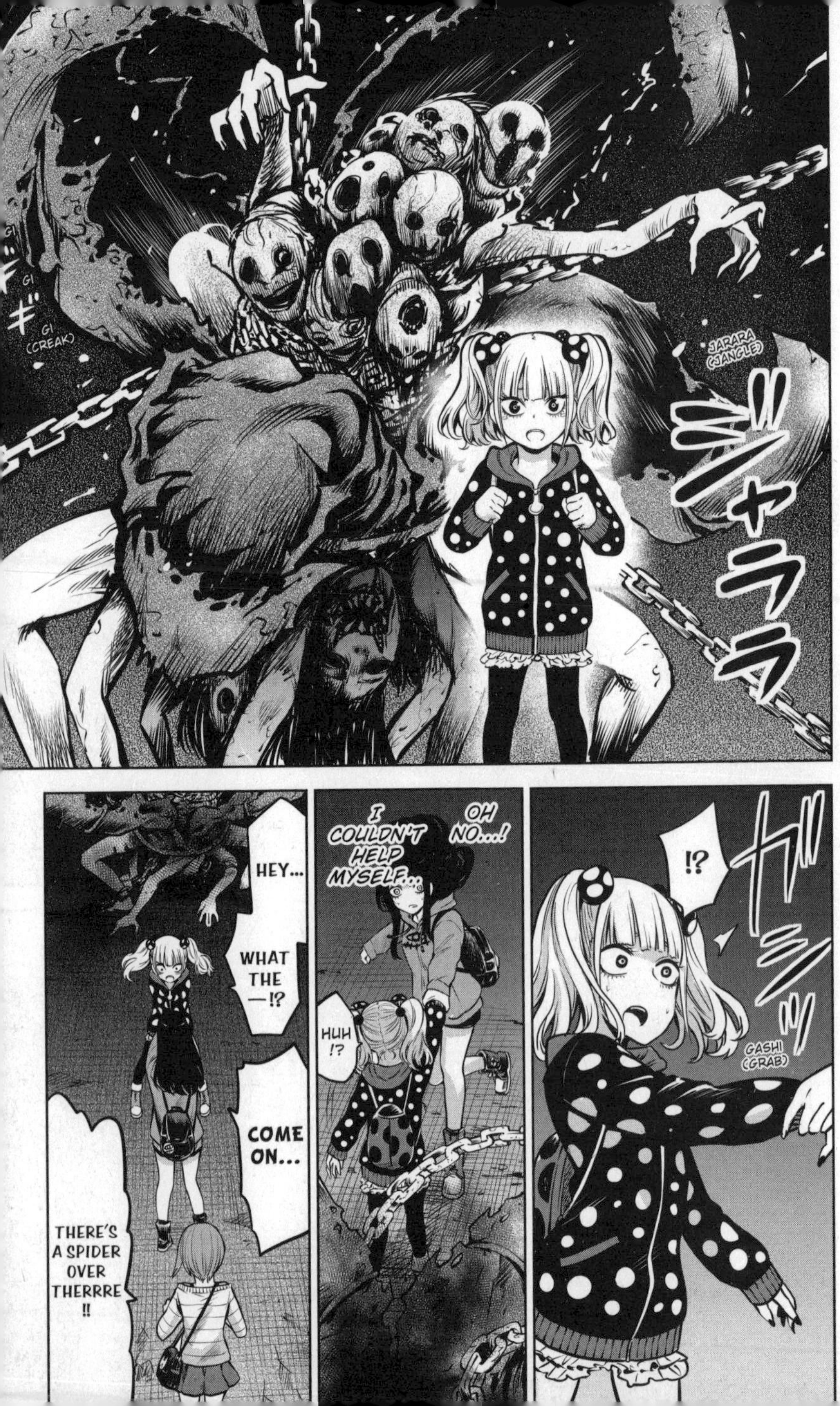
JARARA (JANGLE)
ジャララ
GI GI GI (CREAK)
ガシッ
!?
GASHI (GRAB)
OH NO...!
I COULDN'T HELP MYSELF...
HUH !?
HEY...
WHAT THE —!?
COME ON...
THERE'S A SPIDER OVER THERRRE !!

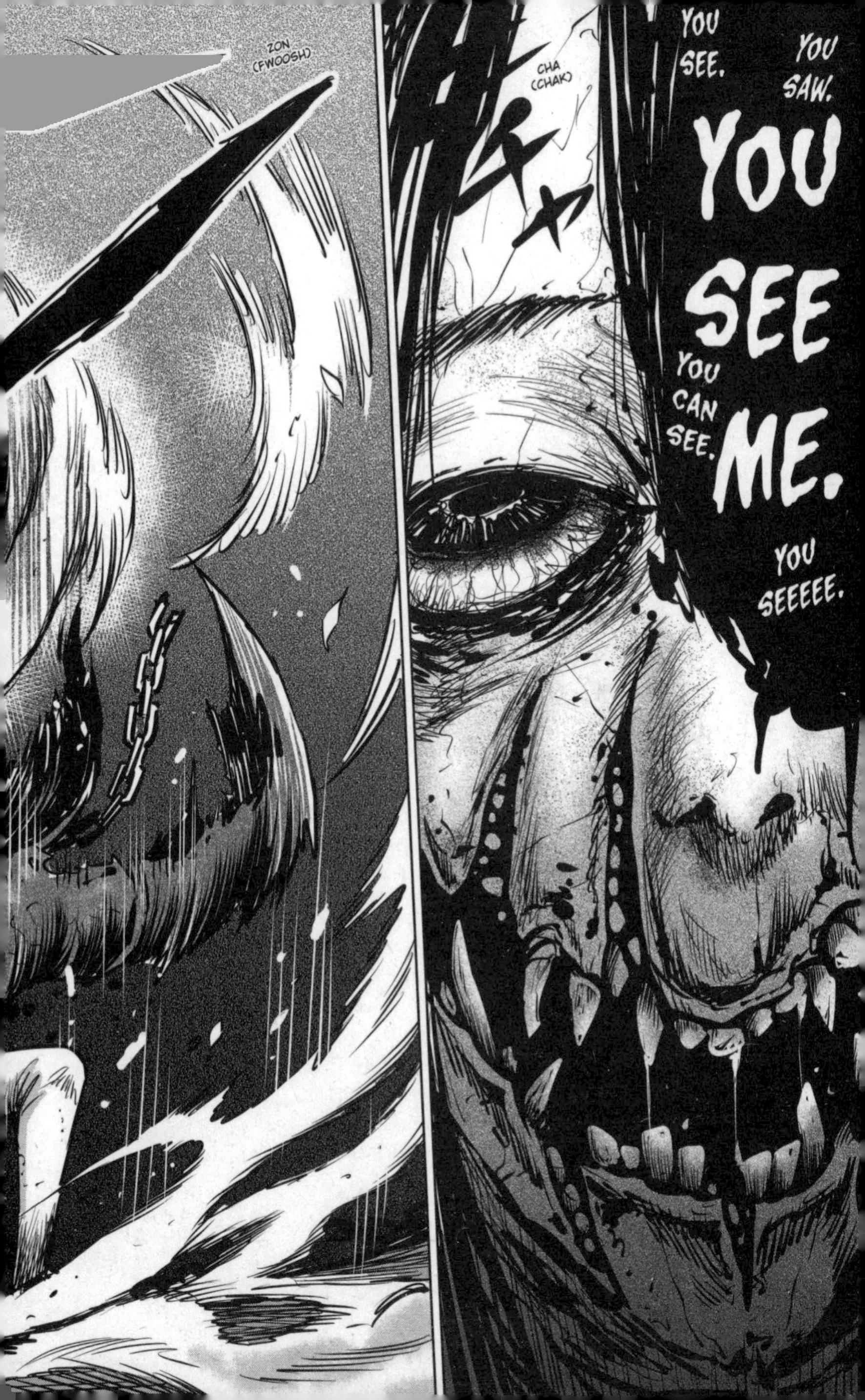
YOU SAW.
YOU SEE.
CHA (CHAK)
YOU SEE ME.
YOU CAN SEE.
YOU SEEEEE.
ZON (FWOOSH)

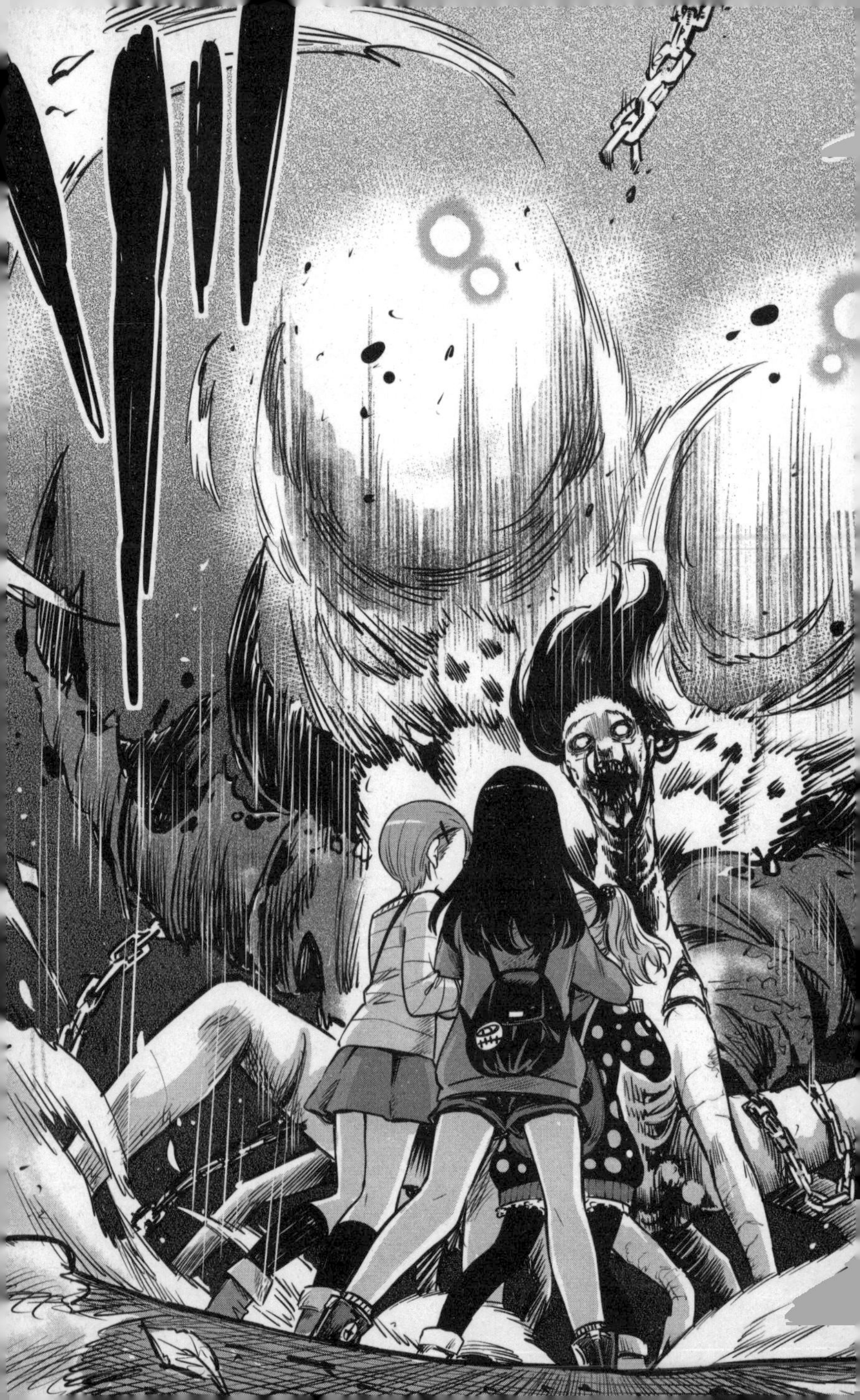

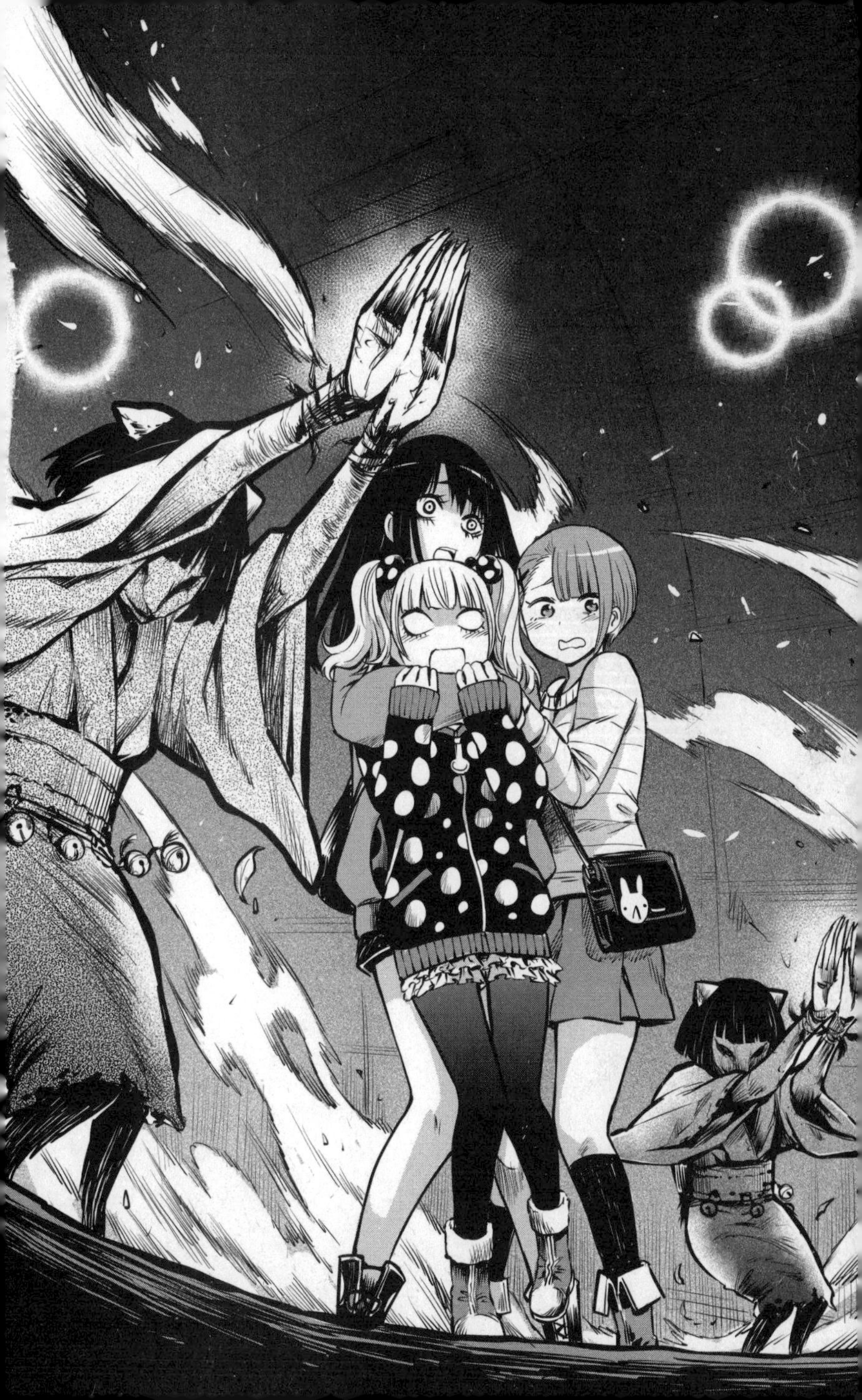

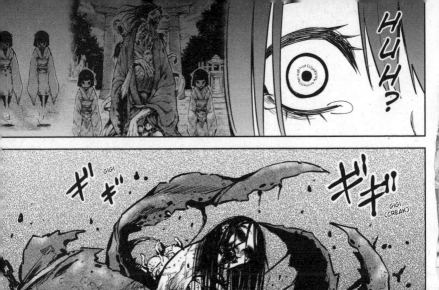

HUH?

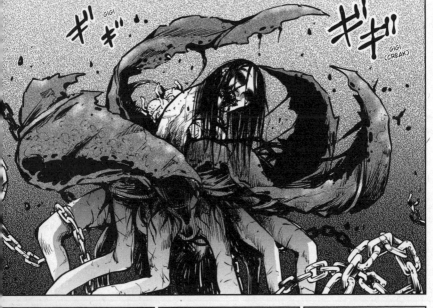

ギ GIGI
ギ
ギギ GIGI (CREAK)

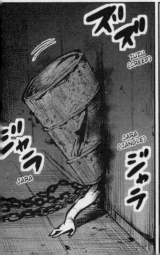

ズズ ZUZU (CREEP)

ジャラ JARA

ジャラ JARA (JANGLE)

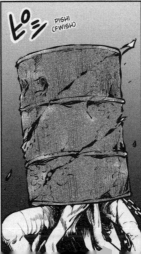

ピシ PISHI (FWISH)

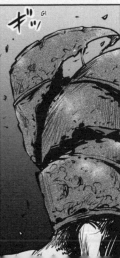

ギッ GI

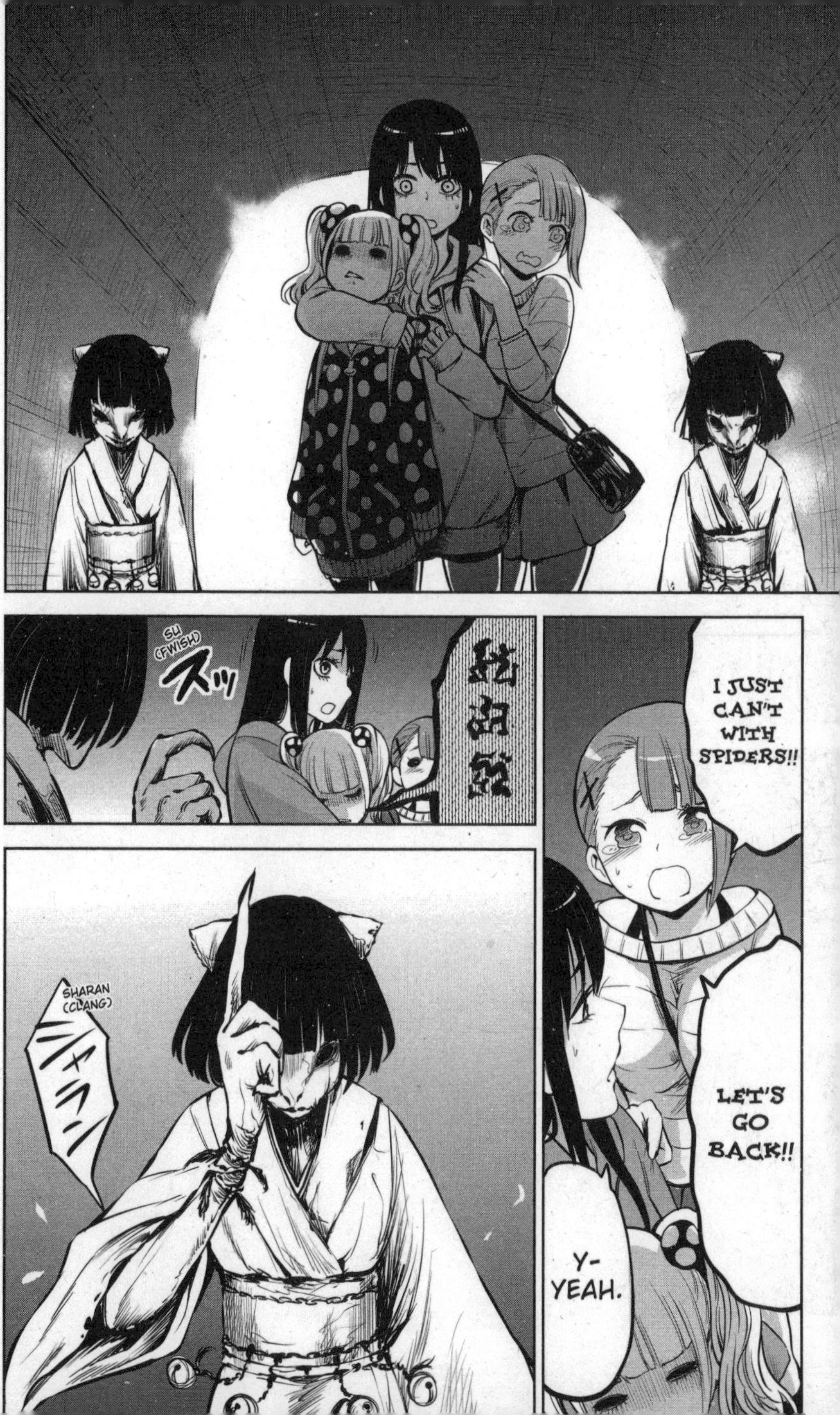
I JUST CAN'T WITH SPIDERS!!
LET'S GO BACK!!
Y- YEAH.
SU (FWISH)
スッ
SHARAN (CLANG)
シャラン

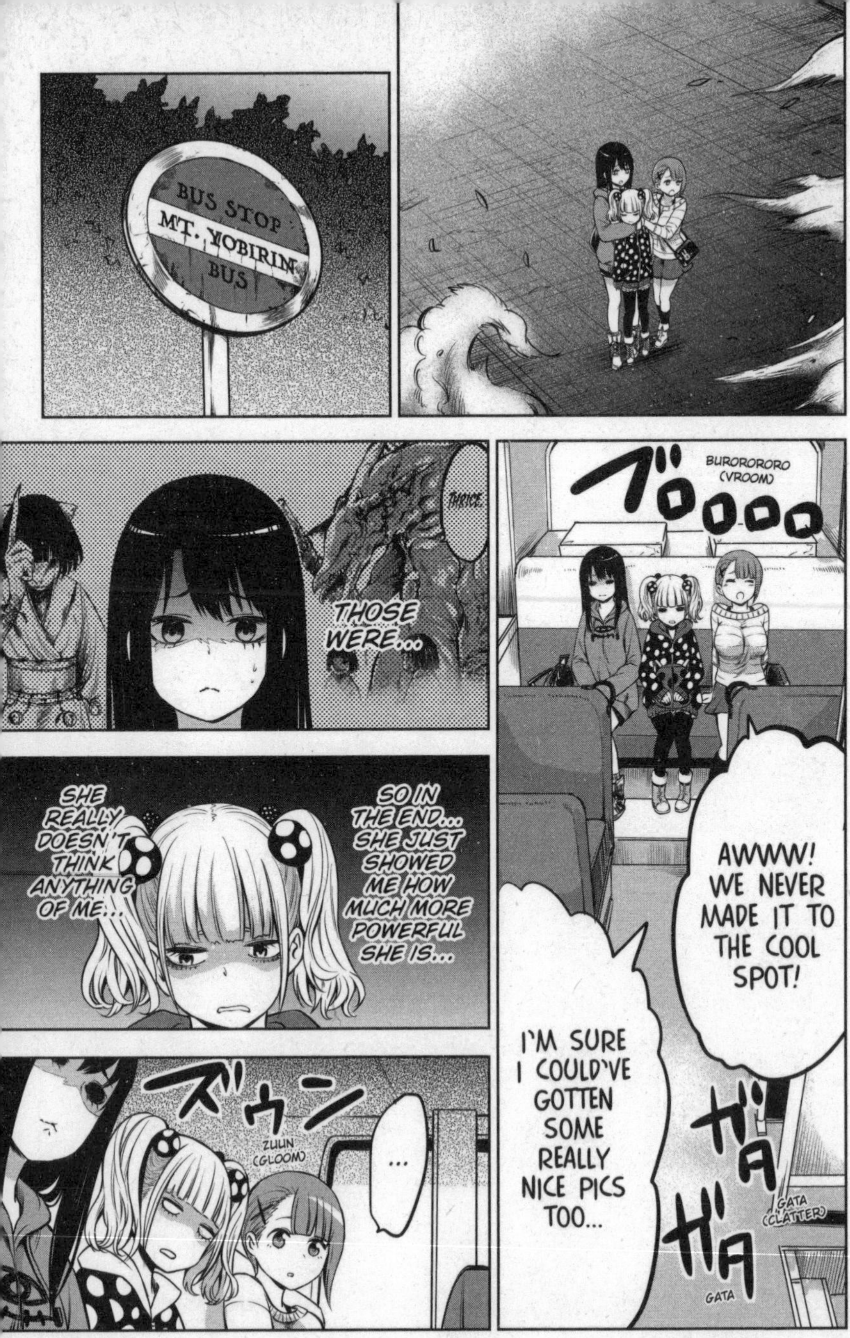
BUS STOP
MT. YOBIRIN
BUS
ブロロロロ
BURORORORO (VROOM)
AWWW! WE NEVER MADE IT TO THE COOL SPOT!
I'M SURE I COULD'VE GOTTEN SOME REALLY NICE PICS TOO...
ガタ ガタ
GATA (CLATTER)
GATA
THRICE
THOSE WERE...
SO IN THE END... SHE JUST SHOWED ME HOW MUCH MORE POWERFUL SHE IS...
SHE REALLY DOESN'T THINK ANYTHING OF ME...
ズウーン
ZUUN (GLOOM)
...

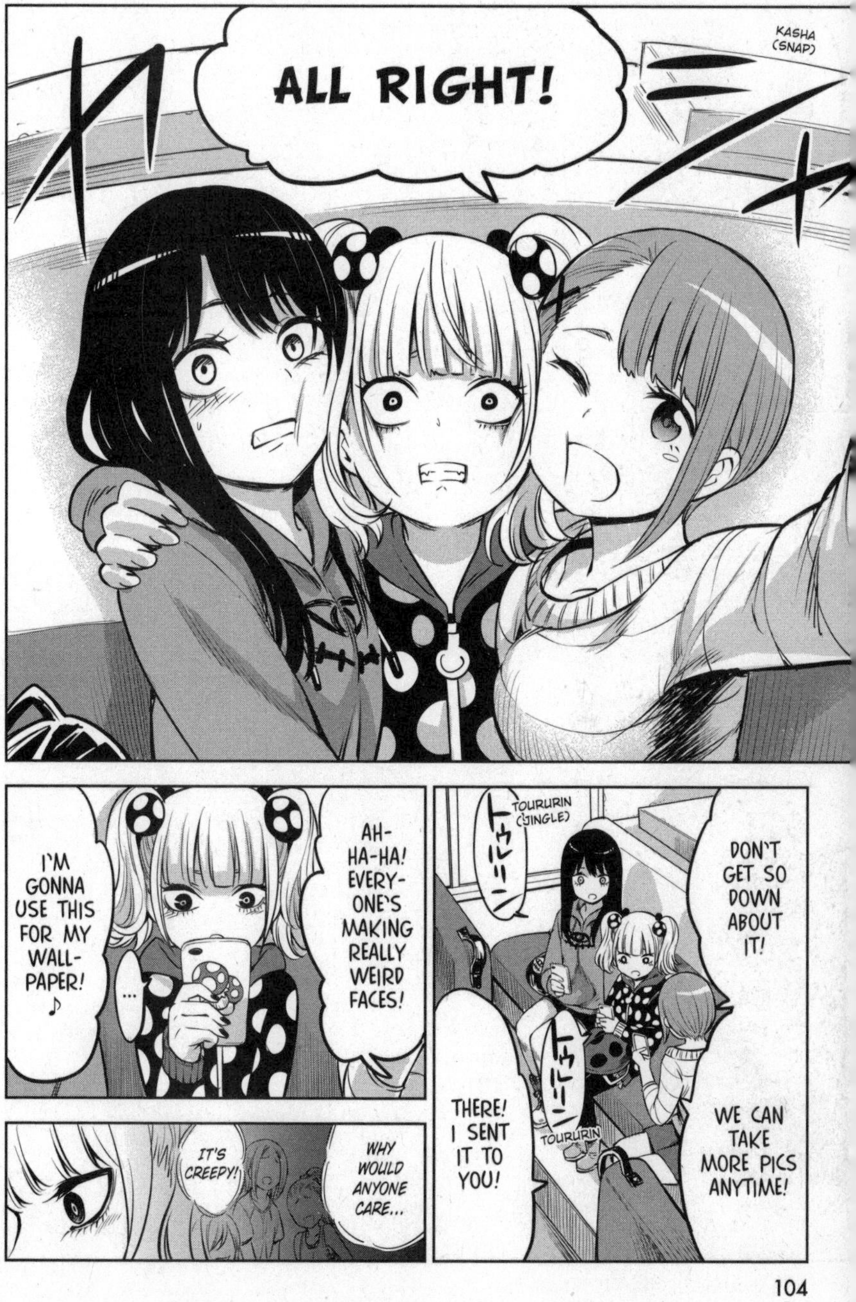
KASHA (SNAP)
ALL RIGHT!
DON'T GET SO DOWN ABOUT IT!
TOURURIN (JINGLE)
WE CAN TAKE MORE PICS ANYTIME!
TOURURIN
THERE! I SENT IT TO YOU!
AH-HA-HA! EVERYONE'S MAKING REALLY WEIRD FACES!
...
I'M GONNA USE THIS FOR MY WALLPAPER! ♪
WHY WOULD ANYONE CARE...
IT'S CREEPY!

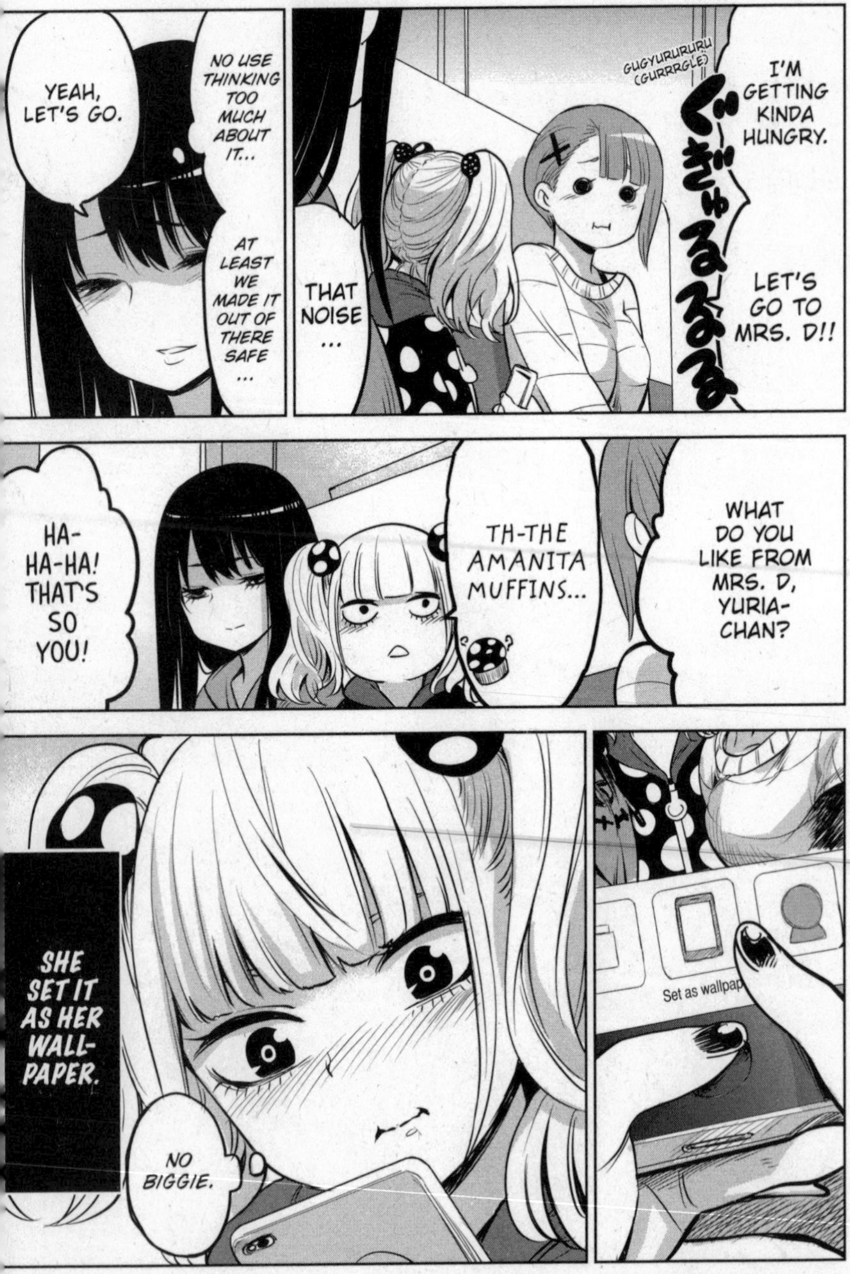
GUGYURURURU (GURRRGLE)
I'M GETTING KINDA HUNGRY.
LET'S GO TO MRS. D!!
THAT NOISE ...
NO USE THINKING TOO MUCH ABOUT IT...
AT LEAST WE MADE IT OUT OF THERE SAFE ...
YEAH, LET'S GO.
WHAT DO YOU LIKE FROM MRS. D, YURIA-CHAN?
TH-THE AMANITA MUFFINS...
HA-HA-HA! THAT'S SO YOU!
Set as wallpap
SHE SET IT AS HER WALL-PAPER.
NO BIGGIE.

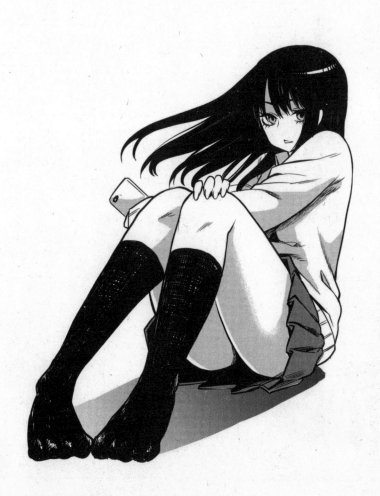

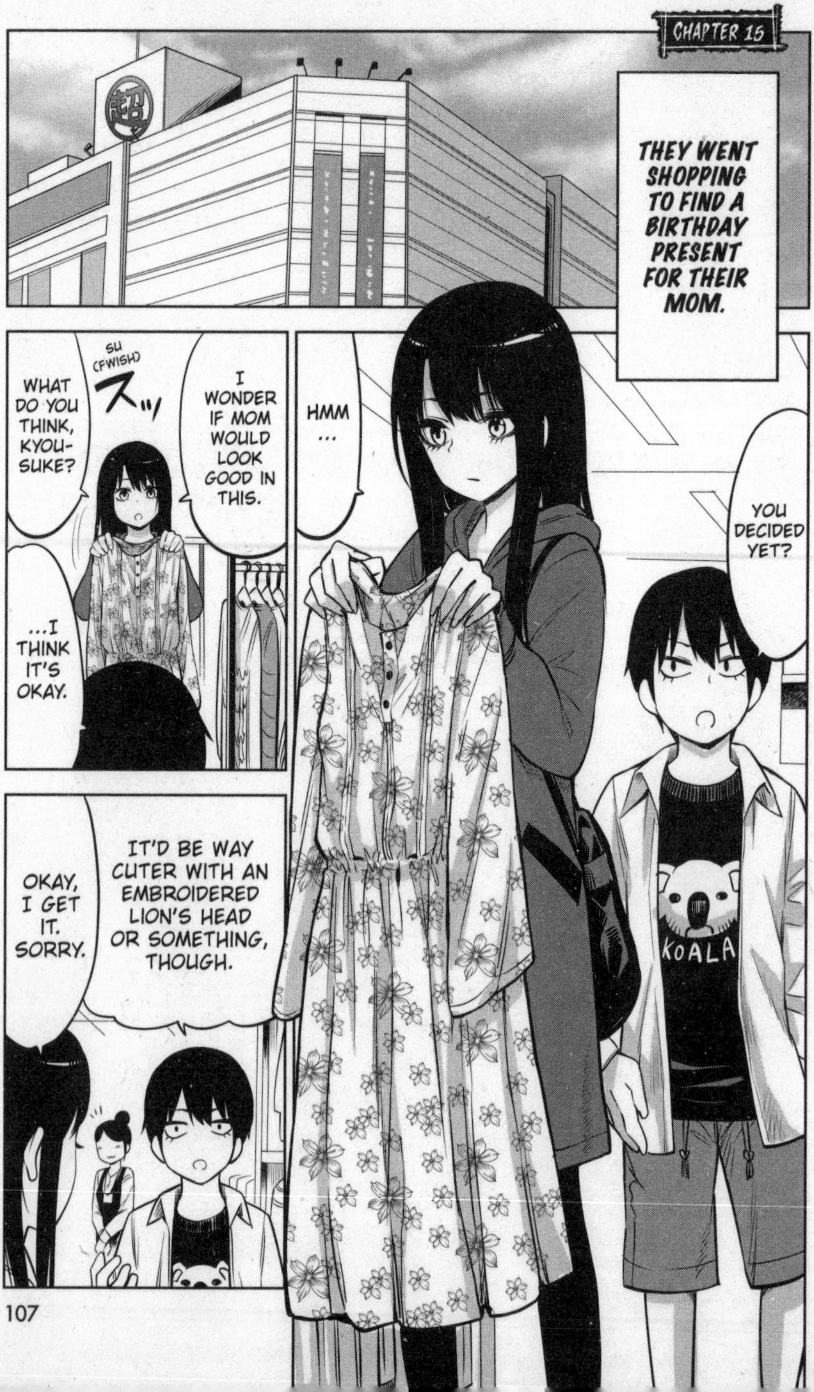
CHAPTER 15
THEY WENT SHOPPING TO FIND A BIRTHDAY PRESENT FOR THEIR MOM.
YOU DECIDED YET?
HMM ...
I WONDER IF MOM WOULD LOOK GOOD IN THIS.
SU (FWISH)
スッ
WHAT DO YOU THINK, KYOU-SUKE?
...I THINK IT'S OKAY.
IT'D BE WAY CUTER WITH AN EMBROIDERED LION'S HEAD OR SOMETHING, THOUGH.
OKAY, I GET IT. SORRY.
KOALA

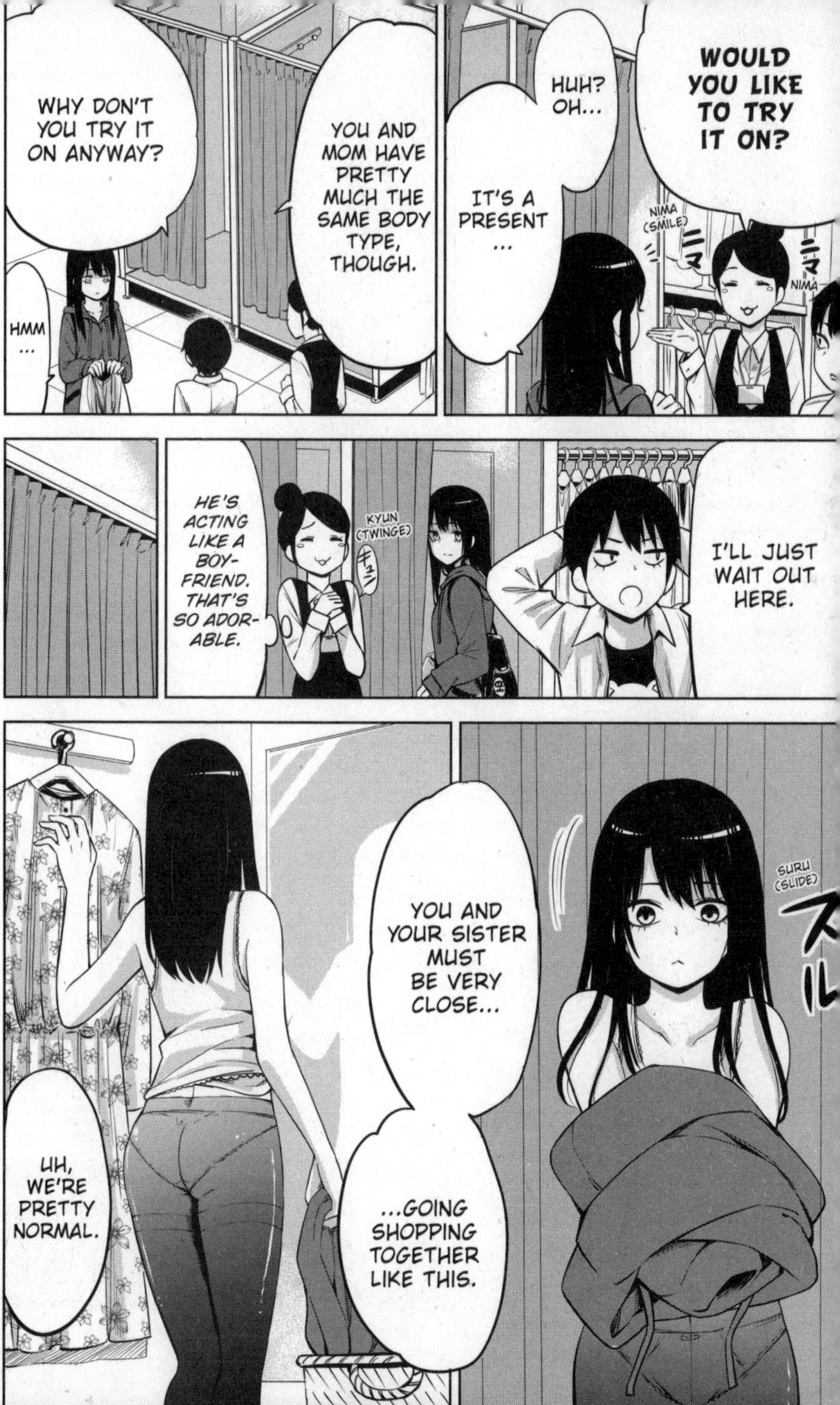
WOULD YOU LIKE TO TRY IT ON?
NIMA (SMILE)
NIMA
HUH? OH...
IT'S A PRESENT ...
YOU AND MOM HAVE PRETTY MUCH THE SAME BODY TYPE, THOUGH.
WHY DON'T YOU TRY IT ON ANYWAY?
HMM ...
I'LL JUST WAIT OUT HERE.
KYUN (TWINGE)
HE'S ACTING LIKE A BOY-FRIEND. THAT'S SO ADOR-ABLE.
SURU (SLIDE)
YOU AND YOUR SISTER MUST BE VERY CLOSE...
...GOING SHOPPING TOGETHER LIKE THIS.
UH, WE'RE PRETTY NORMAL.

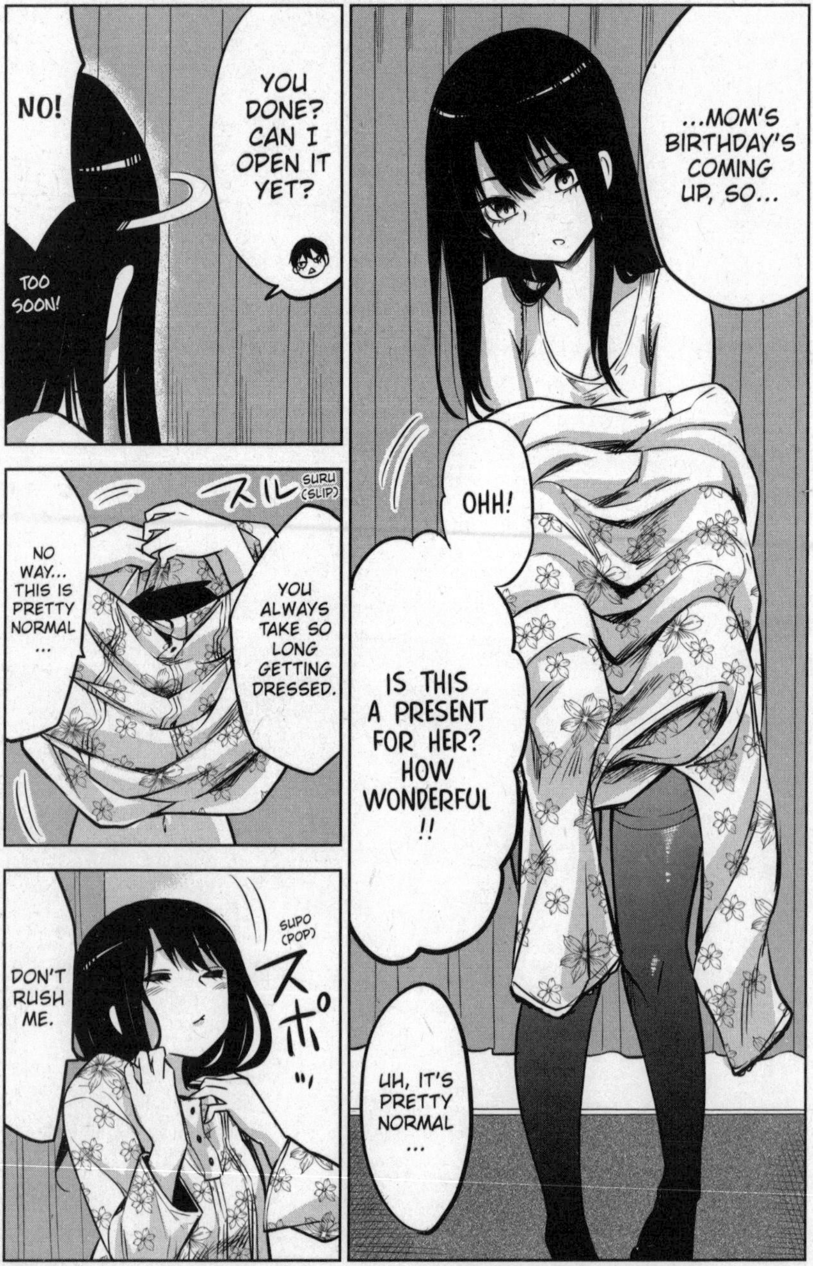
YOU DONE? CAN I OPEN IT YET?
NO!
TOO SOON!
スル SURU (SLIP)
YOU ALWAYS TAKE SO LONG GETTING DRESSED.
NO WAY... THIS IS PRETTY NORMAL ...
スポッ SUPO (POP)
DON'T RUSH ME.
...MOM'S BIRTHDAY'S COMING UP, SO...
OHH!
IS THIS A PRESENT FOR HER? HOW WONDERFUL !!
UH, IT'S PRETTY NORMAL ...

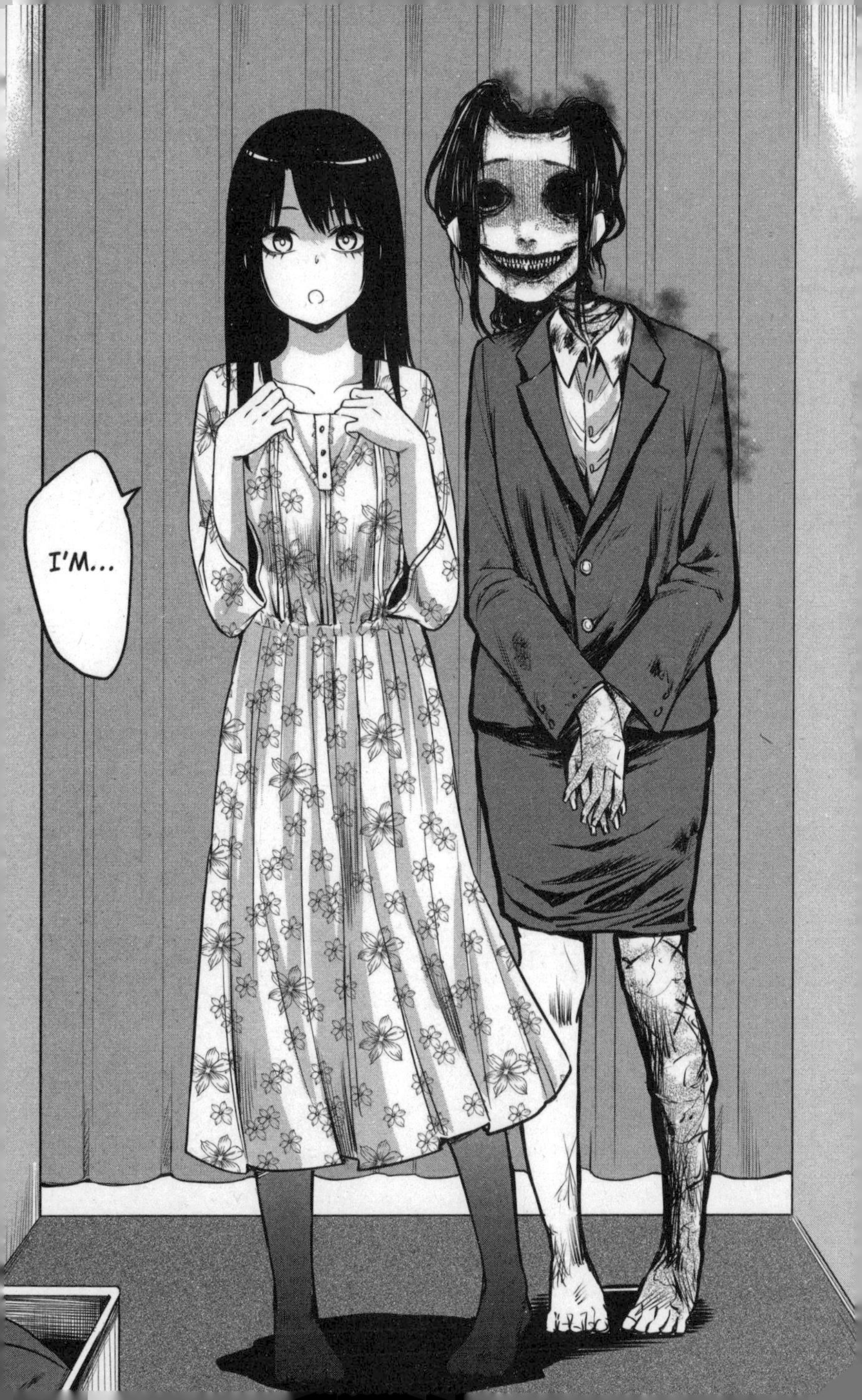
I'M...

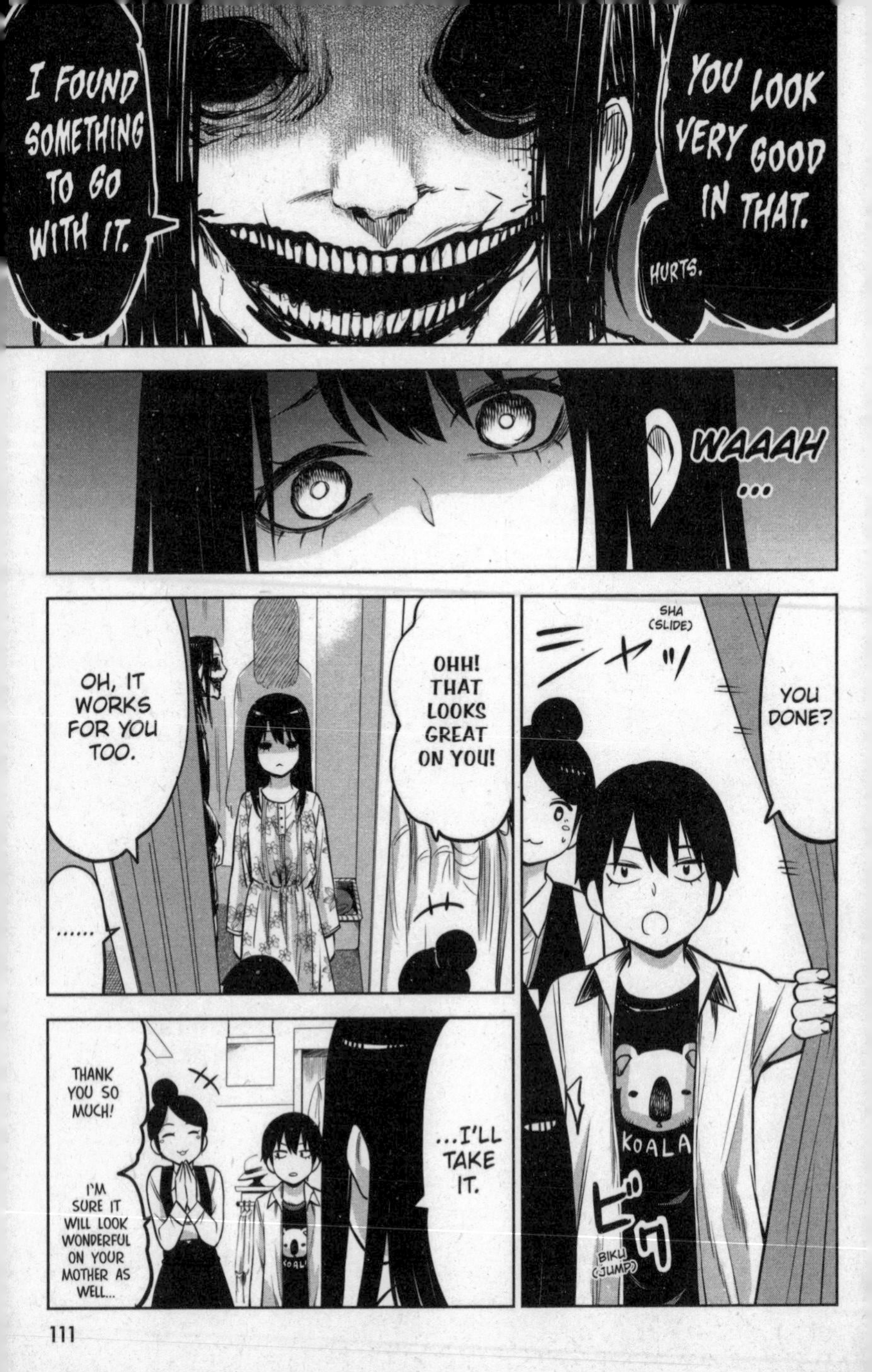
YOU LOOK VERY GOOD IN THAT.
HURTS.
I FOUND SOMETHING TO GO WITH IT.
WAAAH ...
SHA (SLIDE)
YOU DONE?
KOALA
BIKU (JUMP)
OHH! THAT LOOKS GREAT ON YOU!
OH, IT WORKS FOR YOU TOO.
......
...I'LL TAKE IT.
THANK YOU SO MUCH!
I'M SURE IT WILL LOOK WONDERFUL ON YOUR MOTHER AS WELL...

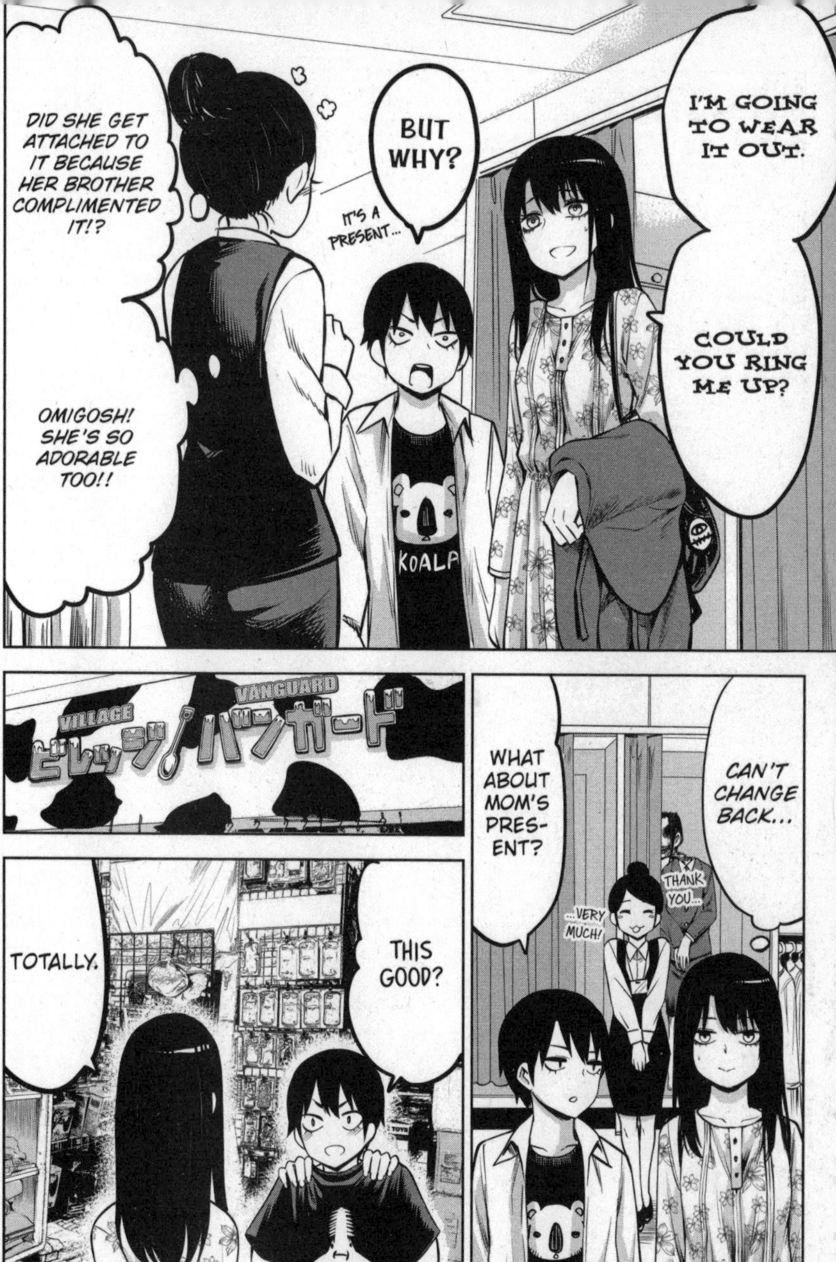
I'M GOING TO WEAR IT OUT.
COULD YOU RING ME UP?
BUT WHY?
IT'S A PRESENT...
DID SHE GET ATTACHED TO IT BECAUSE HER BROTHER COMPLIMENTED IT!?
OMIGOSH! SHE'S SO ADORABLE TOO!!
KOALA
CAN'T CHANGE BACK...
WHAT ABOUT MOM'S PRES-ENT?
THANK YOU...
...VERY MUCH!
KOALA
VANGUARD
VILLAGE
ビレッジ/バンガード
THIS GOOD?
TOTALLY.
NOKOGIRIEL

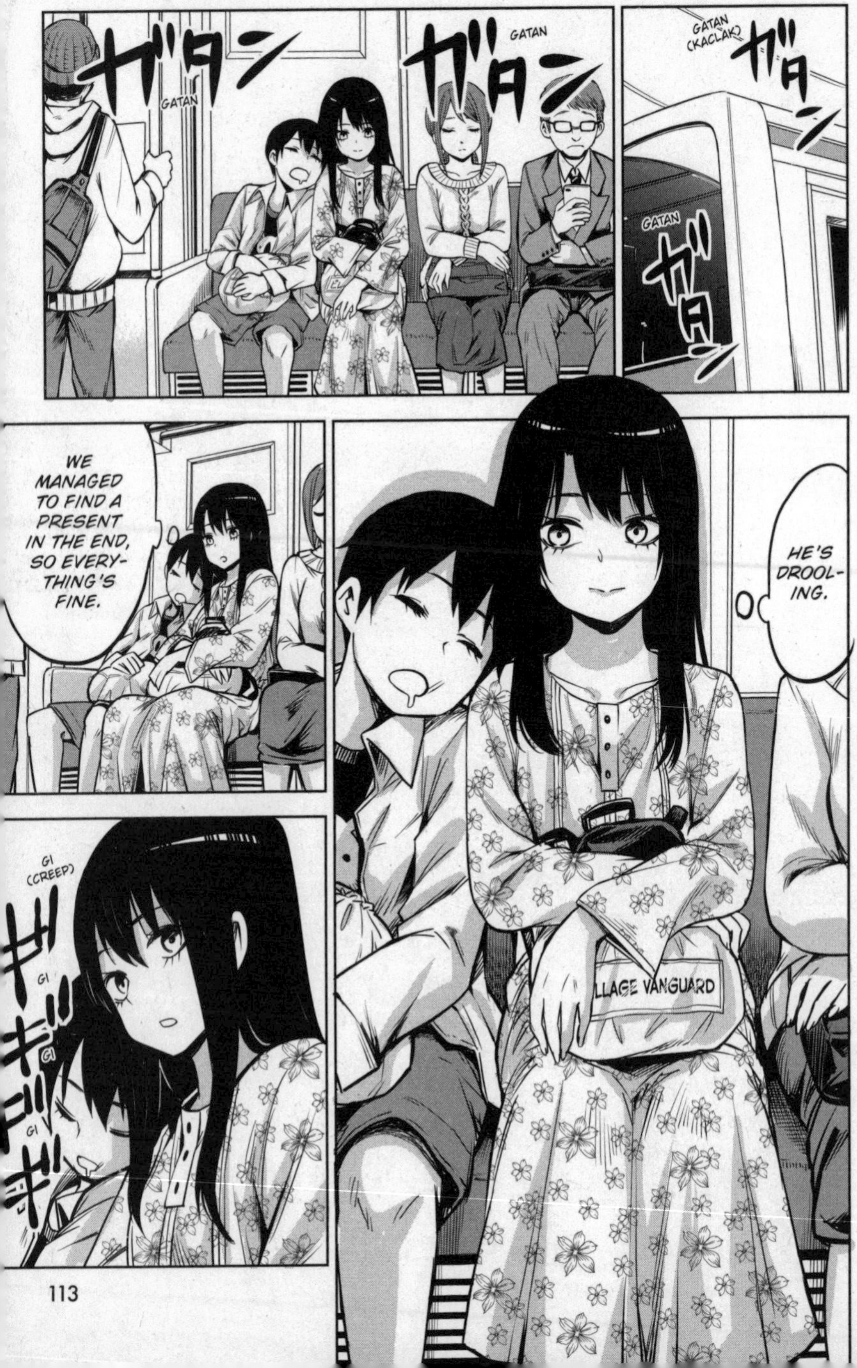
GATAN (KACLAK)
GATAN
GATAN
GATAN
HE'S DROOL-ING.
LLAGE VANGUARD
WE MANAGED TO FIND A PRESENT IN THE END, SO EVERY-THING'S FINE.
GI (CREEP)
GI
GI
GI

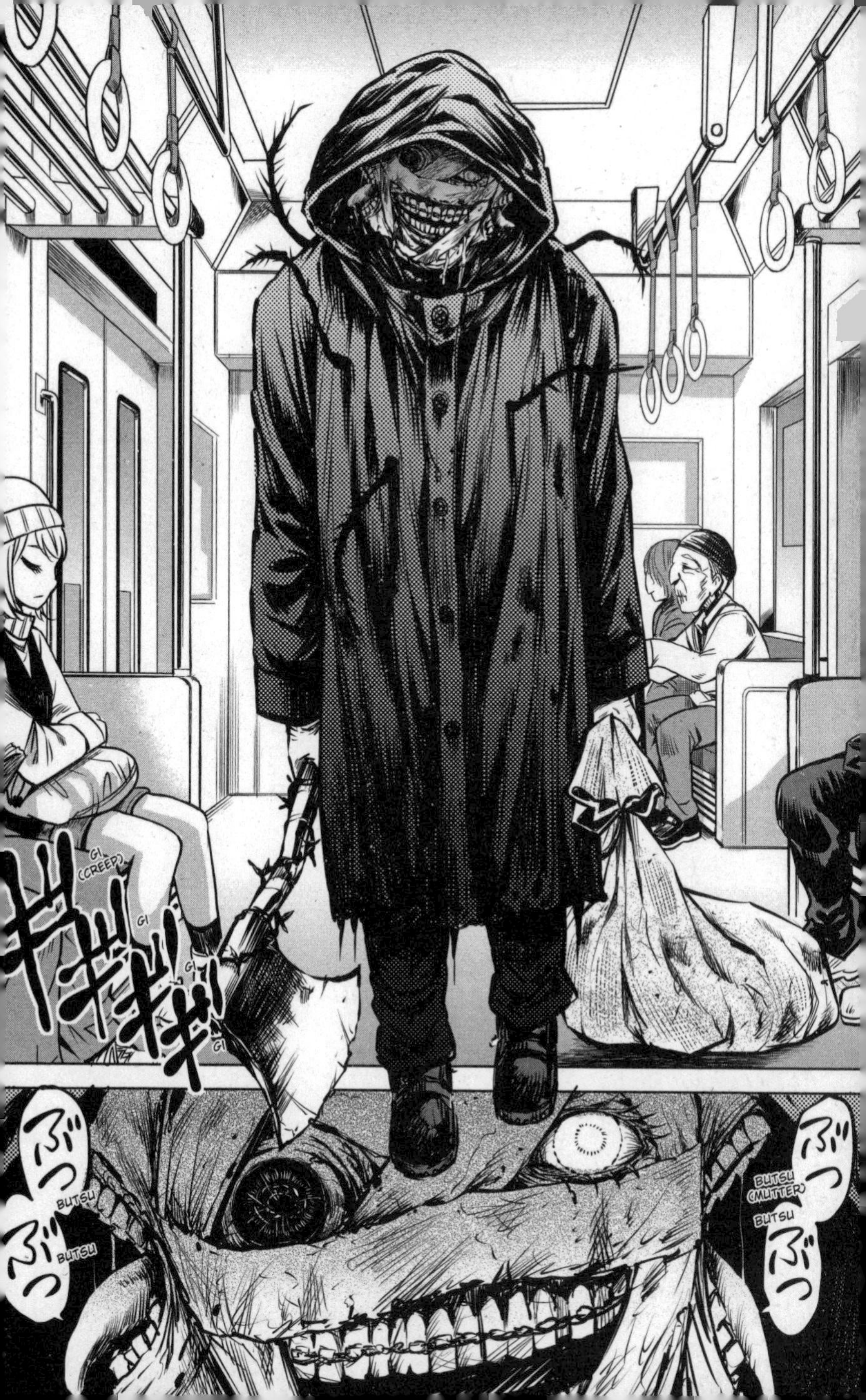
ギッギッギッギッ
GI (CREEP) GI GI GI
ぶつぶつ
BUTSU (MUTTER) BUTSU
ぶつぶつ
BUTSU BUTSU

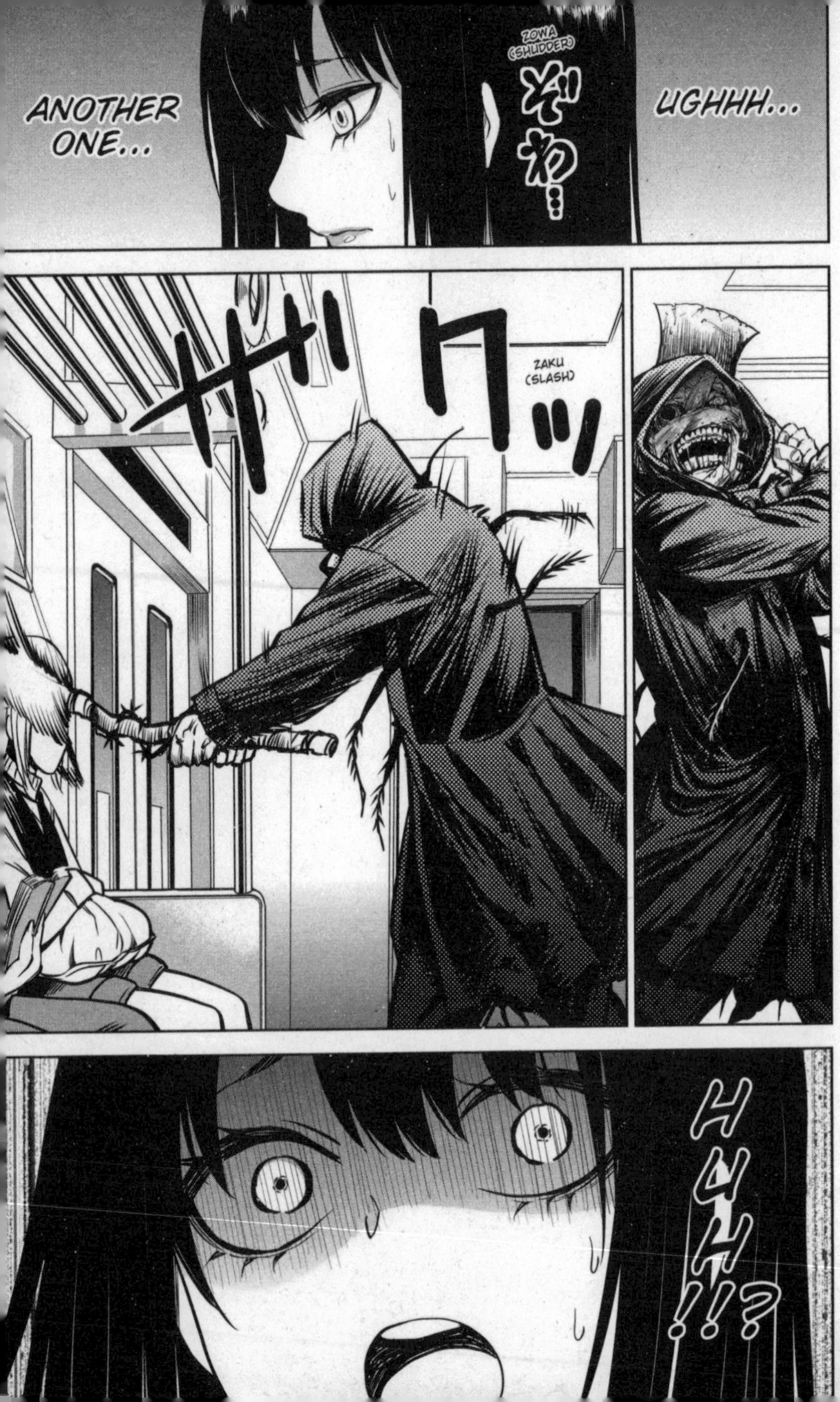
UGHHH...
ZOWA (SHUDDER)
ぞわ...
ANOTHER ONE...
ザクッ
ZAKU (SLASH)
HUH!!?

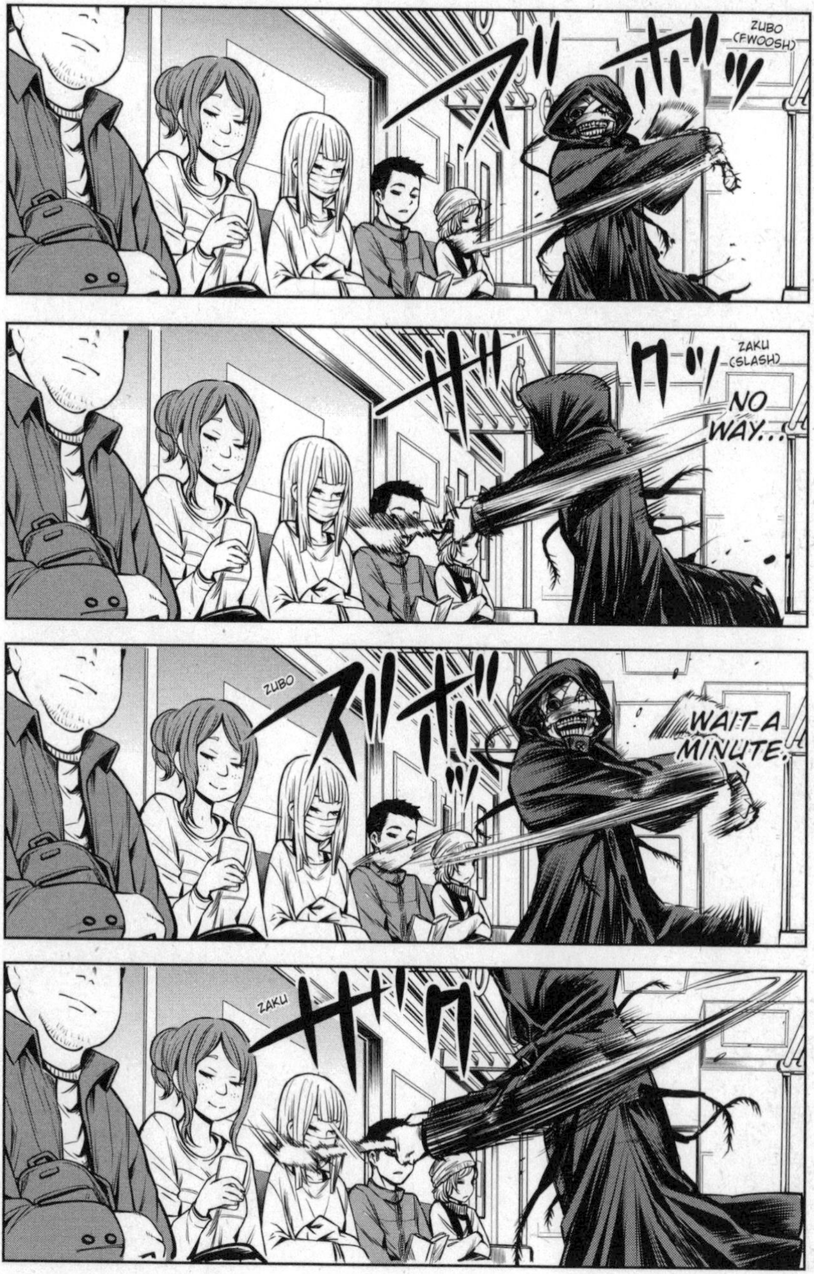
ZUBO (FWOOSH)
ZAKU (SLASH)
NO WAY...
ZUBO
WAIT A MINUTE.
ZAKU

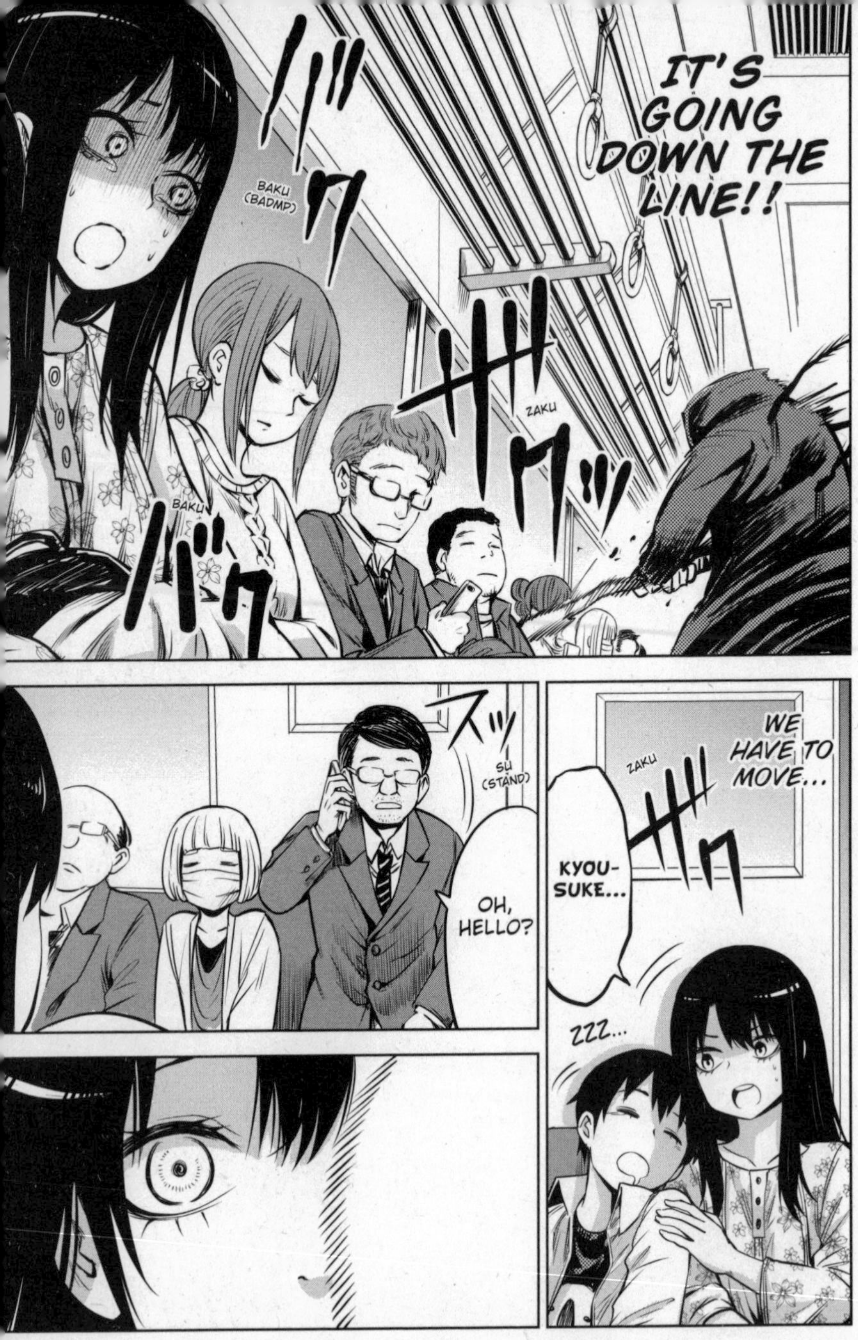
IT'S GOING DOWN THE LINE!!
ZAKU
BAKU (BADMP)
BAKU
WE HAVE TO MOVE...
ZAKU
KYOU-SUKE...
ZZZ...
SU (STAND)
OH, HELLO?

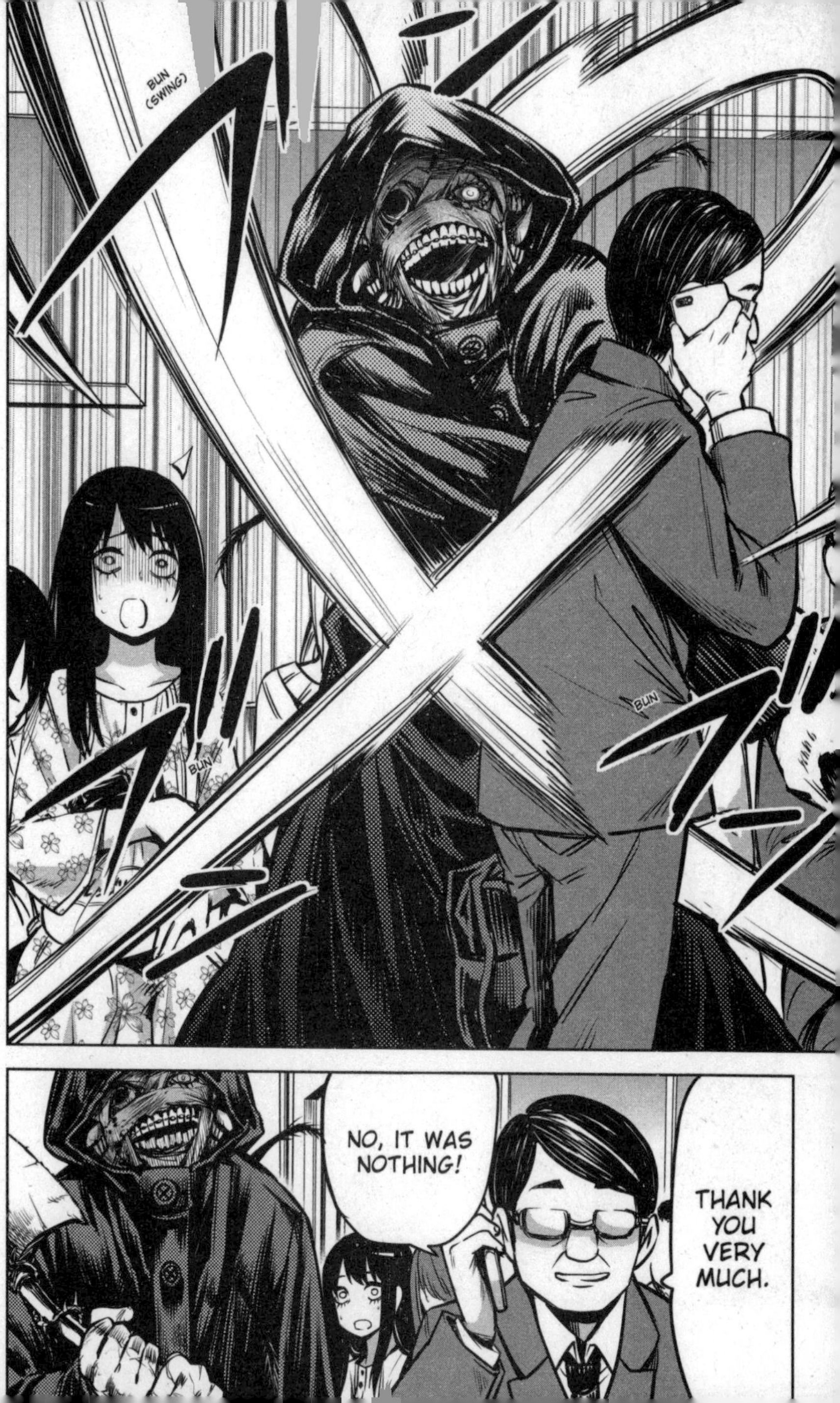
BUN (SWING)
BUN
BUN
NO, IT WAS NOTHING!
THANK YOU VERY MUCH.

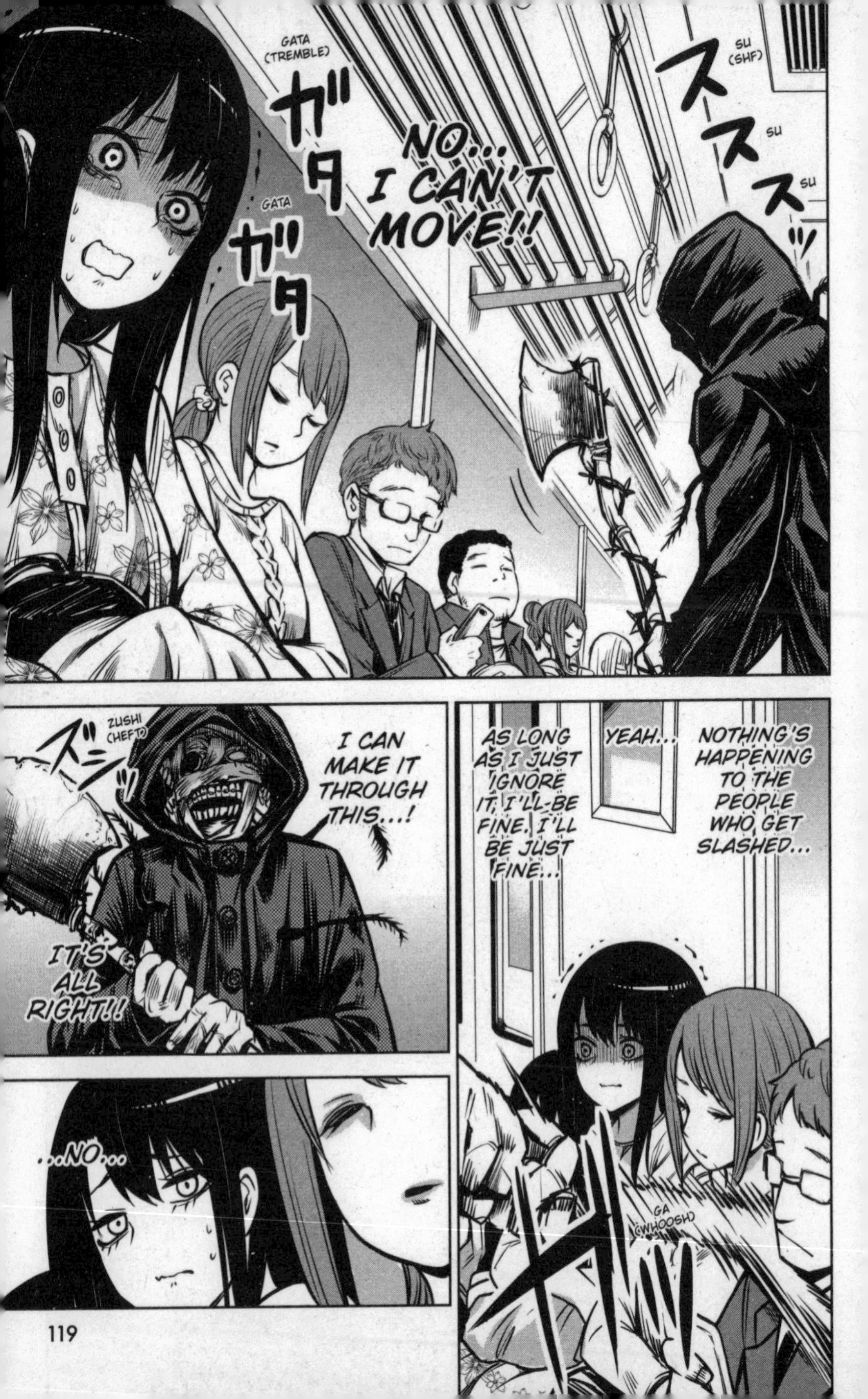

SU (SHF)
SU
SU
NO... I CAN'T MOVE!!
GATA (TREMBLE)
GATA
NOTHING'S HAPPENING TO THE PEOPLE WHO GET SLASHED...
YEAH...
AS LONG AS I JUST IGNORE IT, I'LL BE FINE. I'LL BE JUST FINE...
GA (WHOOSH)
ZUSHI (HEFT)
I CAN MAKE IT THROUGH THIS...!
IT'S ALL RIGHT!!
...NO...

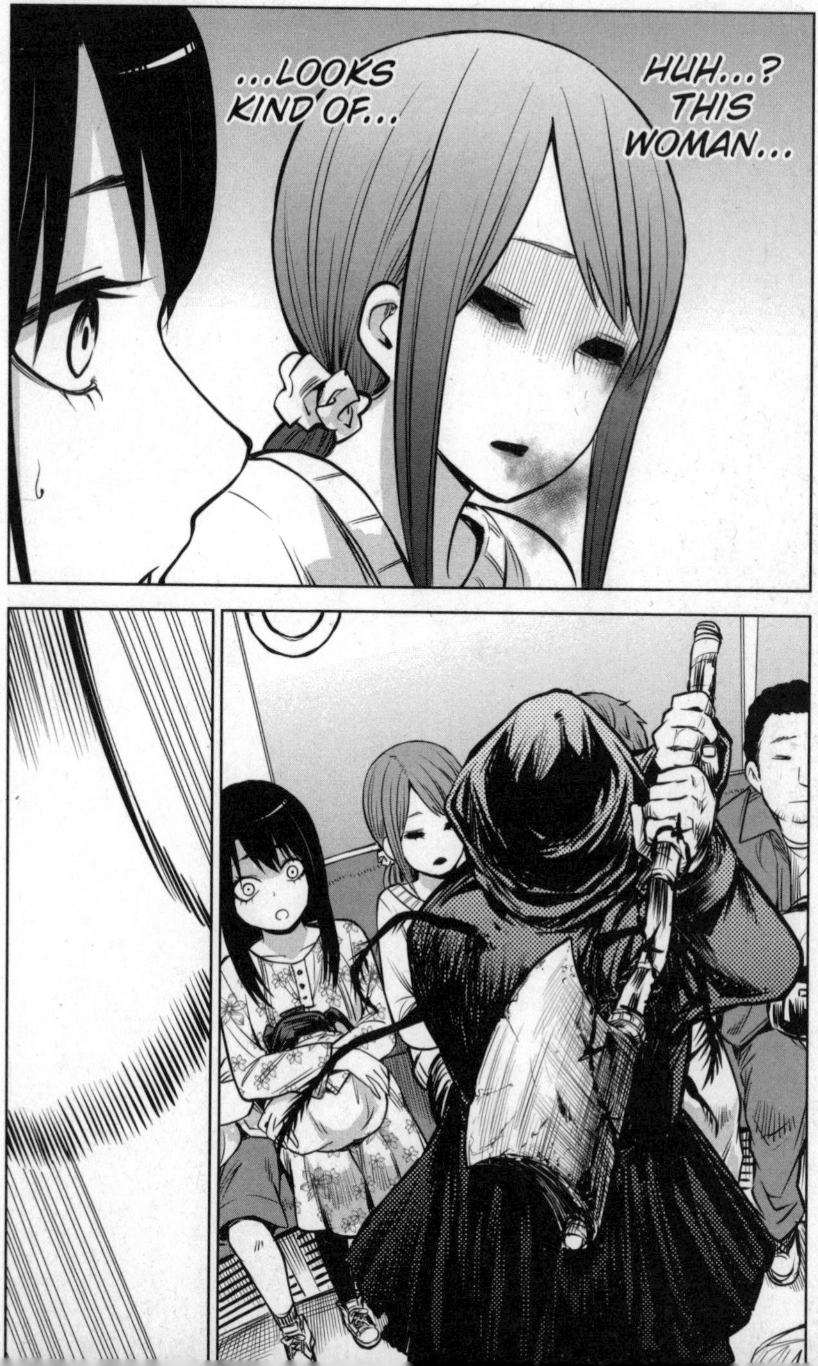
HUH...? THIS WOMAN...
...LOOKS KIND OF...

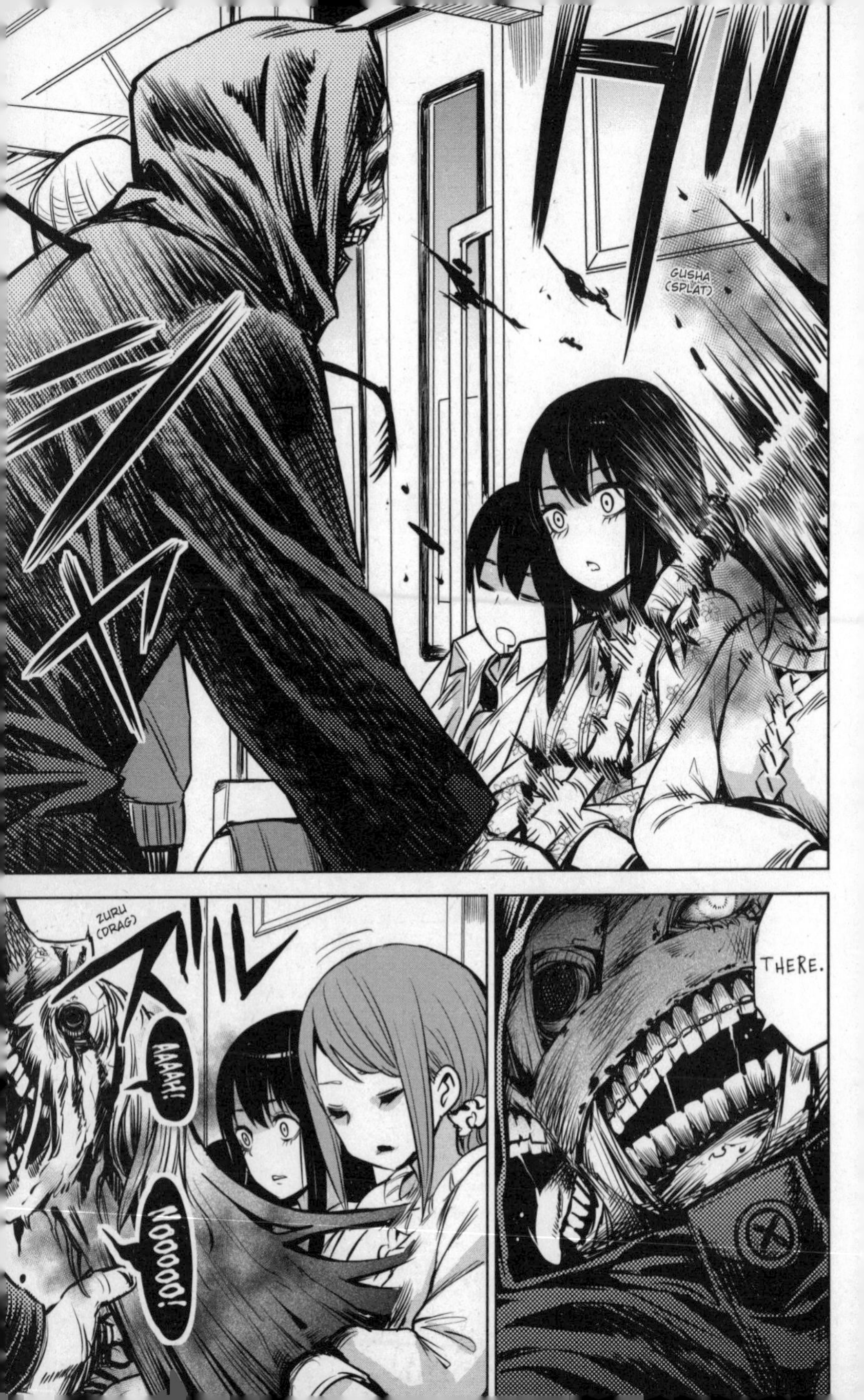
GUSHA
(SPLAT)
THERE.
ZURU
(DRAG)
AAAAH!
NOOOOO!

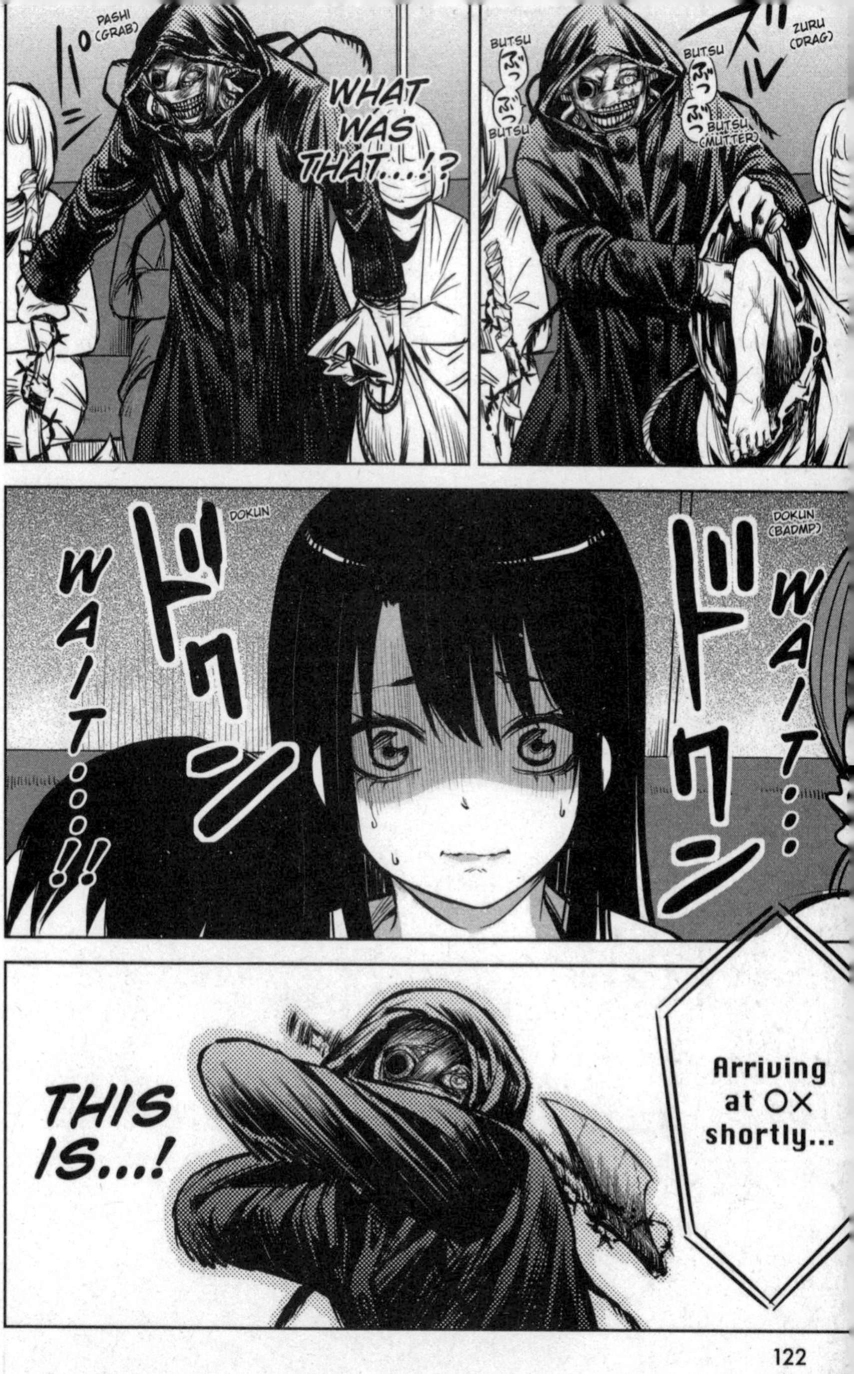
ZURU (DRAG)
ズル
BUTSU
ぶつ
ぶつ
BUTSU
BUTSU
ぶつ
ぶつ
BUTSU (MUTTER)
PASHI (GRAB)
WHAT WAS THAT...!?
DOKUN (BADMP)
ドクン
WAIT...
DOKUN
ドクン
WAIT...!!
Arriving at ○× shortly...
THIS IS...!

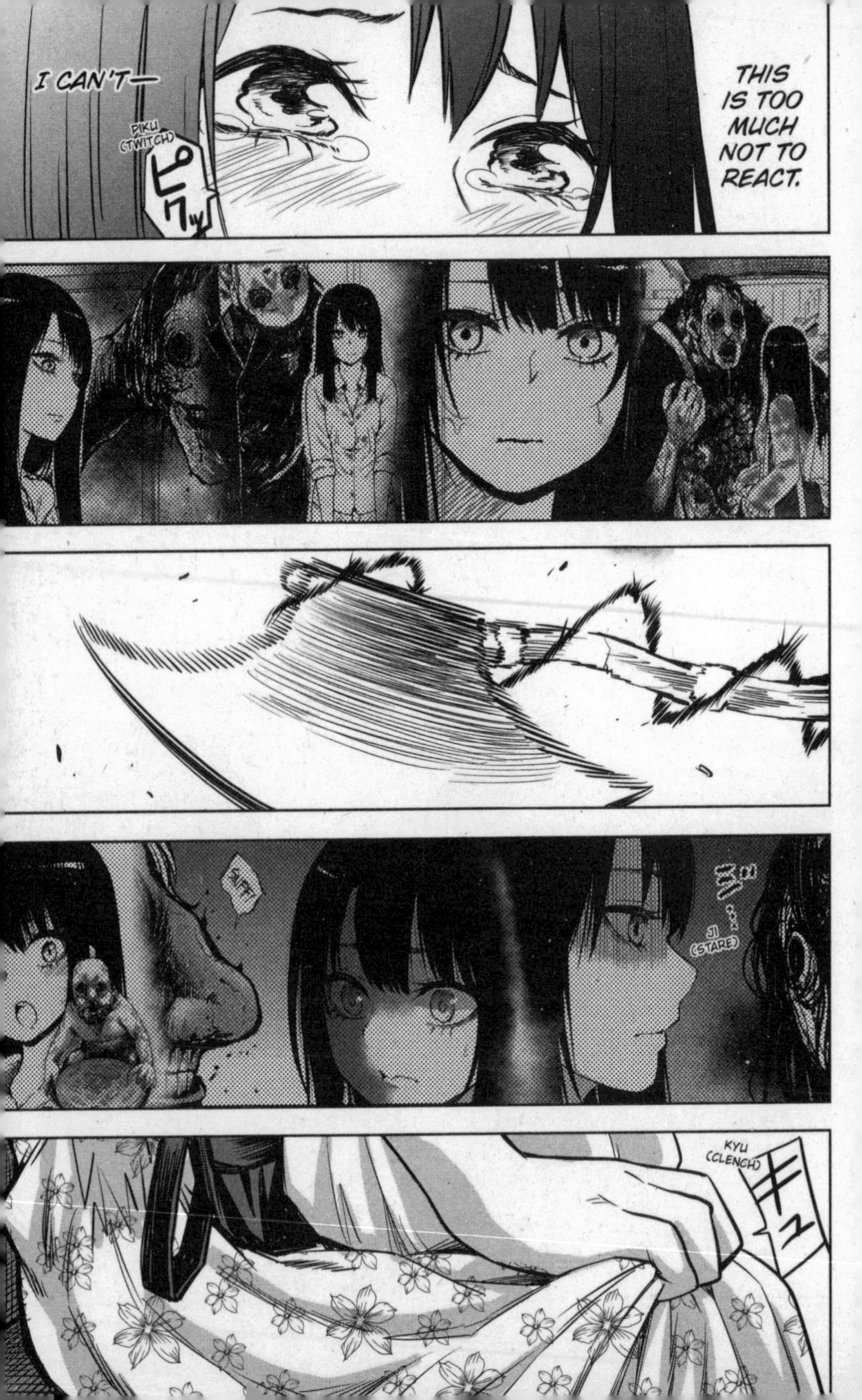
THIS IS TOO MUCH NOT TO REACT.
PIKU (TWITCH)
ピクッ
I CAN'T—
JI (STARE)
SNIFF
KYU (CLENCH)

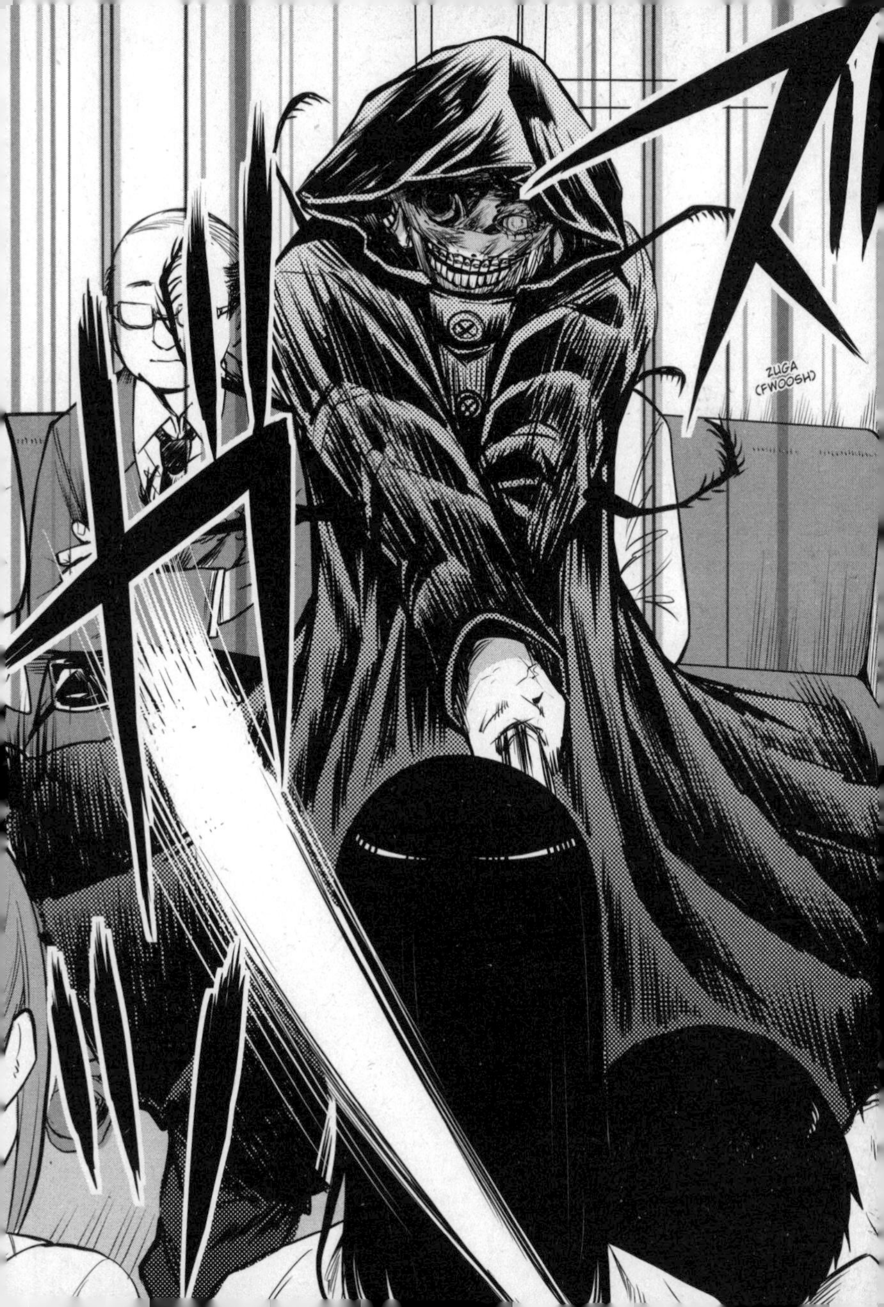
ZUGA
(FWOOSH)

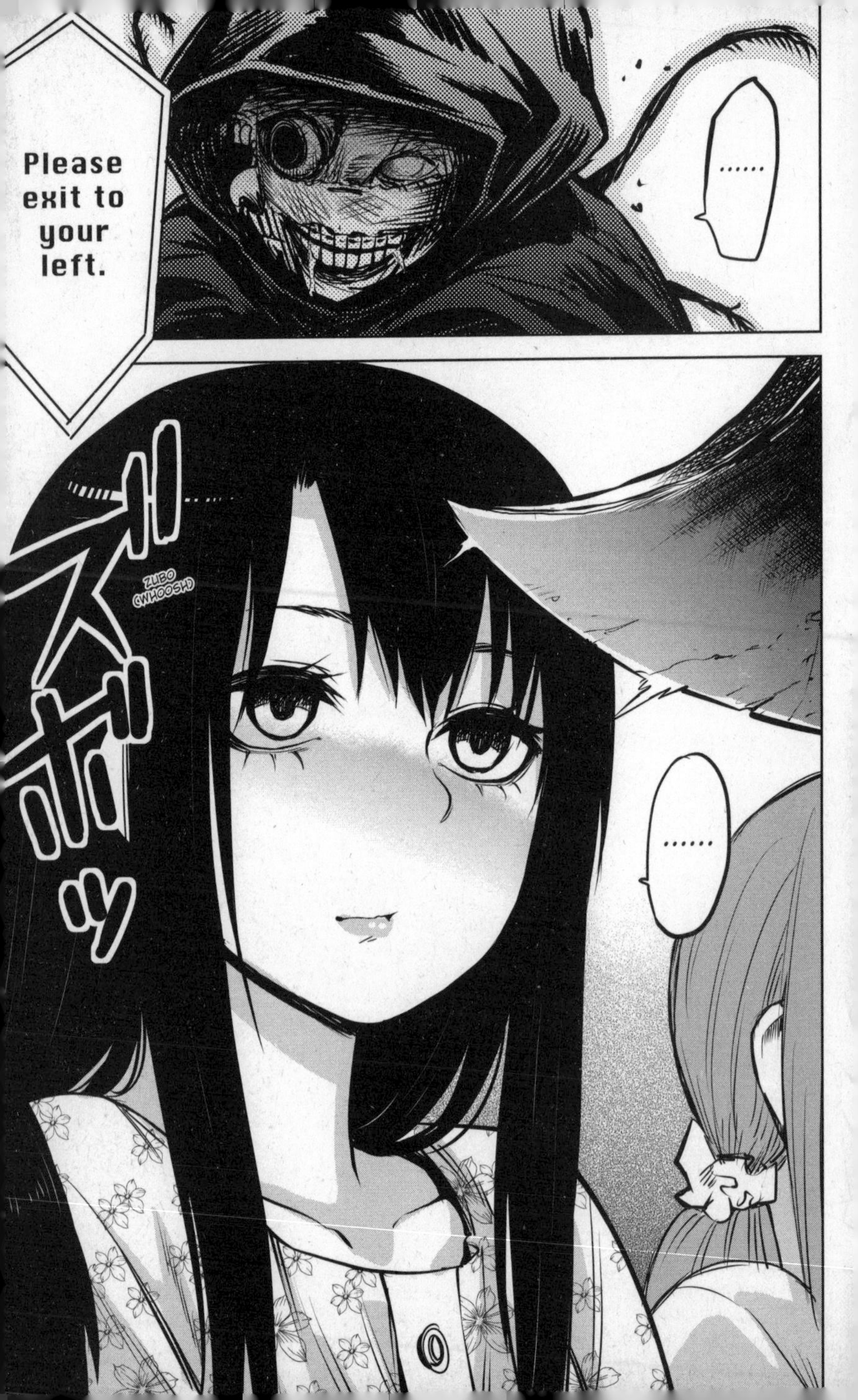
......
Please exit to your left.
......
ZUBO (WHOOSH)

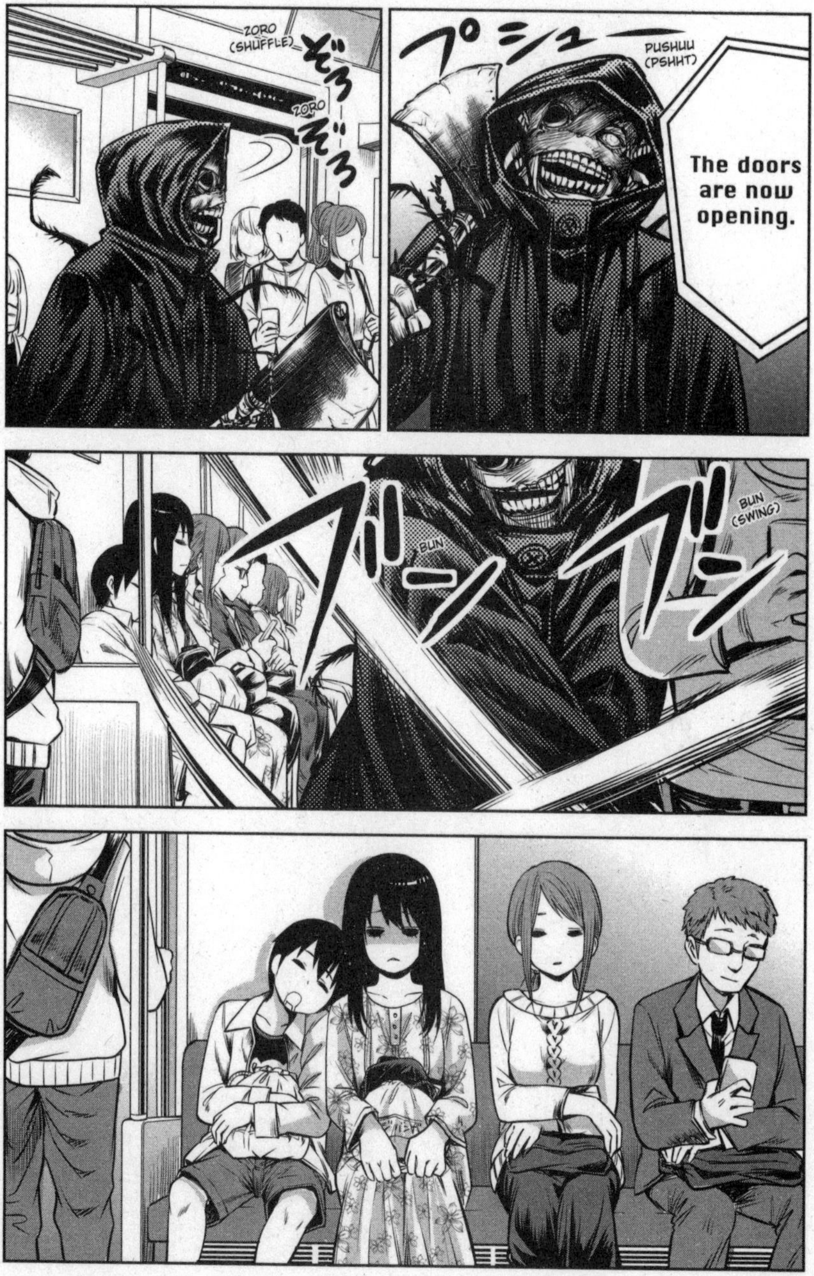
プシュー
PUSHUU
(PSHHT)
The doors are now opening.
ZORO
(SHUFFLE)
ぞろ
ZORO
ぞろ
ブン
BUN
(SWING)
ブーン
BUN

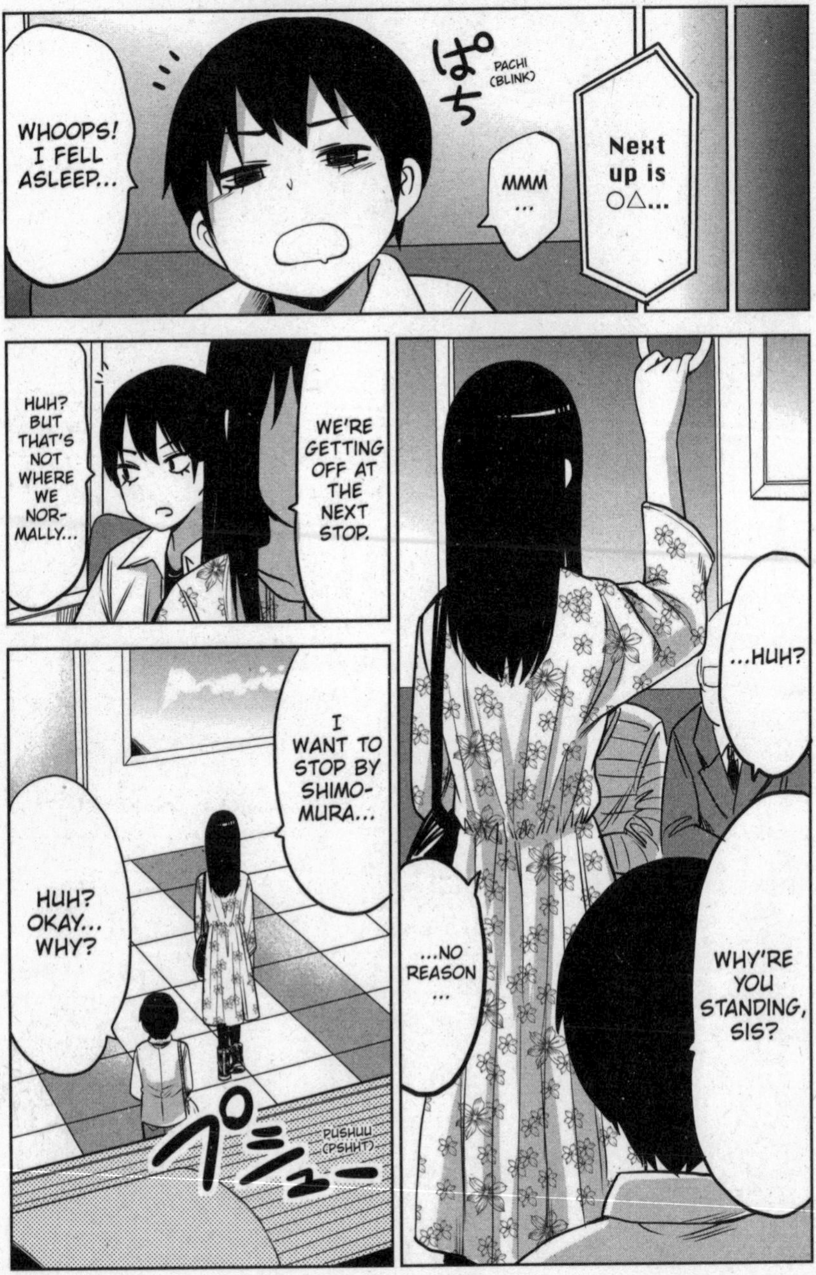
Next up is ○△...
MMM...
ぱち
PACHI (BLINK)
WHOOPS! I FELL ASLEEP...
...HUH?
WHY'RE YOU STANDING, SIS?
...NO REASON...
WE'RE GETTING OFF AT THE NEXT STOP.
HUH? BUT THAT'S NOT WHERE WE NOR-MALLY...
I WANT TO STOP BY SHIMO-MURA...
HUH? OKAY... WHY?
プシュー
PUSHUU (PSHHT)

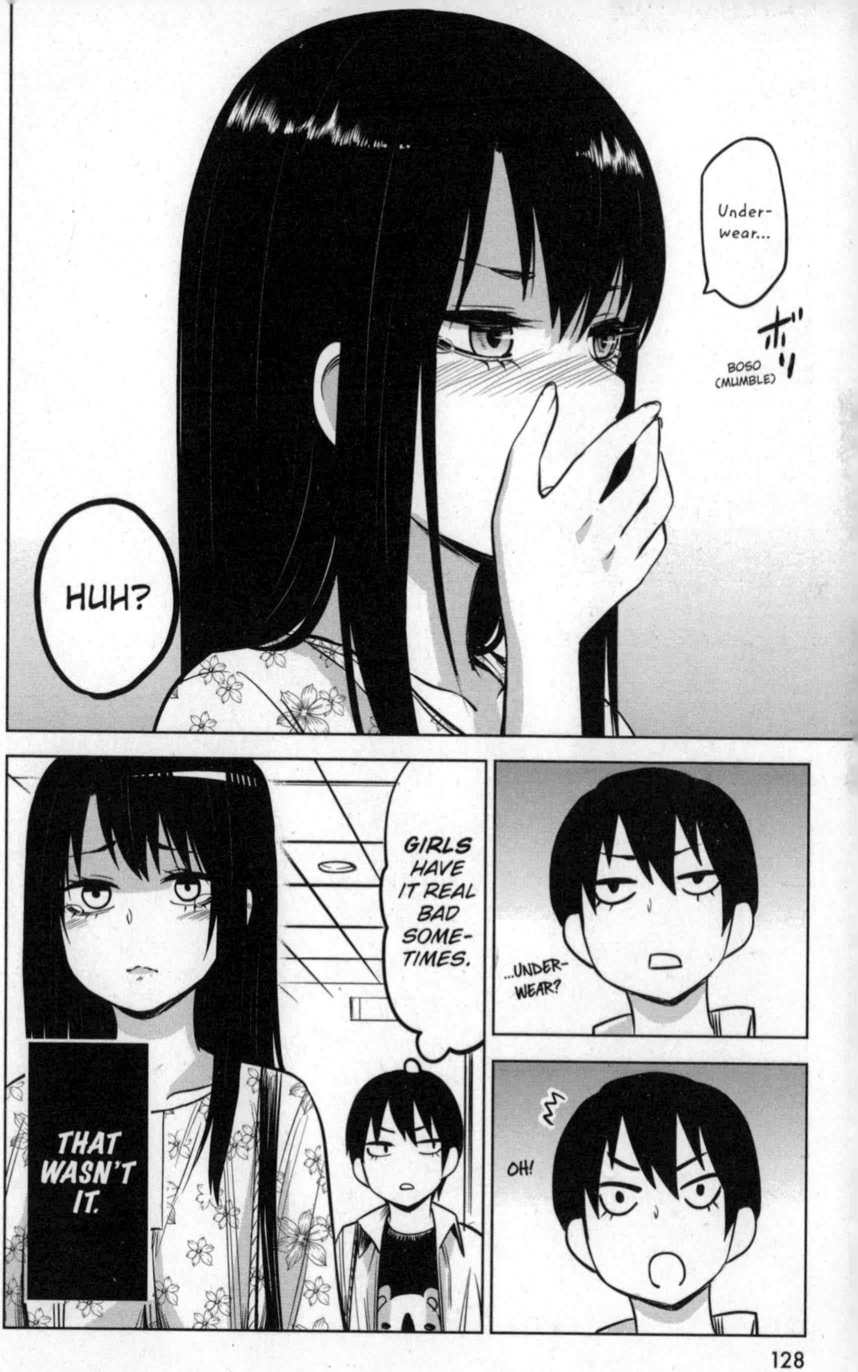
Under-wear...
BOSO (MUMBLE)
HUH?
...UNDER-WEAR?
OH!
GIRLS HAVE IT REAL BAD SOME-TIMES.
THAT WASN'T IT.

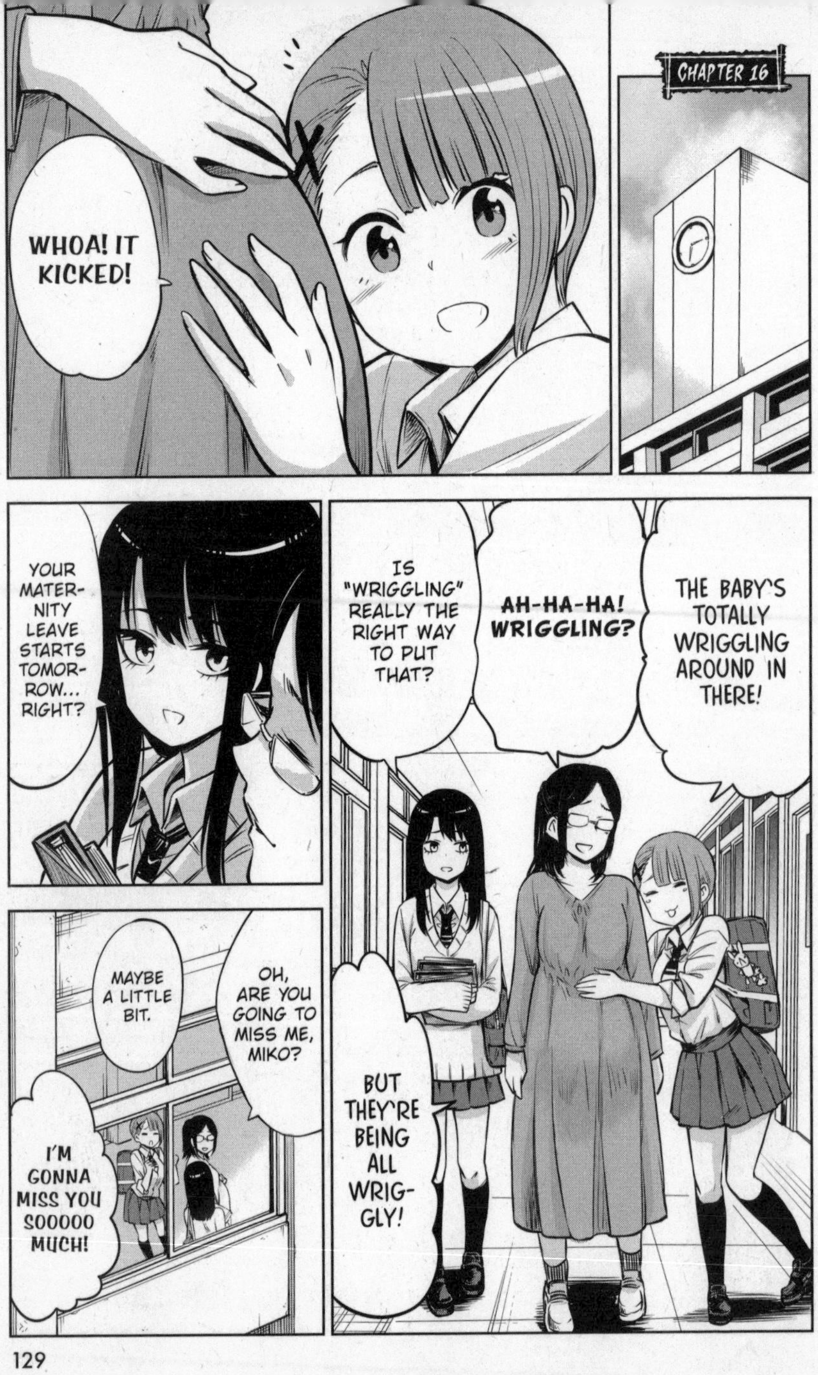
CHAPTER 16
WHOA! IT KICKED!
THE BABY'S TOTALLY WRIGGLING AROUND IN THERE!
AH-HA-HA! WRIGGLING?
IS "WRIGGLING" REALLY THE RIGHT WAY TO PUT THAT?
BUT THEY'RE BEING ALL WRIG-GLY!
YOUR MATER-NITY LEAVE STARTS TOMOR-ROW... RIGHT?
OH, ARE YOU GOING TO MISS ME, MIKO?
MAYBE A LITTLE BIT.
I'M GONNA MISS YOU SOOOOO MUCH!

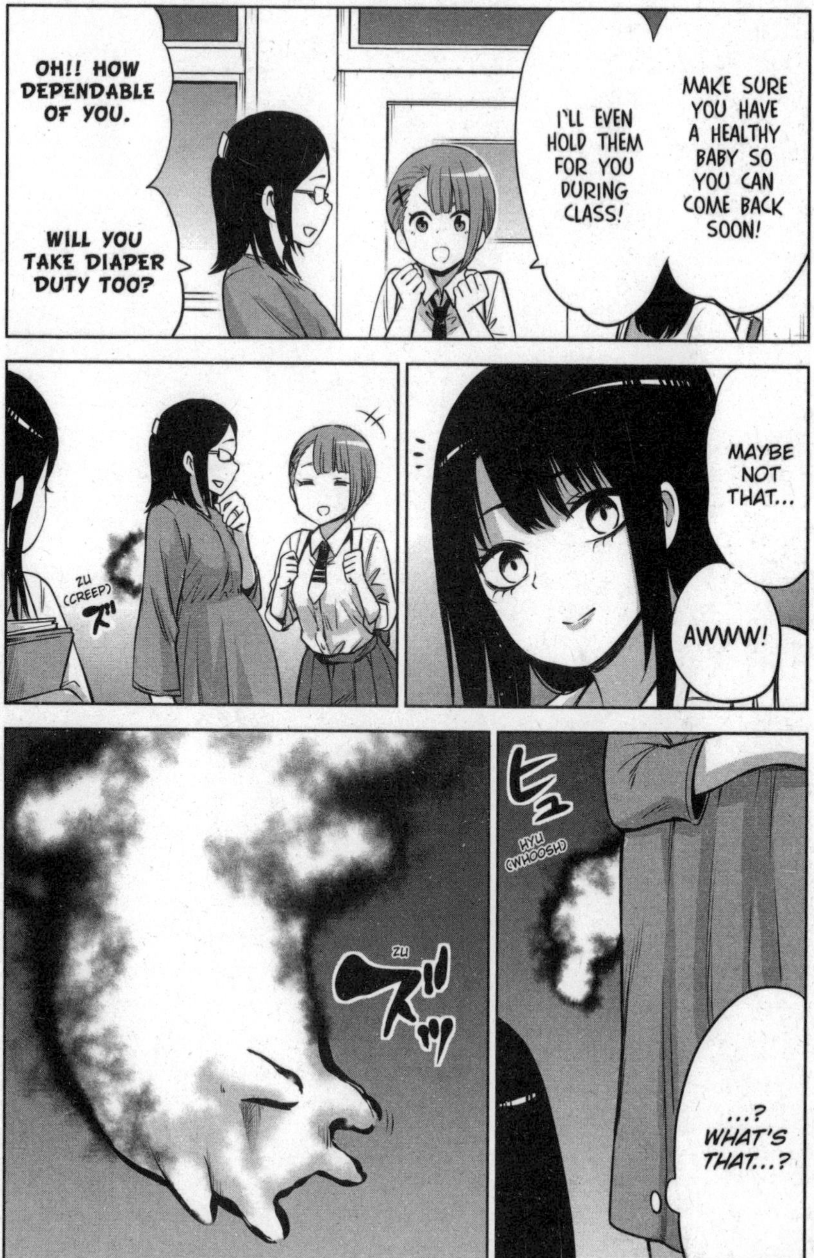
MAKE SURE YOU HAVE A HEALTHY BABY SO YOU CAN COME BACK SOON!
I'LL EVEN HOLD THEM FOR YOU DURING CLASS!
OH!! HOW DEPENDABLE OF YOU.
WILL YOU TAKE DIAPER DUTY TOO?
MAYBE NOT THAT...
AWWW!
ZU (CREEP)
ズッ
ヒュ
HYU (WHOOSH)
...? WHAT'S THAT...?
ZU
ズッ

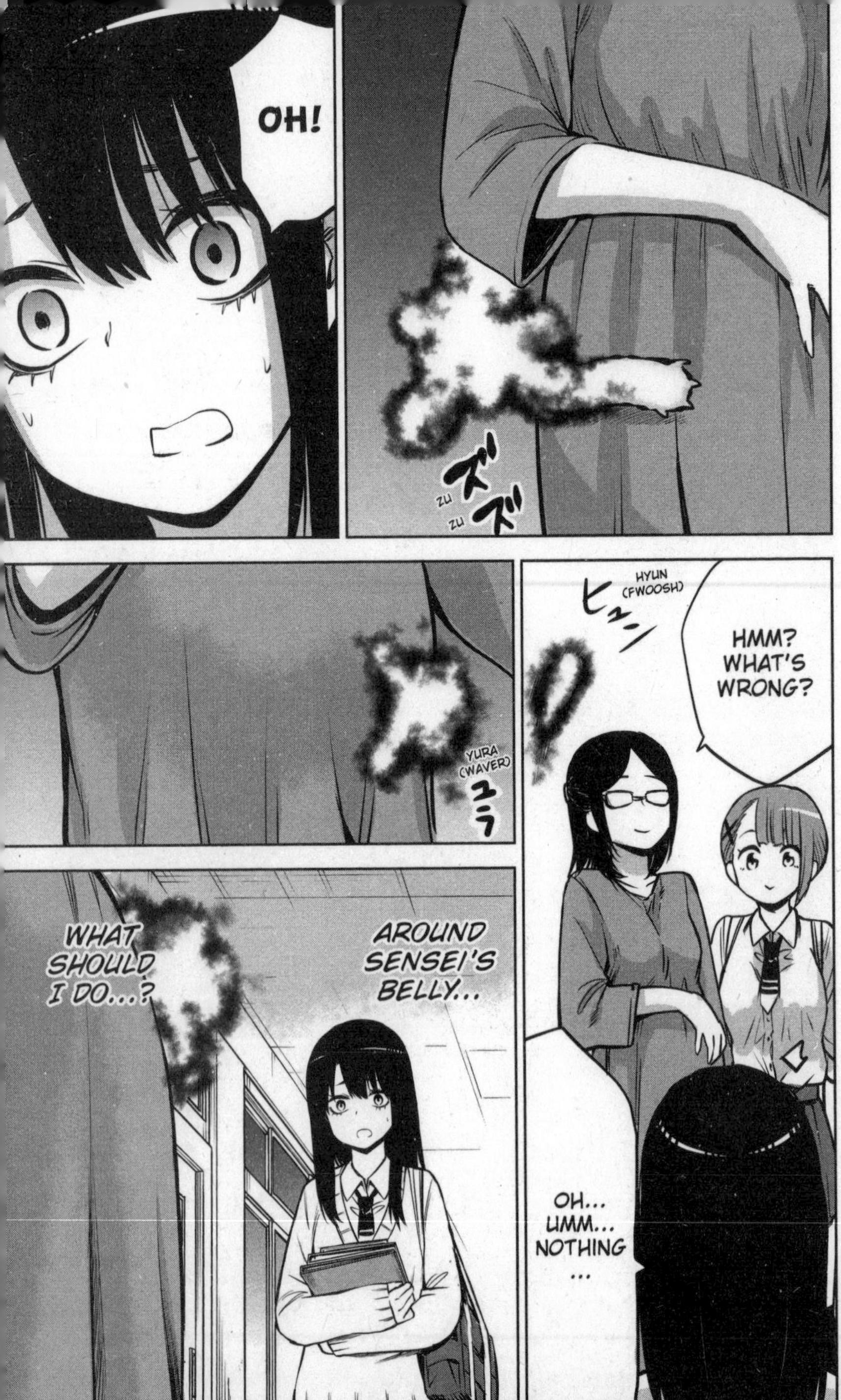
ズズ
ZU ZU
OH!
ヒュン
HYUN (FWOOSH)
HMM? WHAT'S WRONG?
OH... UMM... NOTHING ...
ユラ
YURA (WAVER)
AROUND SENSEI'S BELLY...
WHAT SHOULD I DO...?

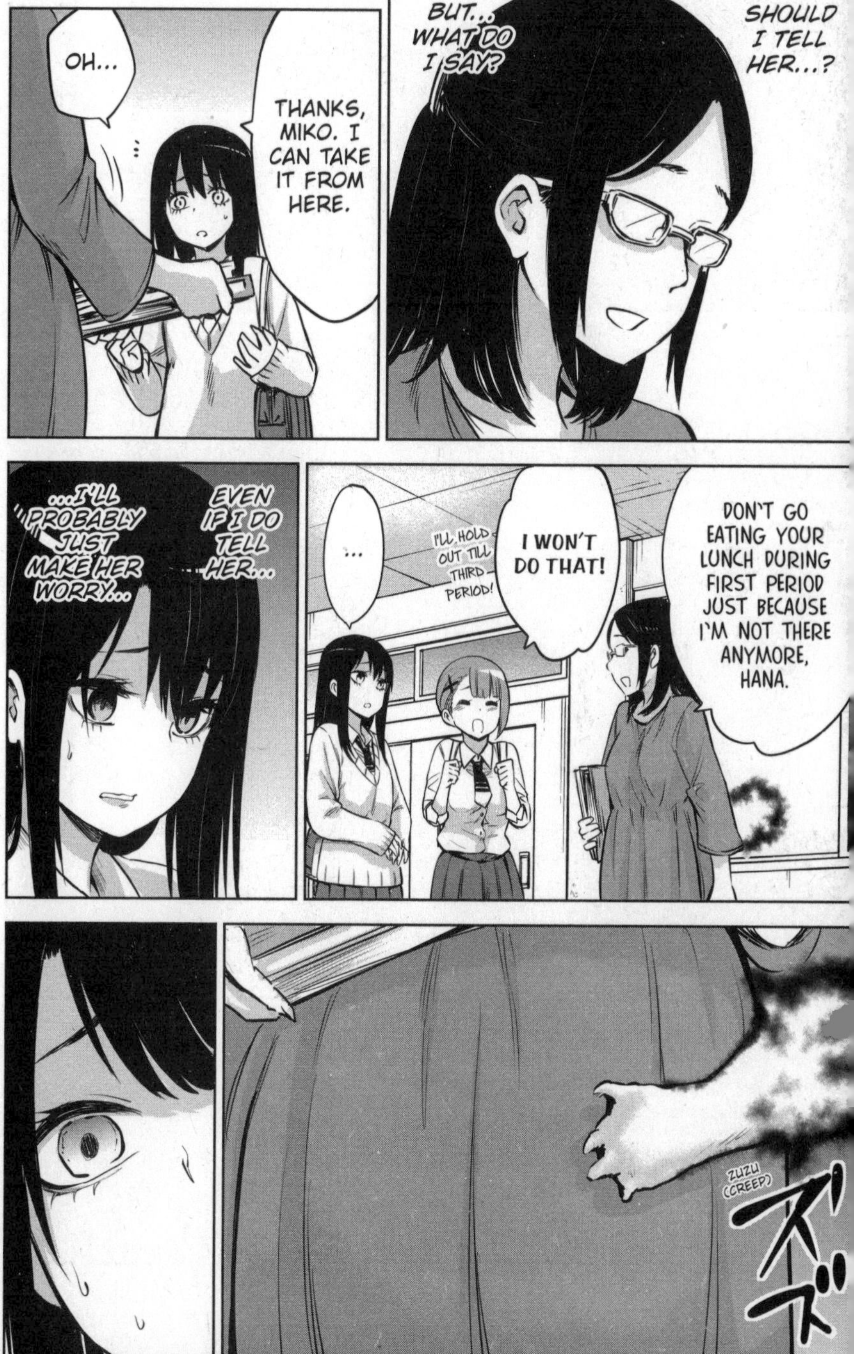
SHOULD I TELL HER...?
BUT... WHAT DO I SAY?
THANKS, MIKO. I CAN TAKE IT FROM HERE.
OH...
DON'T GO EATING YOUR LUNCH DURING FIRST PERIOD JUST BECAUSE I'M NOT THERE ANYMORE, HANA.
I WON'T DO THAT!
I'LL HOLD OUT TILL THIRD PERIOD!
...
EVEN IF I DO TELL HER...
...I'LL PROBABLY JUST MAKE HER WORRY...
ZUZU (CREEP)

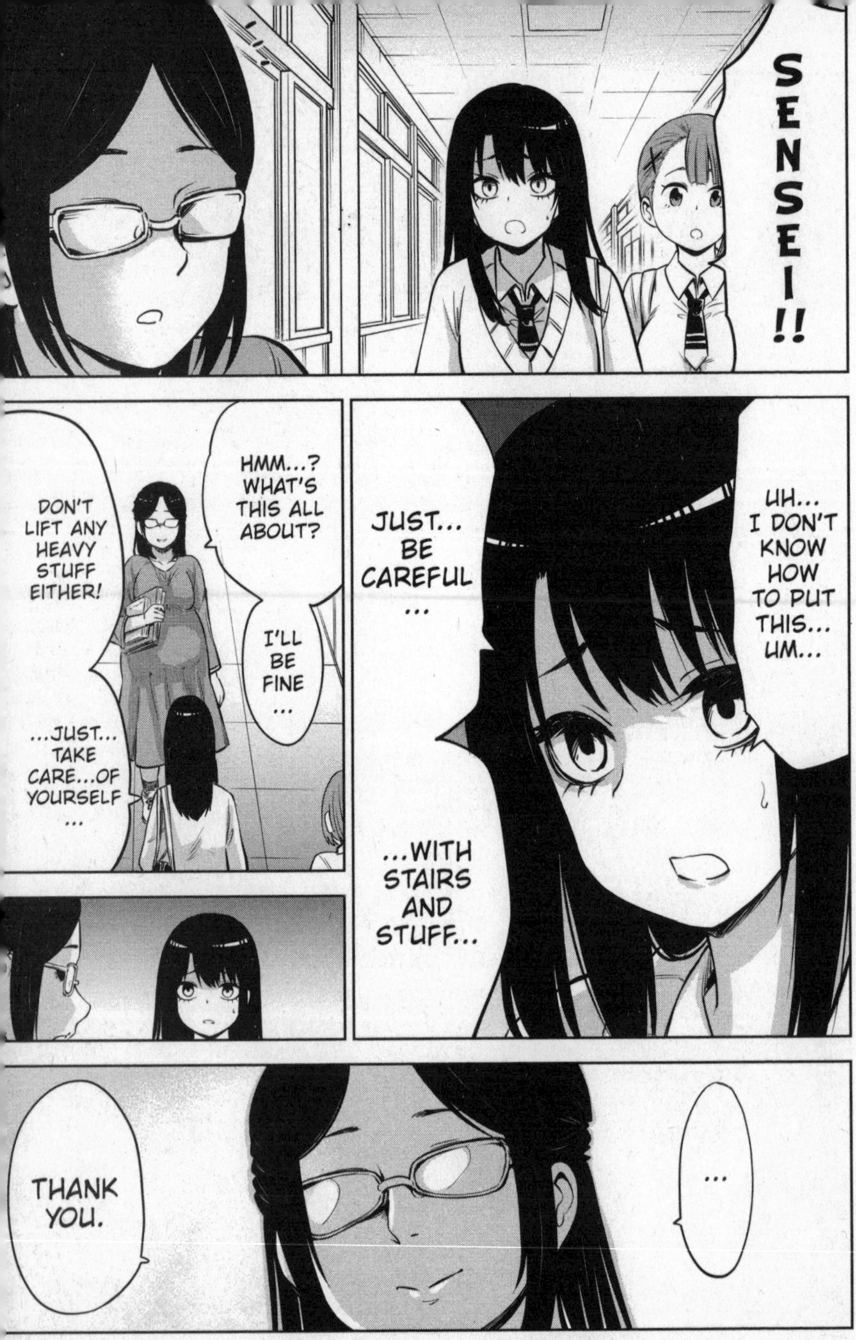
SENSEI!!
UH... I DON'T KNOW HOW TO PUT THIS... UM...
JUST... BE CAREFUL...
...WITH STAIRS AND STUFF...
HMM...? WHAT'S THIS ALL ABOUT?
I'LL BE FINE...
DON'T LIFT ANY HEAVY STUFF EITHER!
...JUST... TAKE CARE...OF YOURSELF...
...
THANK YOU.

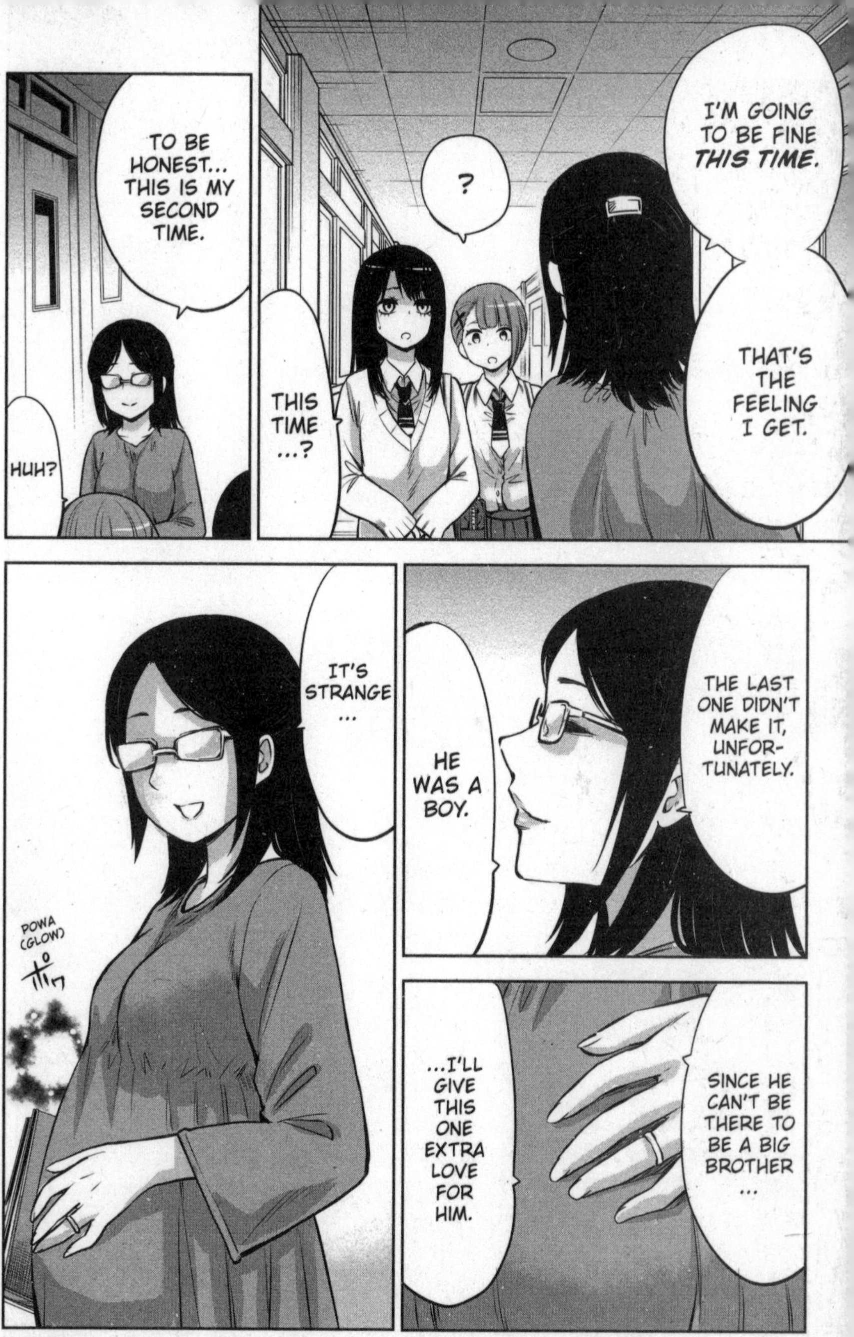
I'M GOING TO BE FINE *THIS TIME.*
?
THAT'S THE FEELING I GET.
THIS TIME ...?
TO BE HONEST... THIS IS MY SECOND TIME.
HUH?
THE LAST ONE DIDN'T MAKE IT, UNFOR-TUNATELY.
HE WAS A BOY.
SINCE HE CAN'T BE THERE TO BE A BIG BROTHER ...
...I'LL GIVE THIS ONE EXTRA LOVE FOR HIM.
IT'S STRANGE ...
POWA (GLOW)

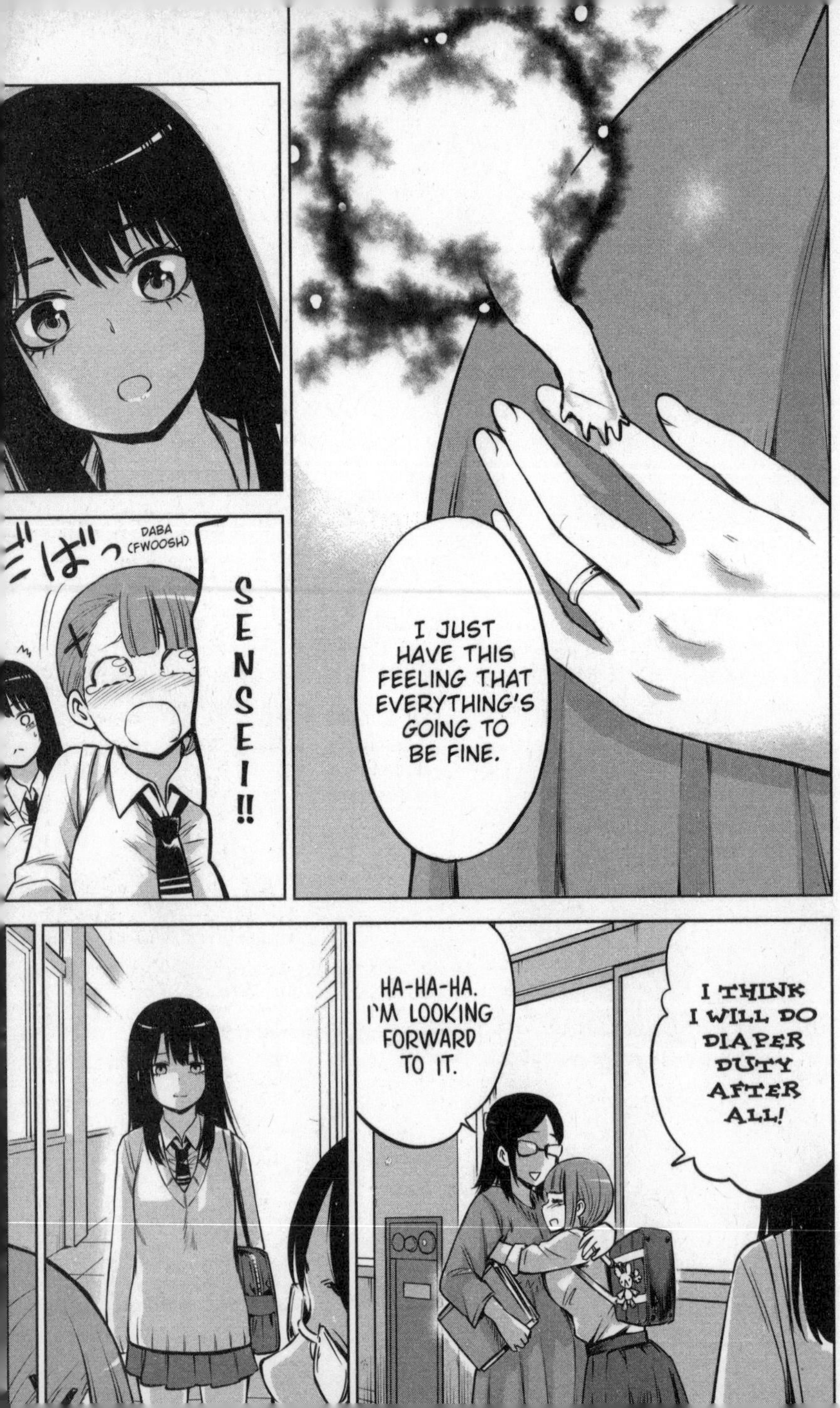
I JUST HAVE THIS FEELING THAT EVERYTHING'S GOING TO BE FINE.
DABA (FWOOSH)
SENSEI!!
I THINK I WILL DO DIAPER DUTY AFTER ALL!
HA-HA-HA. I'M LOOKING FORWARD TO IT.

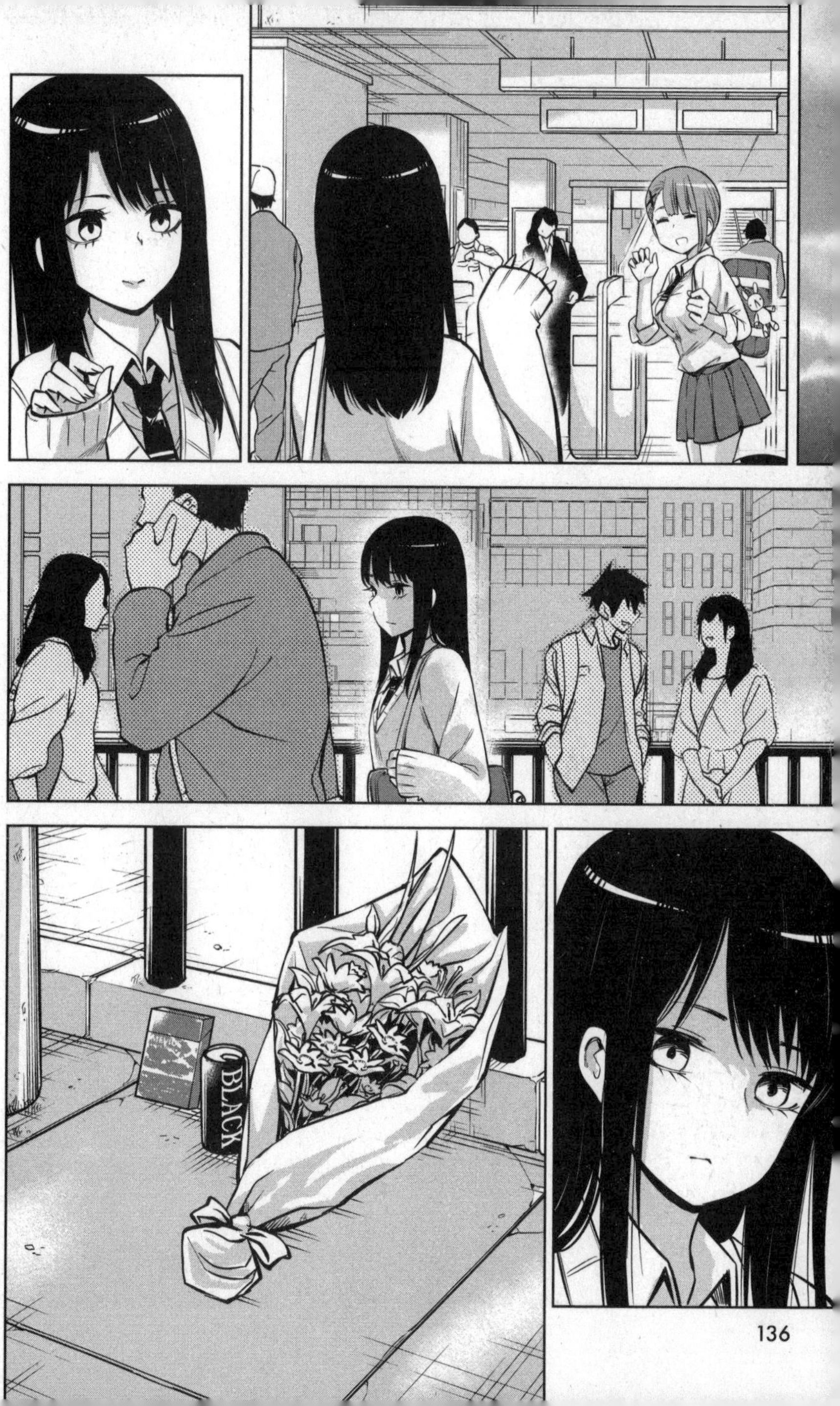
BLACK

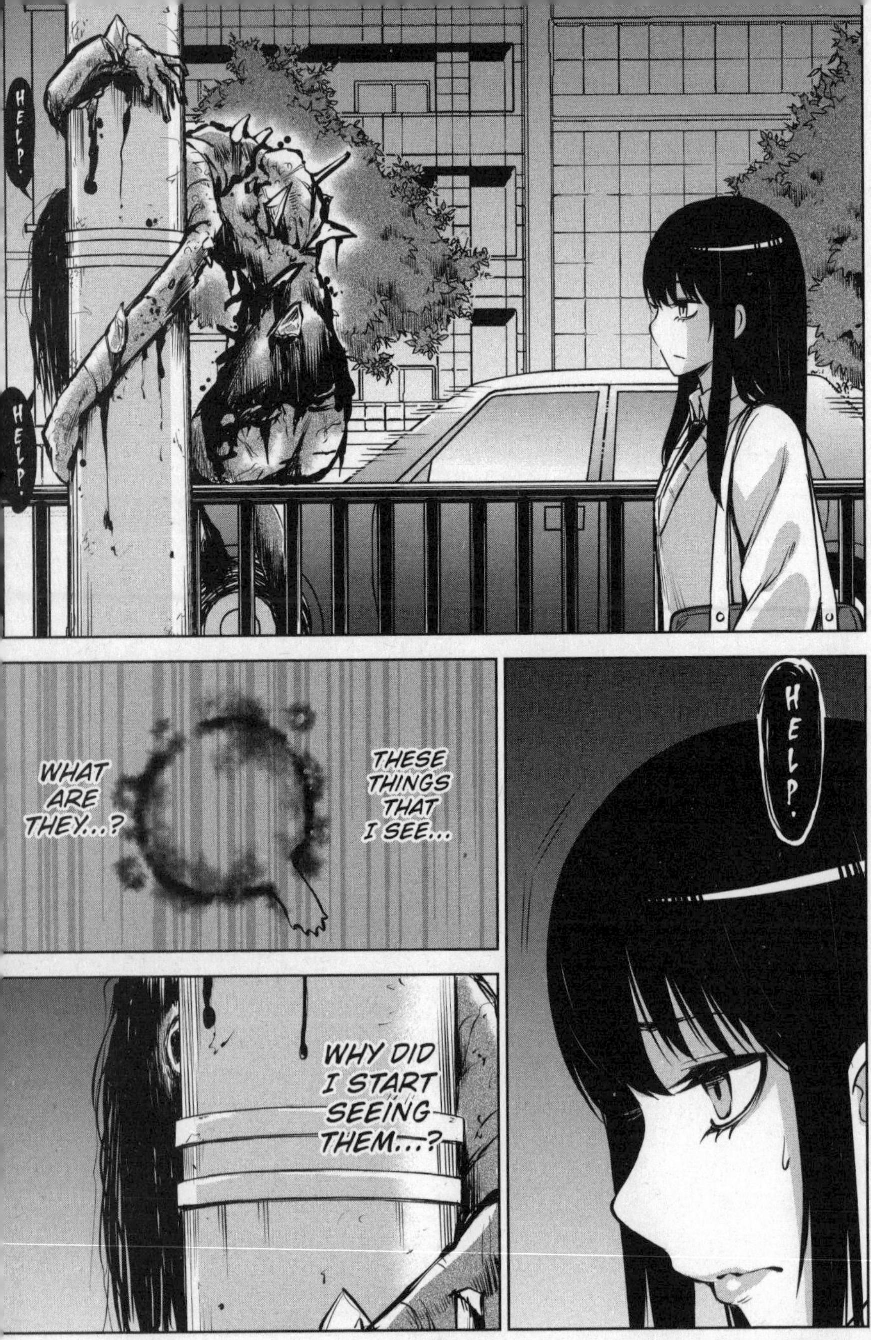
HELP.
HELP.
HELP.
THESE THINGS THAT I SEE...
WHAT ARE THEY...?
WHY DID I START SEEING THEM...?

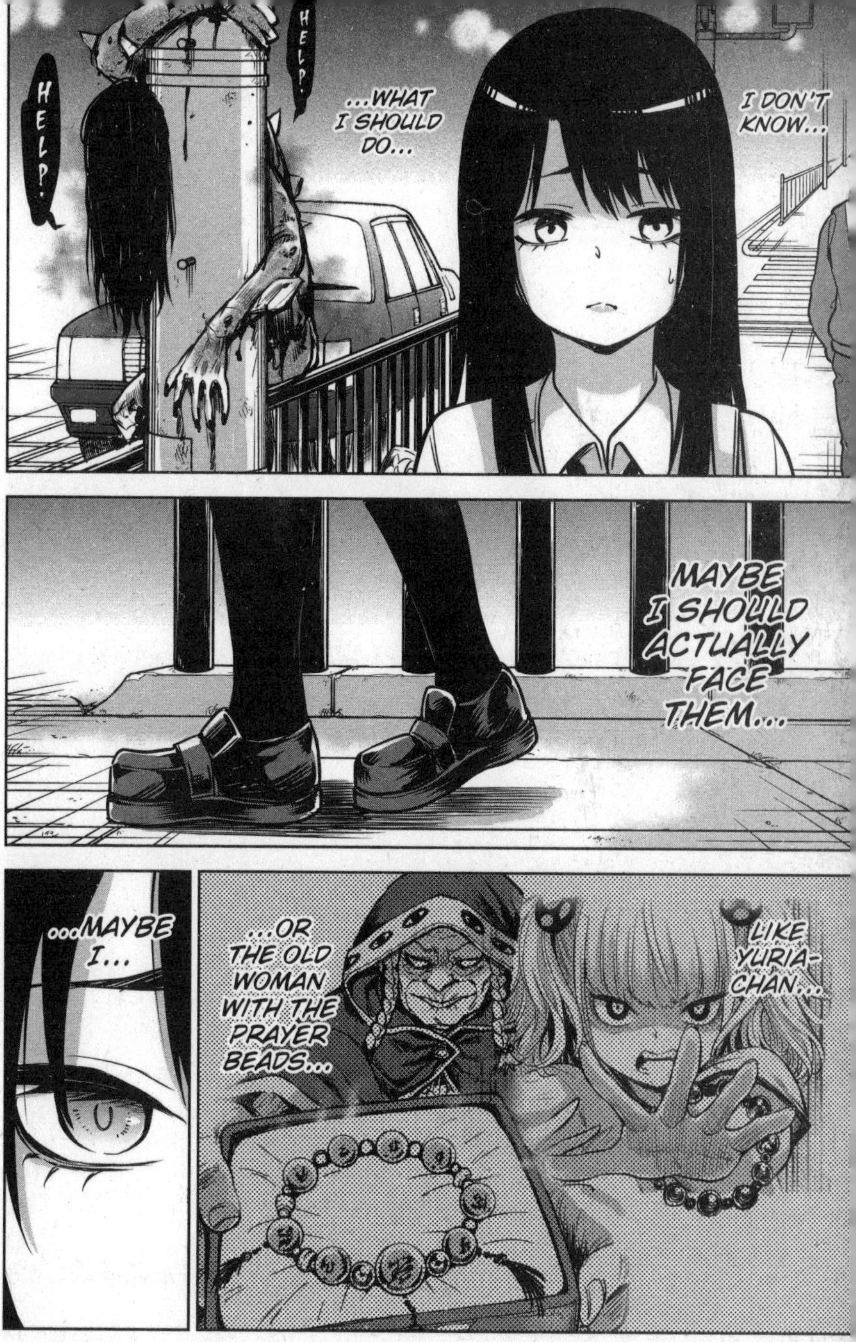
I DON'T KNOW...
...WHAT I SHOULD DO...
HELP.
HELP?
MAYBE I SHOULD ACTUALLY FACE THEM...
LIKE YURIA-CHAN...
...OR THE OLD WOMAN WITH THE PRAYER BEADS...
...MAYBE I...

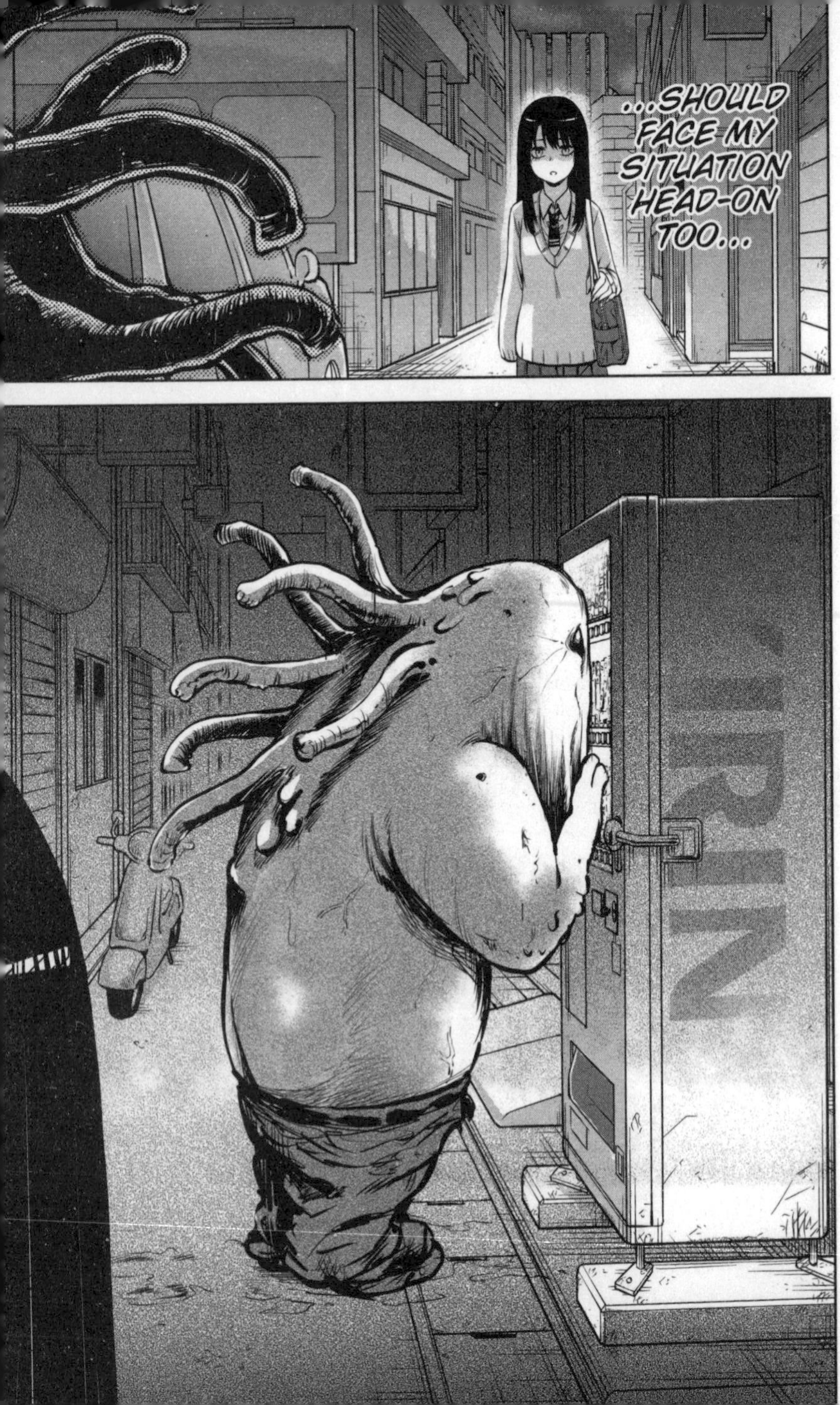
...SHOULD FACE MY SITUATION HEAD-ON TOO...

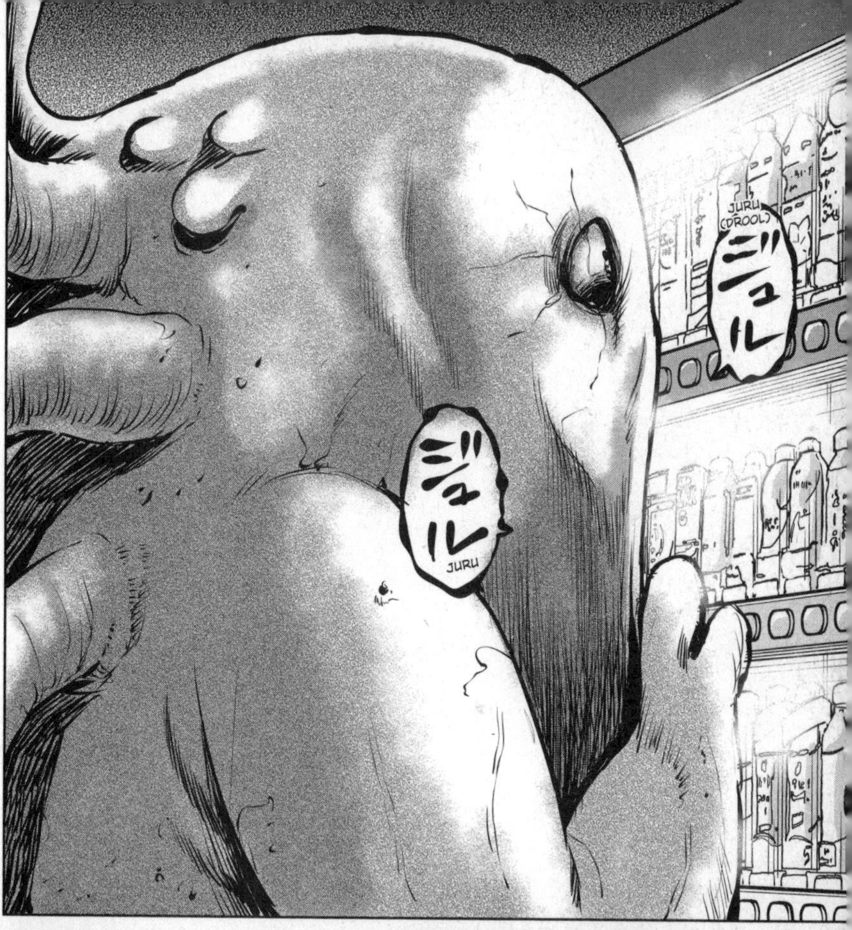
ジュル
JURU (DROOL)
ジュル
JURU

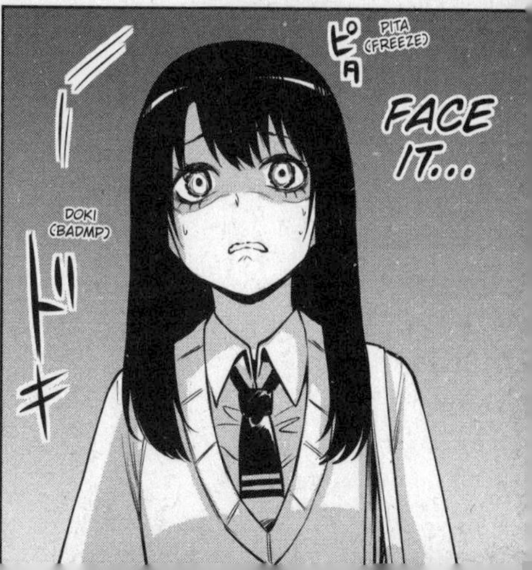
ピタ
PITA (FREEZE)
FACE IT...
ドキ
DOKI (BADMP)

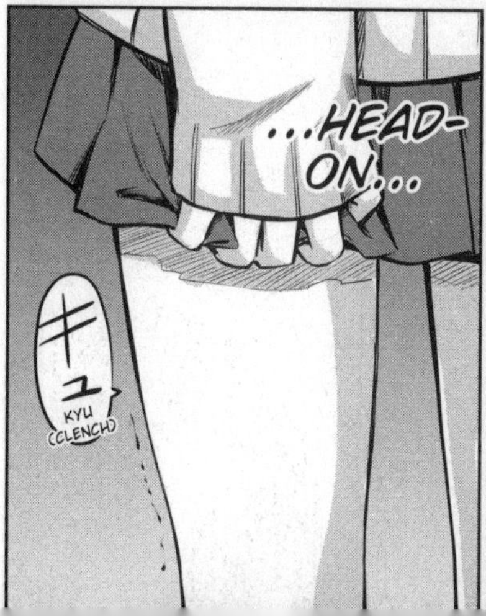
...HEAD-ON...
キュ
KYU (CLENCH)

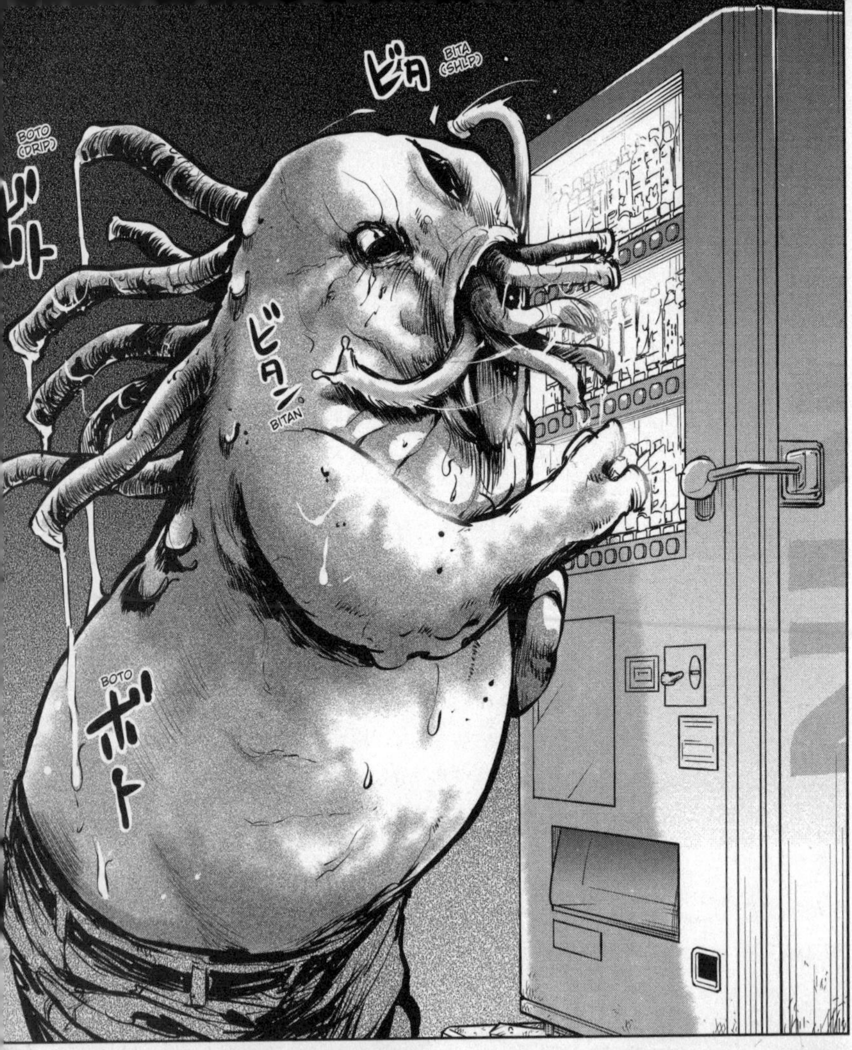
ビタ
BITA (SHLP)
BOTO (DRIP)
ビタン
BITAN
ボト
BOTO
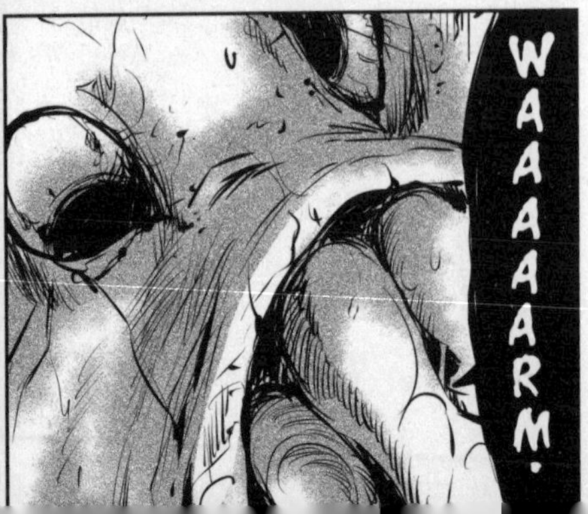
WAAAAARM.
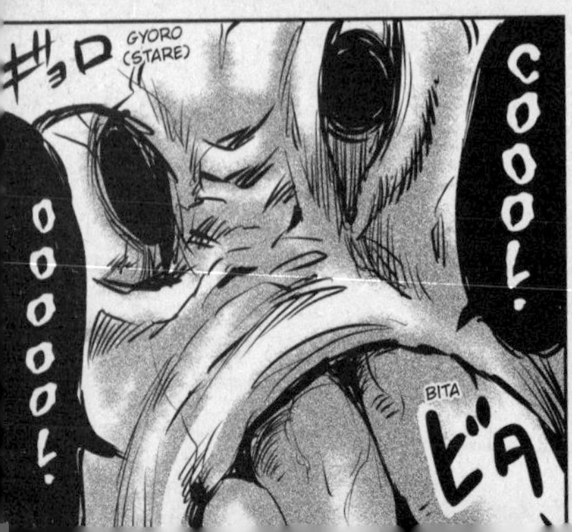
ギョロ
GYORO (STARE)
COOOOL.
OOOOOL.
BITA
ビタ

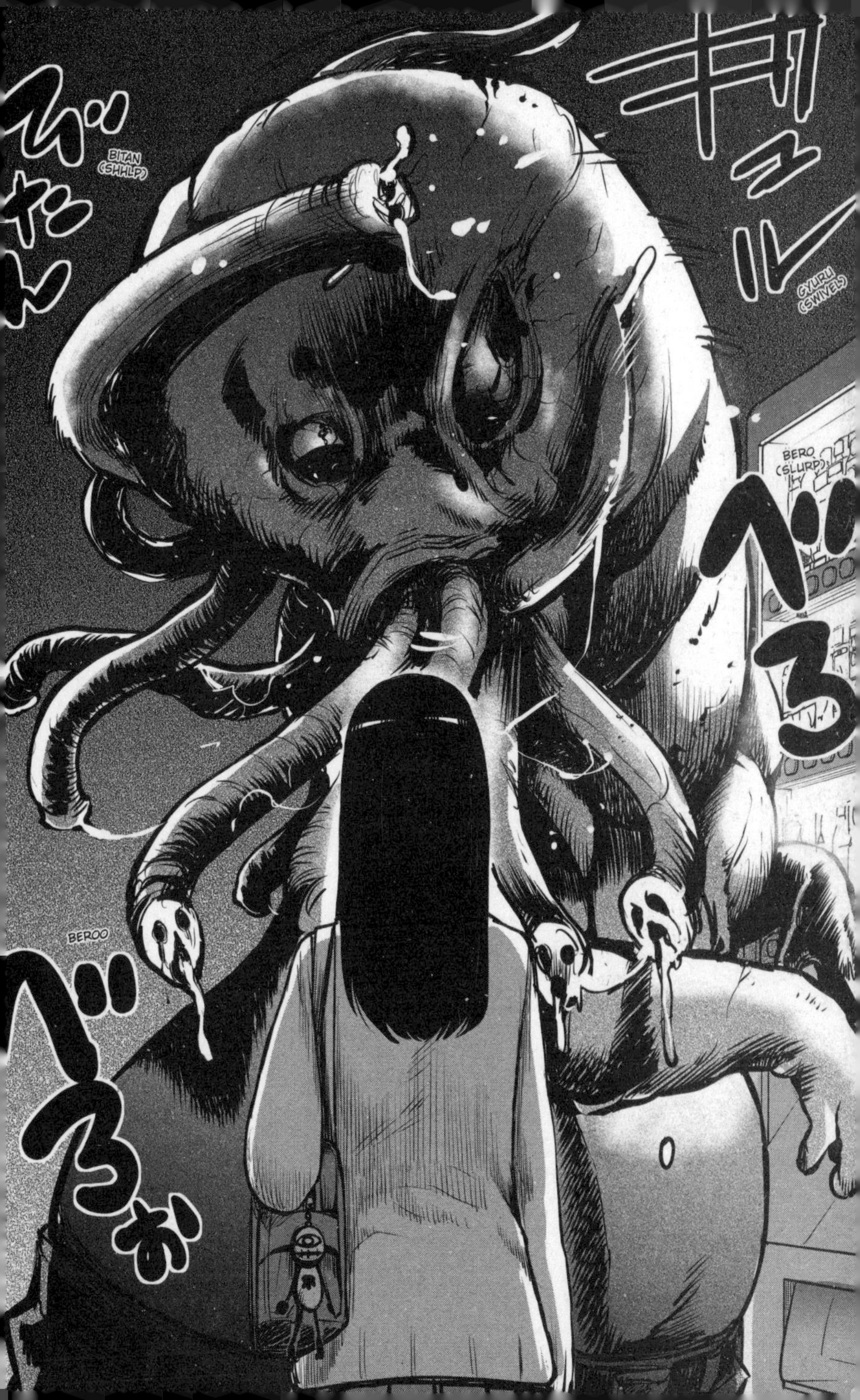
ギュル
GYURU (SWIVEL)
びたん
BITAN (SHHLP)
べろ
BERO (SLURP)
べろぉ
BEROO

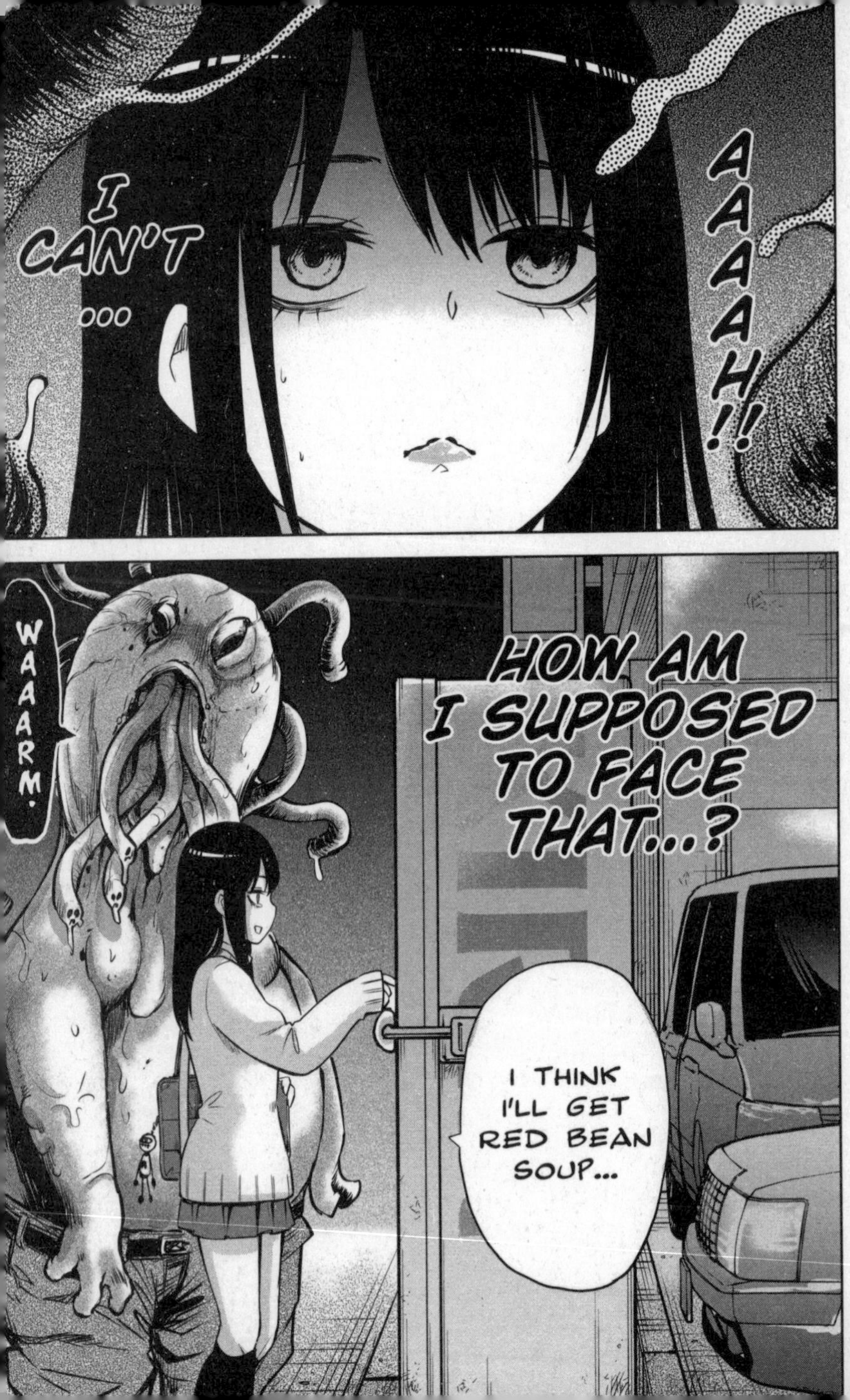
AAAAAH!!
I CAN'T...
HOW AM I SUPPOSED TO FACE THAT...?
WAAAARM.
I THINK I'LL GET RED BEAN SOUP...

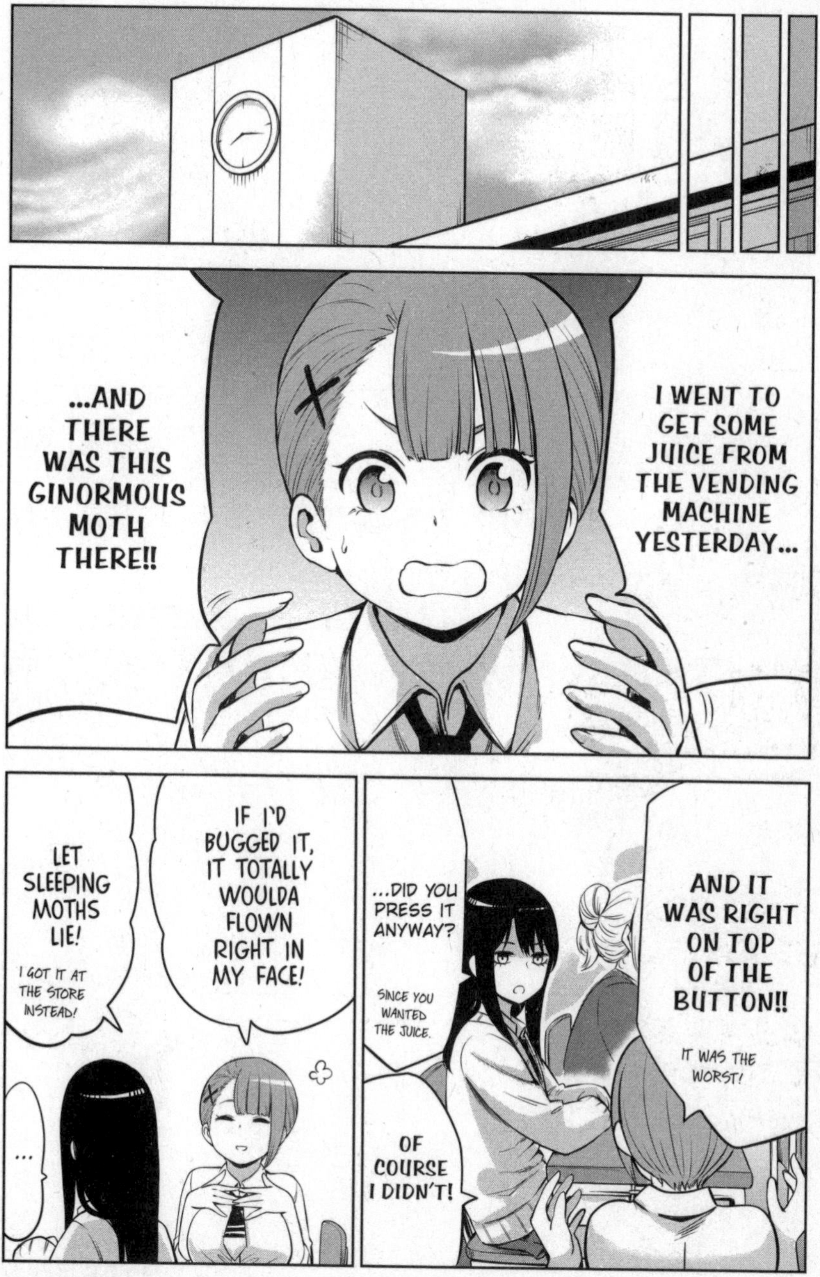
I WENT TO GET SOME JUICE FROM THE VENDING MACHINE YESTERDAY...
...AND THERE WAS THIS GINORMOUS MOTH THERE!!
AND IT WAS RIGHT ON TOP OF THE BUTTON!!
IT WAS THE WORST!
...DID YOU PRESS IT ANYWAY?
SINCE YOU WANTED THE JUICE.
OF COURSE I DIDN'T!
IF I'D BUGGED IT, IT TOTALLY WOULDA FLOWN RIGHT IN MY FACE!
LET SLEEPING MOTHS LIE!
I GOT IT AT THE STORE INSTEAD!
...

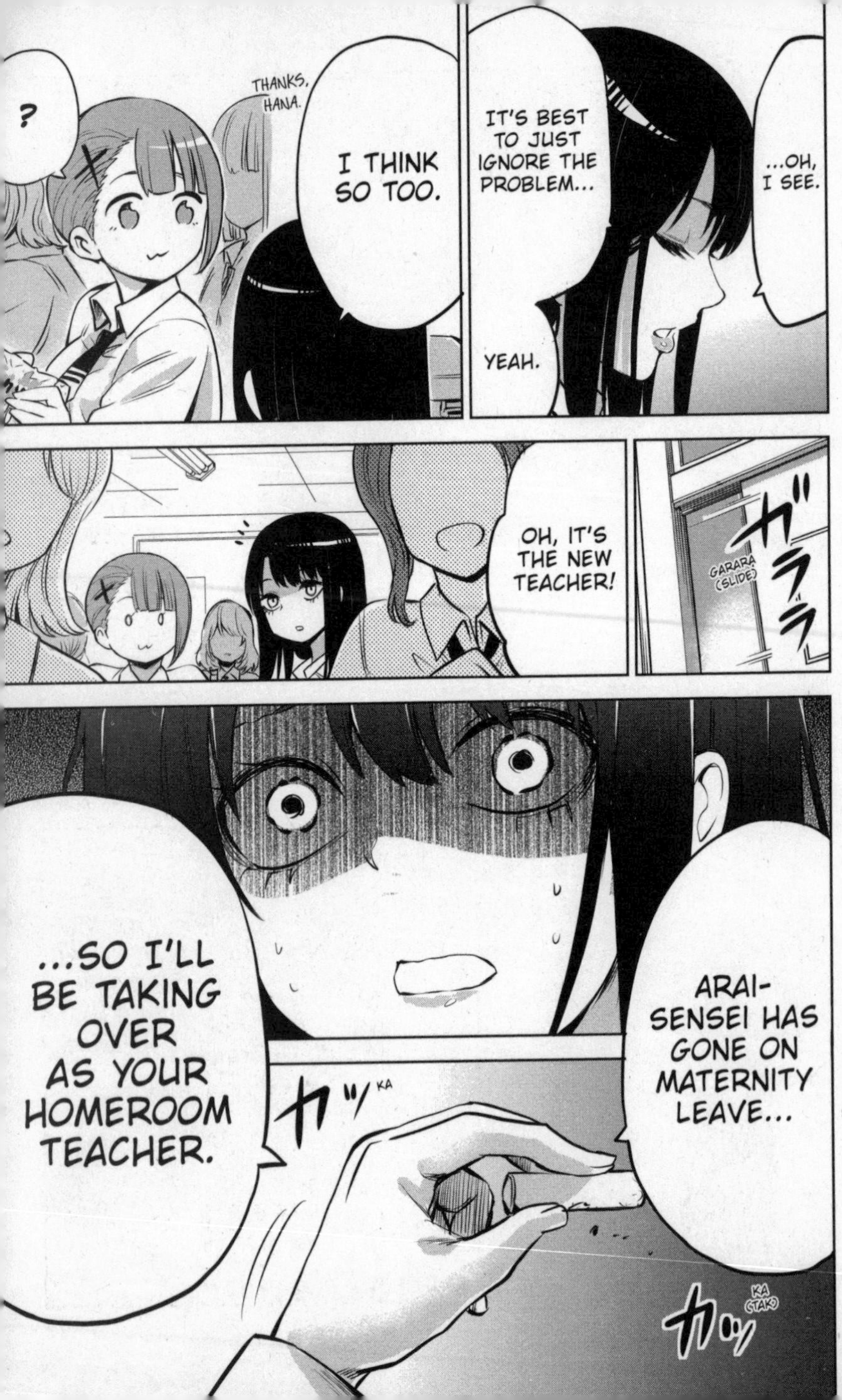
...OH, I SEE.
IT'S BEST TO JUST IGNORE THE PROBLEM...
YEAH.
I THINK SO TOO.
THANKS, HANA.
?
ガララ
GARARA (SLIDE)
OH, IT'S THE NEW TEACHER!
ARAI-SENSEI HAS GONE ON MATERNITY LEAVE...
カッ
KA (TAK)
...SO I'LL BE TAKING OVER AS YOUR HOMEROOM TEACHER.
カッ
KA

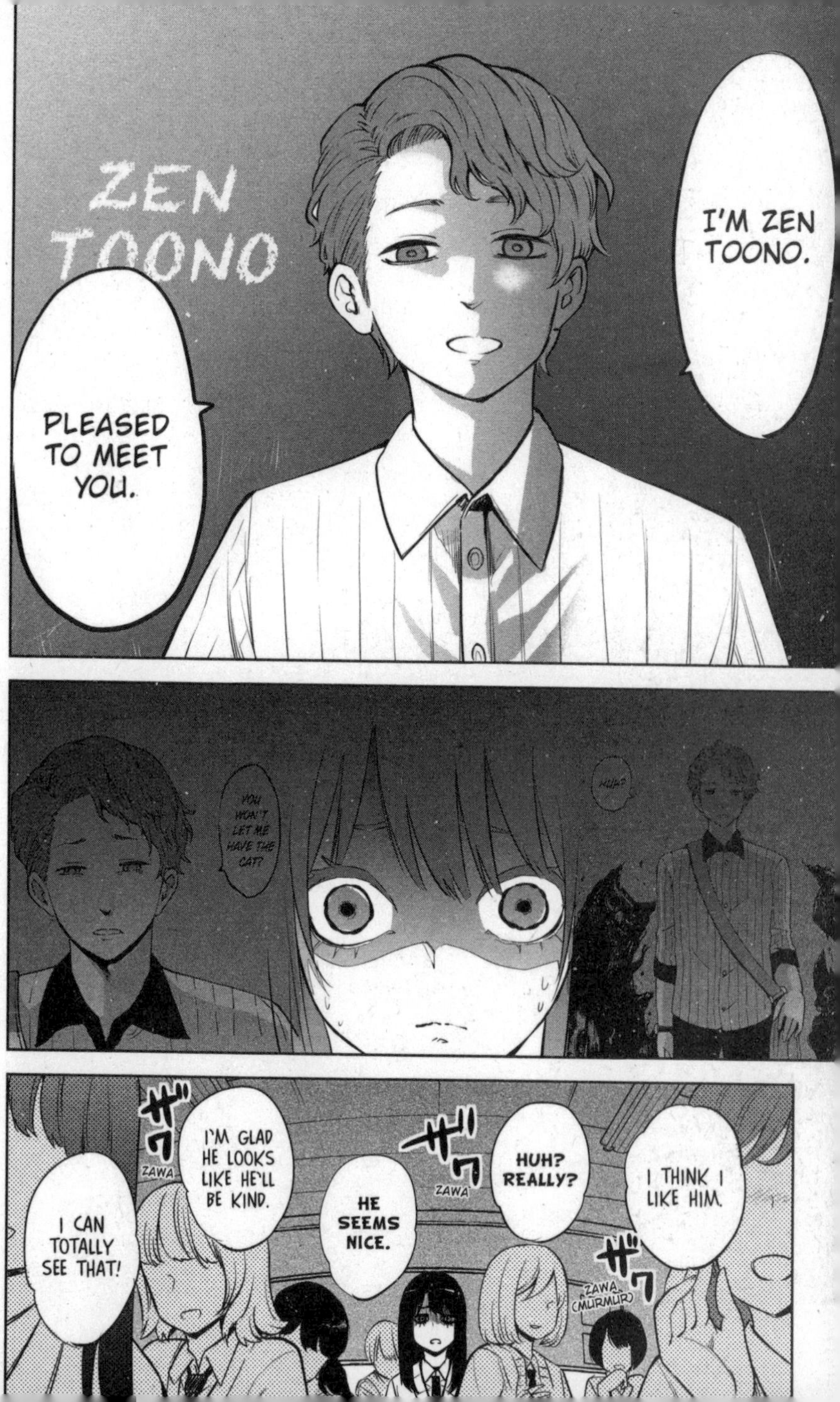
I'M ZEN TOONO.
ZEN TOONO
PLEASED TO MEET YOU.
HUH?
YOU WON'T LET ME HAVE THE CAT?
I THINK I LIKE HIM.
HUH? REALLY?
ザワ
ZAWA
HE SEEMS NICE.
I'M GLAD HE LOOKS LIKE HE'LL BE KIND.
ザワ
ZAWA
I CAN TOTALLY SEE THAT!
ザワ
ZAWA (MURMUR)

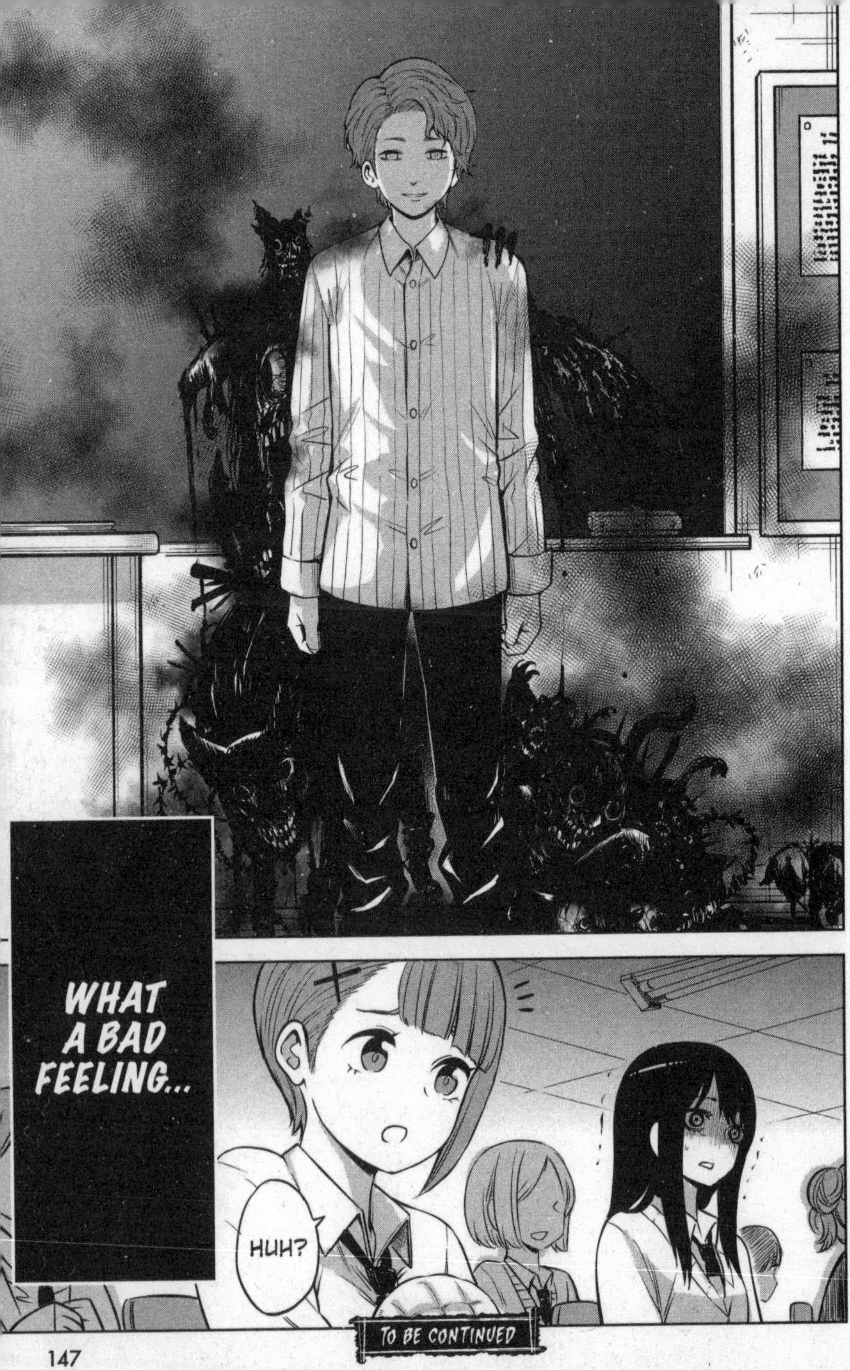
HUH?
WHAT A BAD FEELING...
TO BE CONTINUED

AT THE BAKERY (NO SIGHT VER.)

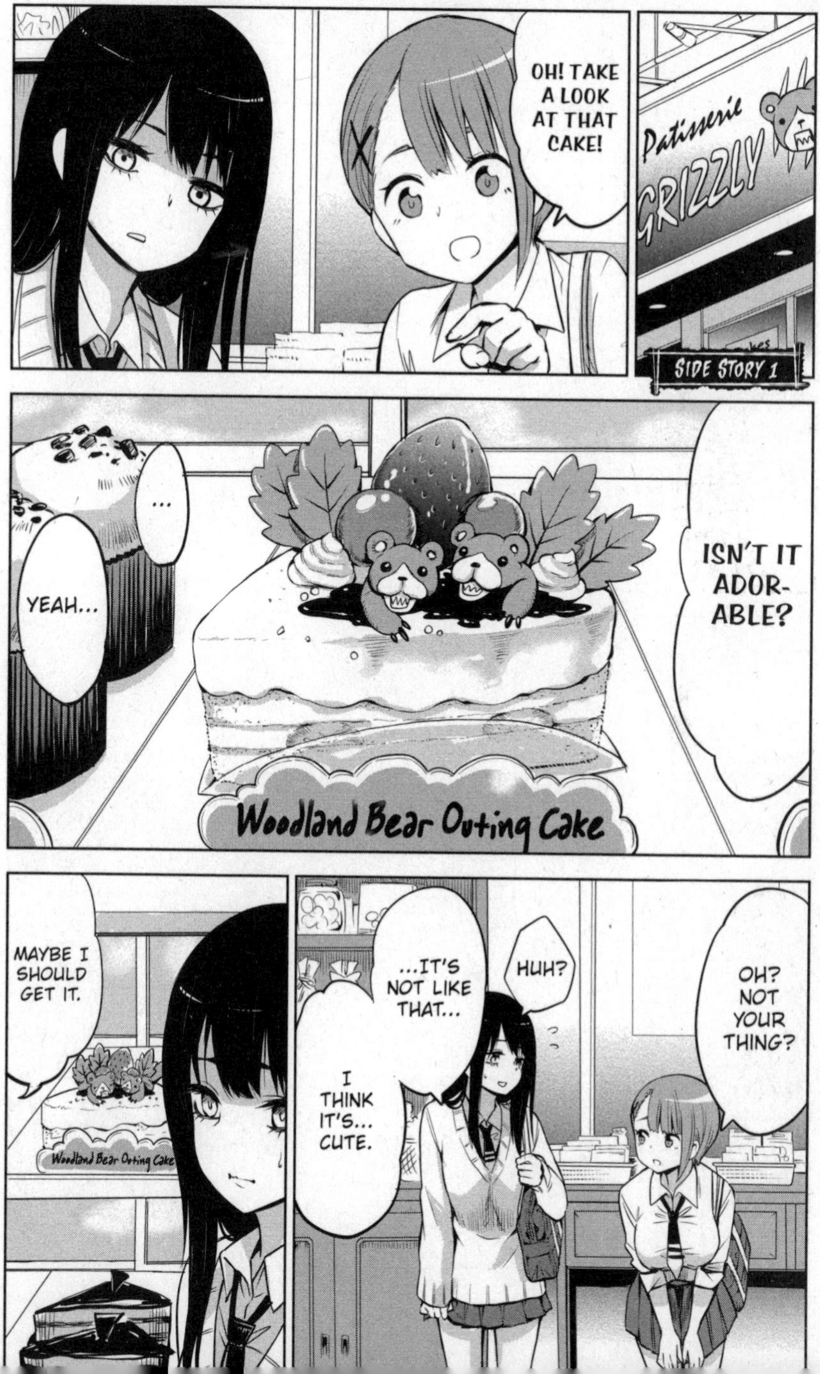
Patisserie GRIZZLY
SIDE STORY 1
OH! TAKE A LOOK AT THAT CAKE!
ISN'T IT ADORABLE?
...
YEAH...
Woodland Bear Outing Cake
OH? NOT YOUR THING?
HUH?
...IT'S NOT LIKE THAT...
I THINK IT'S... CUTE.
MAYBE I SHOULD GET IT.
Woodland Bear Outing Cake

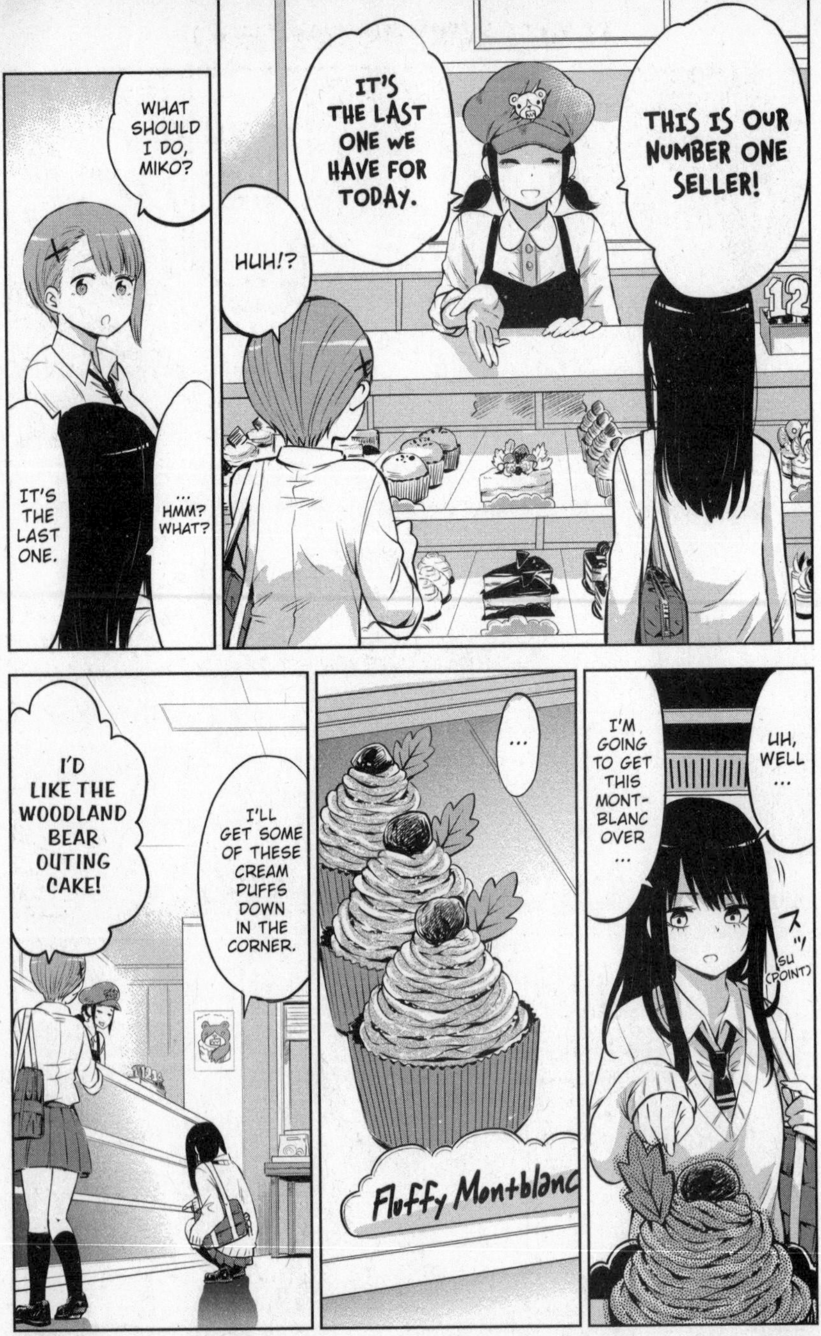
THIS IS OUR NUMBER ONE SELLER!
IT'S THE LAST ONE WE HAVE FOR TODAY.
HUH!?
WHAT SHOULD I DO, MIKO?
... HMM? WHAT?
IT'S THE LAST ONE.
UH, WELL ...
I'M GOING TO GET THIS MONT-BLANC OVER ...
スッ
SU (POINT)
...
Fluffy Montblanc
I'LL GET SOME OF THESE CREAM PUFFS DOWN IN THE CORNER.
I'D LIKE THE WOODLAND BEAR OUTING CAKE!

AT THE BAKERY (SIGHT VER.)

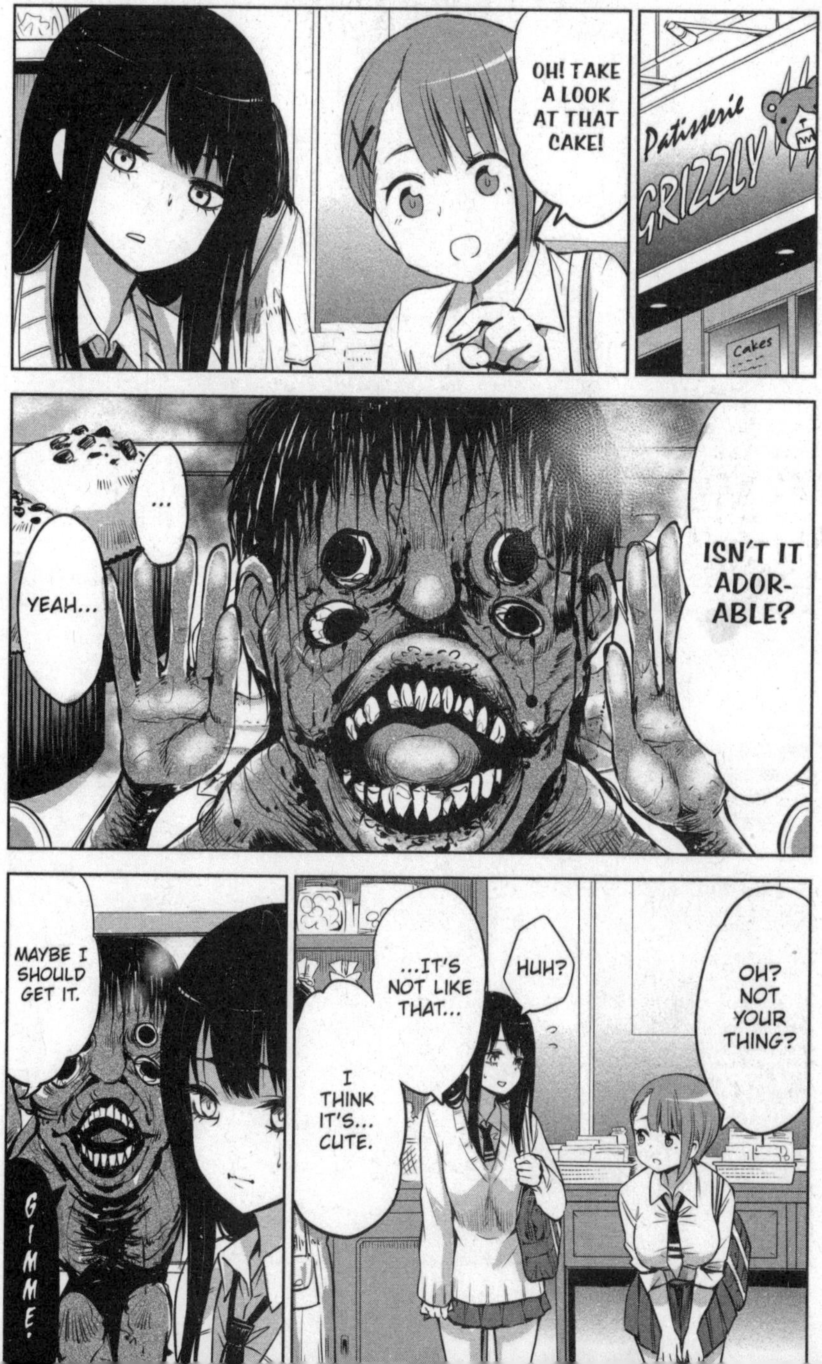
Patisserie GRIZZLY
Cakes
OH! TAKE A LOOK AT THAT CAKE!
ISN'T IT ADOR-ABLE?
...
YEAH...
OH? NOT YOUR THING?
HUH?
...IT'S NOT LIKE THAT...
I THINK IT'S... CUTE.
MAYBE I SHOULD GET IT.
GIMME.

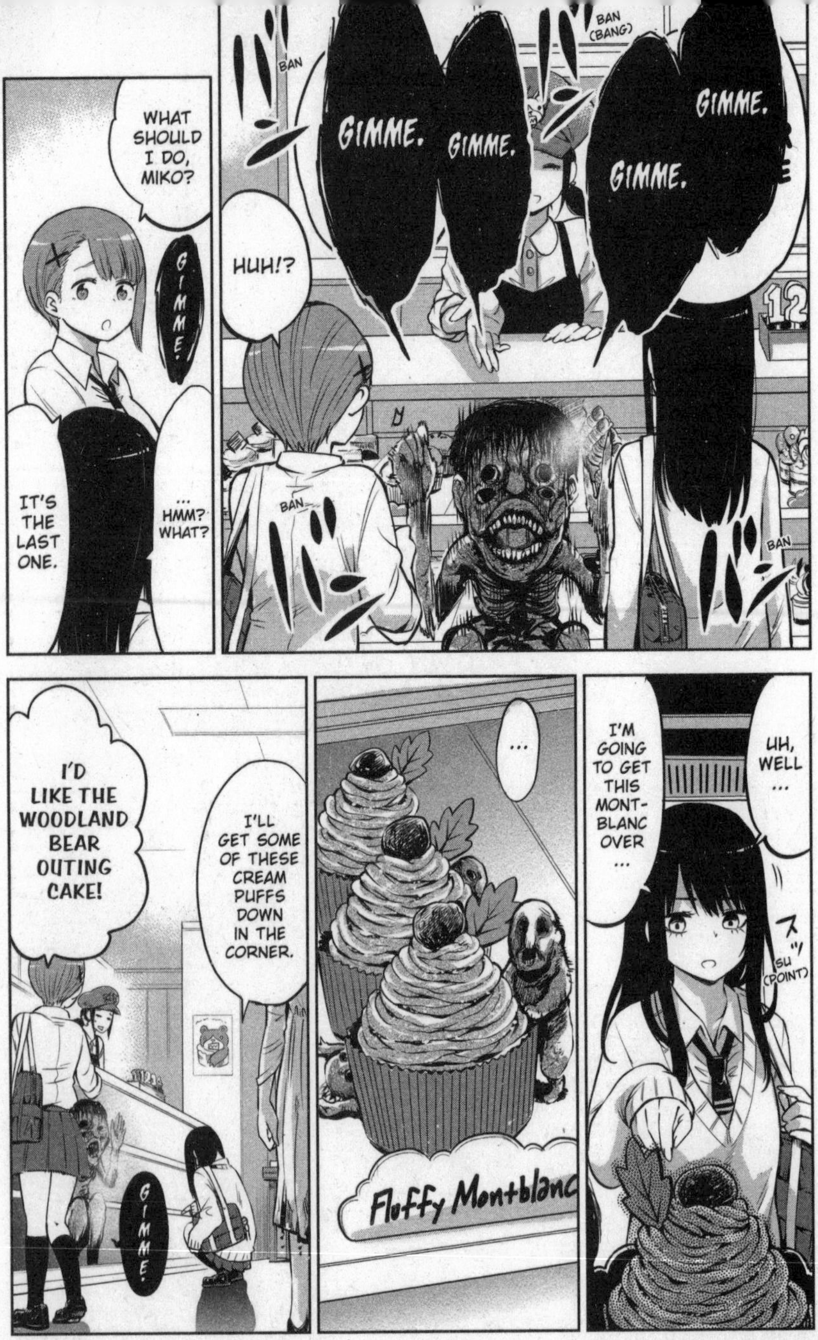
BAN (BANG)
GIMME.
GIMME.
GIMME.
GIMME.
BAN
HUH!?
BAN
BAN
WHAT SHOULD I DO, MIKO?
GIMME.
... HMM? WHAT?
IT'S THE LAST ONE.
UH, WELL ...
I'M GOING TO GET THIS MONT-BLANC OVER ...
SU (POINT)
...
Fluffy Montblanc
I'LL GET SOME OF THESE CREAM PUFFS DOWN IN THE CORNER.
I'D LIKE THE WOODLAND BEAR OUTING CAKE!
GIMME.

ON THE PARANORMAL TV SHOW (NO SIGHT VER.)

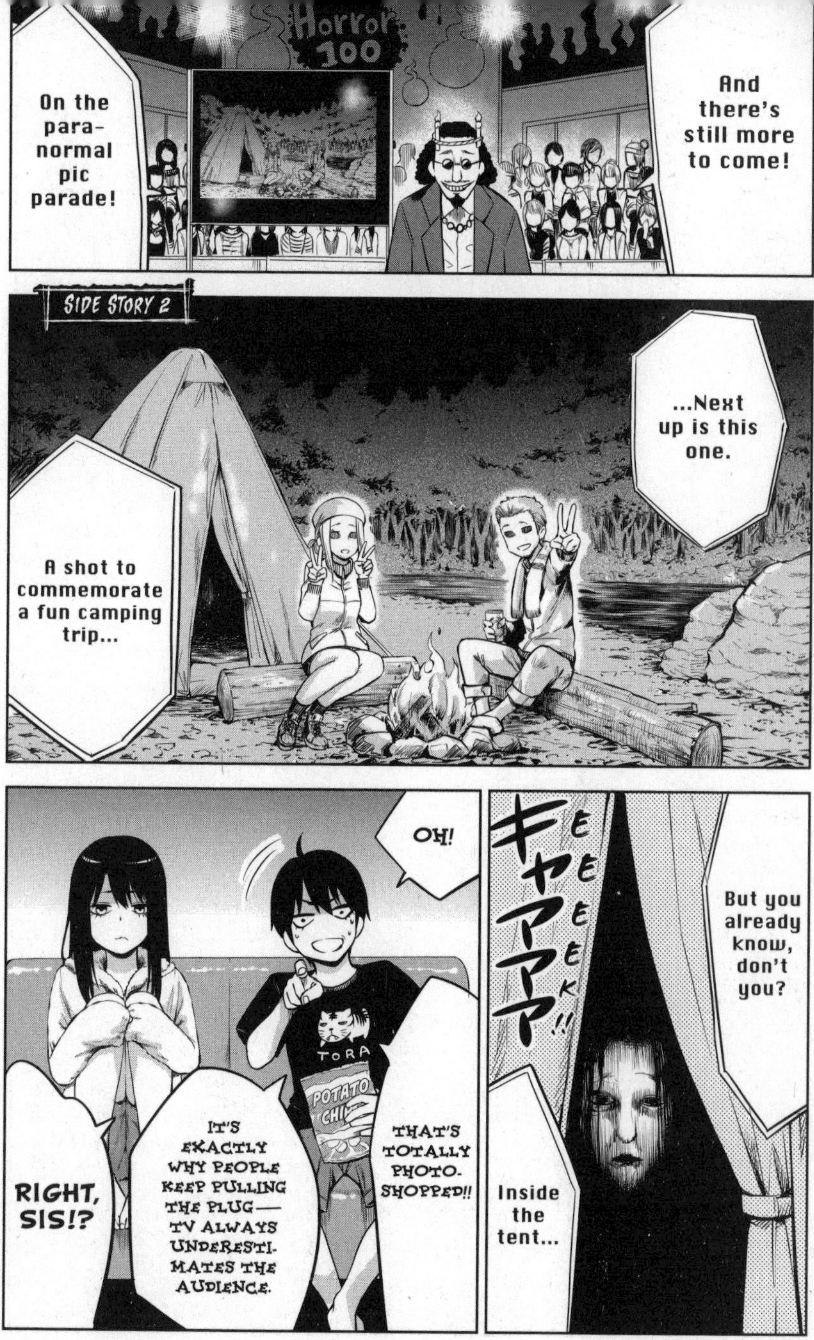

Horror 100
And there's still more to come!
On the para-normal pic parade!
SIDE STORY 2
...Next up is this one.
A shot to commemorate a fun camping trip...
But you already know, don't you?
Inside the tent...
キャアア
EEEEEK!!
OH!
THAT'S TOTALLY PHOTO-SHOPPED!!
IT'S EXACTLY WHY PEOPLE KEEP PULLING THE PLUG— TV ALWAYS UNDERESTI-MATES THE AUDIENCE.
RIGHT, SIS!?
TORA
POTATO CHIPS

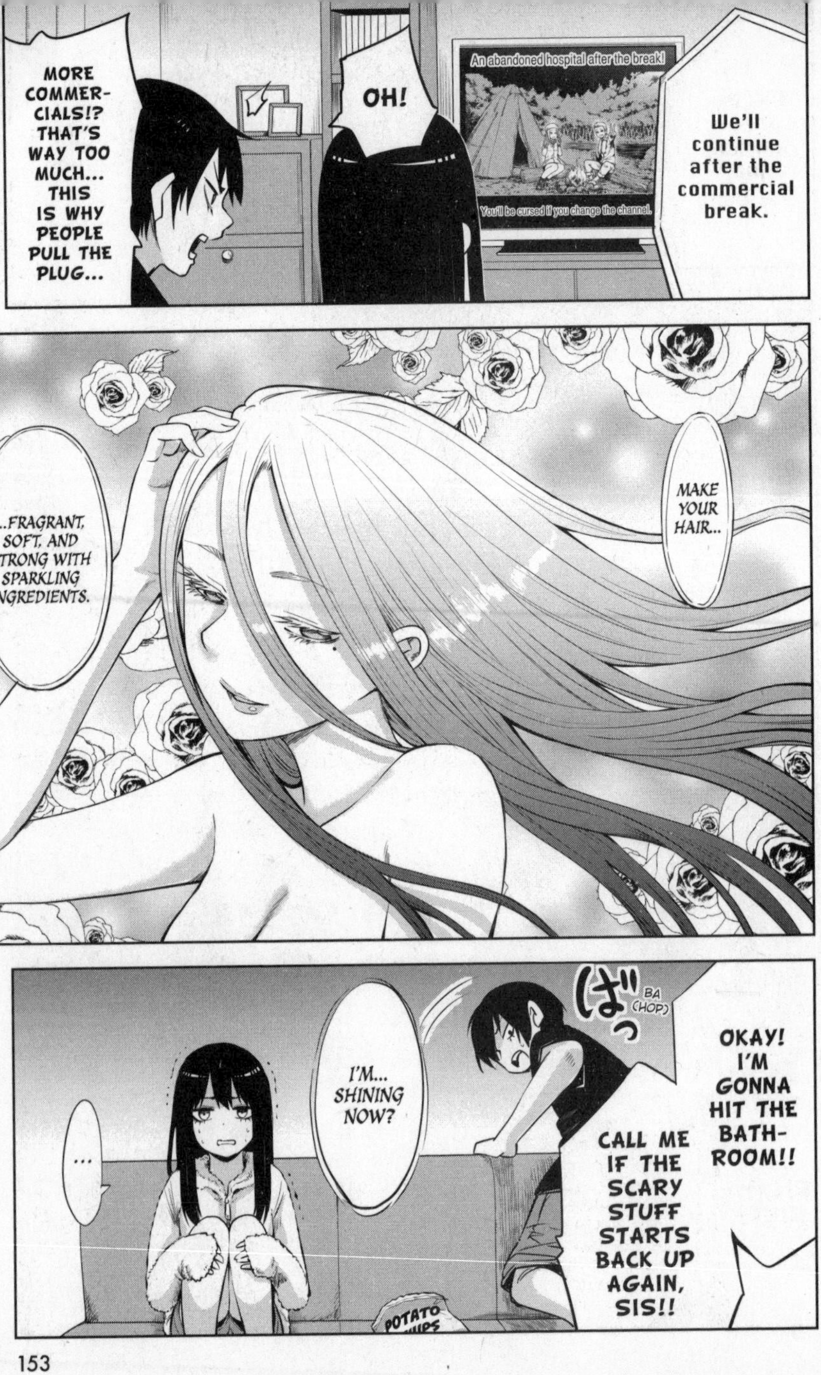
We'll continue after the commercial break.
An abandoned hospital after the break!
You'll be cursed if you change the channel.
OH!
MORE COMMERCIALS!? THAT'S WAY TOO MUCH... THIS IS WHY PEOPLE PULL THE PLUG...
MAKE YOUR HAIR...
...FRAGRANT, SOFT, AND STRONG WITH SPARKLING INGREDIENTS.
OKAY! I'M GONNA HIT THE BATHROOM!!
CALL ME IF THE SCARY STUFF STARTS BACK UP AGAIN, SIS!!
ばっ
BA (HOP)
I'M... SHINING NOW?
...
POTATO

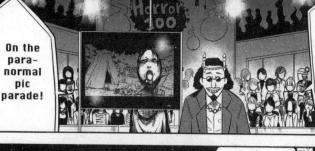

On the paranormal pic parade!

And there's still more to come!

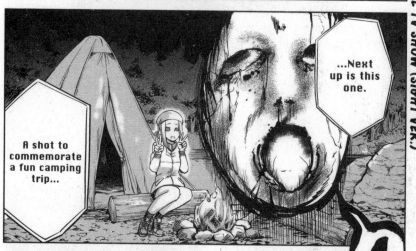

...Next up is this one.

A shot to commemorate a fun camping trip...

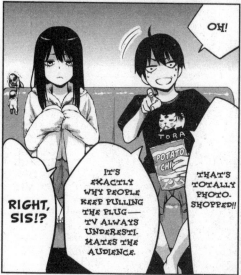

OH!

RIGHT, SIS!?

IT'S EXACTLY WHY PEOPLE KEEP PULLING THE PLUG— TV ALWAYS UNDERESTIMATES THE AUDIENCE.

THAT'S TOTALLY PHOTO-SHOPPED!!

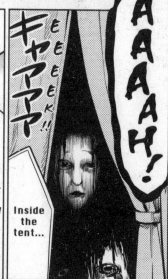

AAAAH!

EEEEK!!

Inside the tent...

154

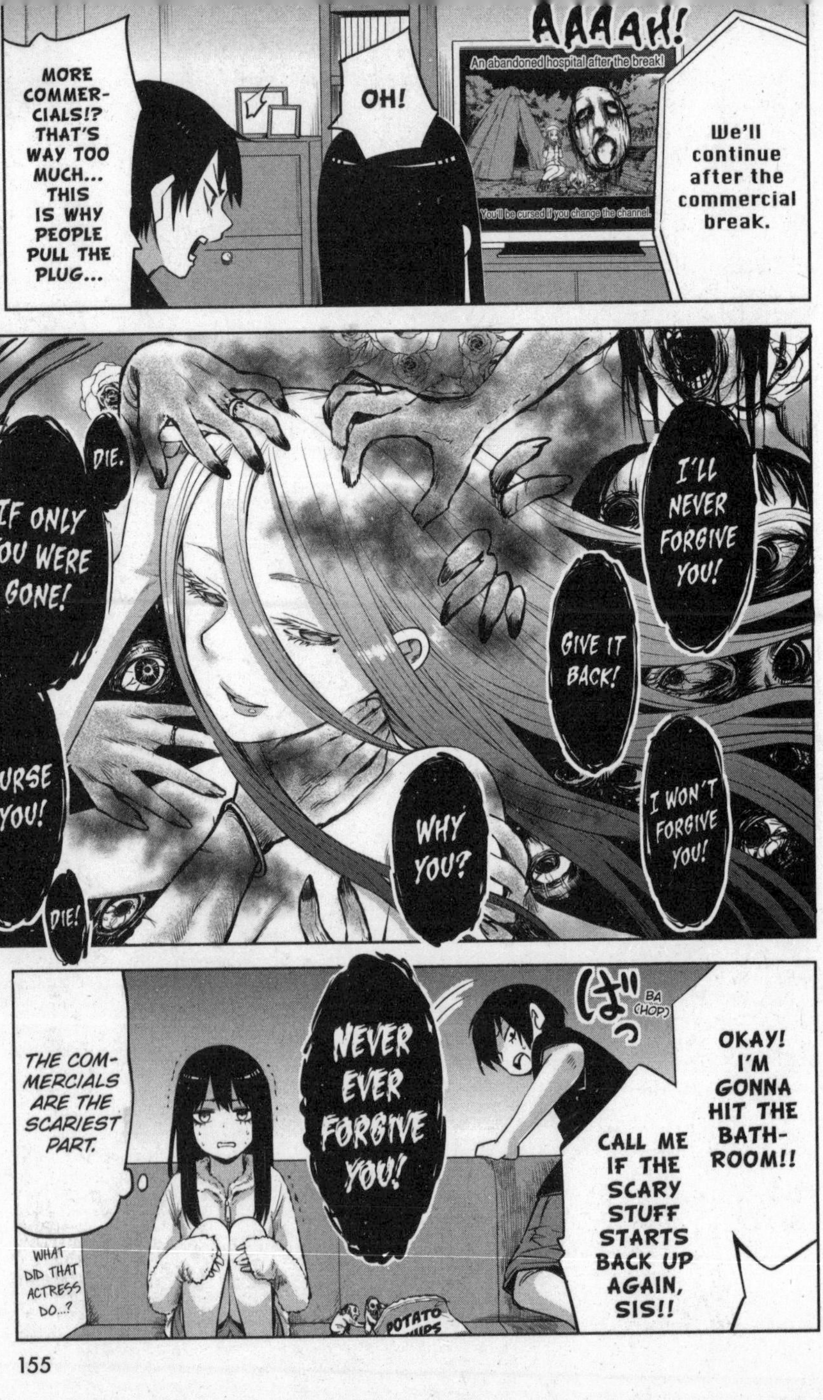
AAAAH!
An abandoned hospital after the break!
You'll be cursed if you change the channel.
We'll continue after the commercial break.
OH!
MORE COMMERCIALS!? THAT'S WAY TOO MUCH... THIS IS WHY PEOPLE PULL THE PLUG...
I'LL NEVER FORGIVE YOU!
GIVE IT BACK!
I WON'T FORGIVE YOU!
WHY YOU?
DIE.
IF ONLY YOU WERE GONE!
CURSE YOU!
DIE!
OKAY! I'M GONNA HIT THE BATHROOM!!
ばっ
BA (HOP)
CALL ME IF THE SCARY STUFF STARTS BACK UP AGAIN, SIS!!
NEVER EVER FORGIVE YOU!
THE COMMERCIALS ARE THE SCARIEST PART.
WHAT DID THAT ACTRESS DO...?
POTATO CHIPS

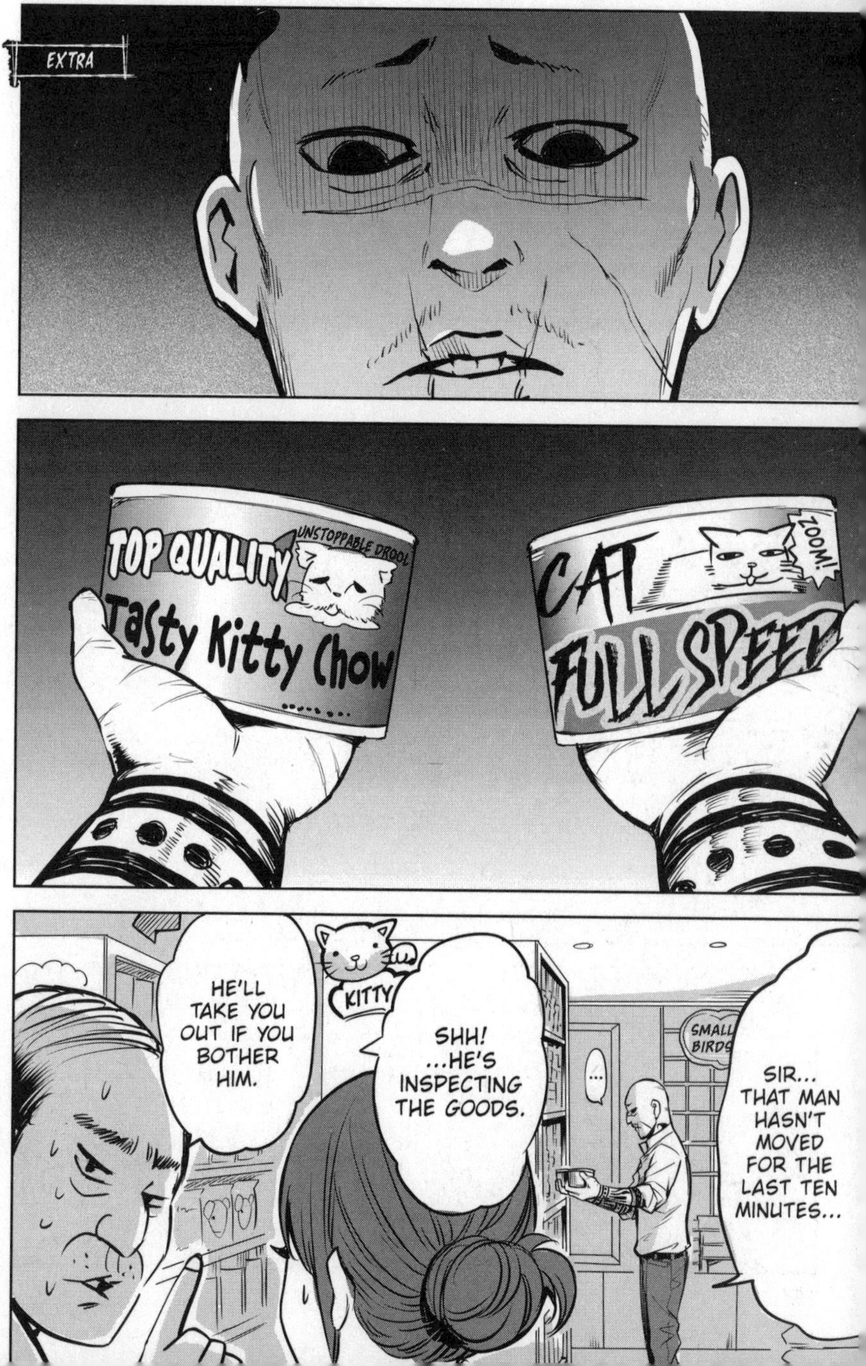
EXTRA
ZOOM!
CAT
TOP QUALITY
UNSTOPPABLE DROOL
Tasty Kitty Chow
SIR... THAT MAN HASN'T MOVED FOR THE LAST TEN MINUTES...
...
SHH! ...HE'S INSPECTING THE GOODS.
KITTY
HE'LL TAKE YOU OUT IF YOU BOTHER HIM.

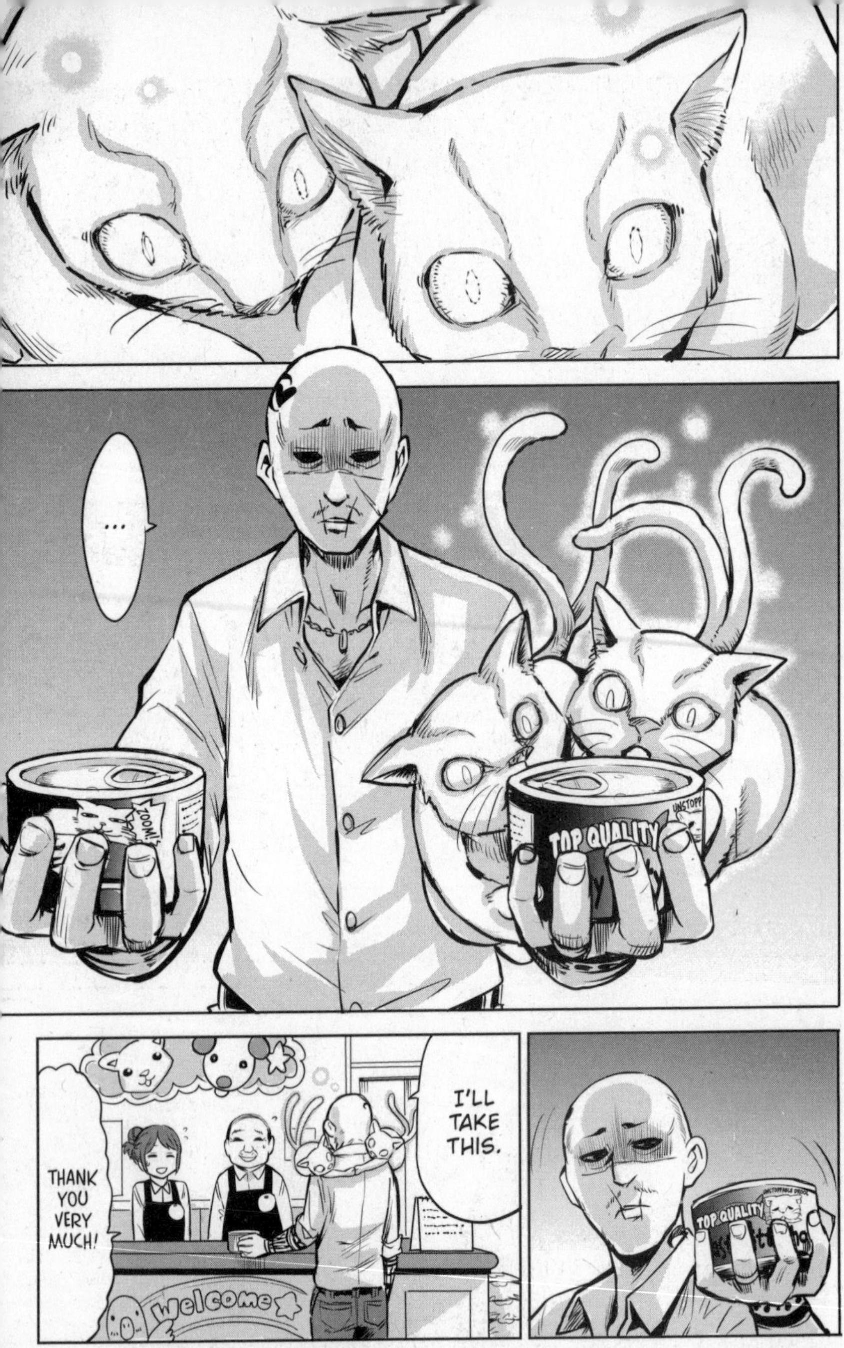
...
ZOOM!
TOP QUALITY
TOP QUALITY
I'LL TAKE THIS.
THANK YOU VERY MUCH!
Welcome

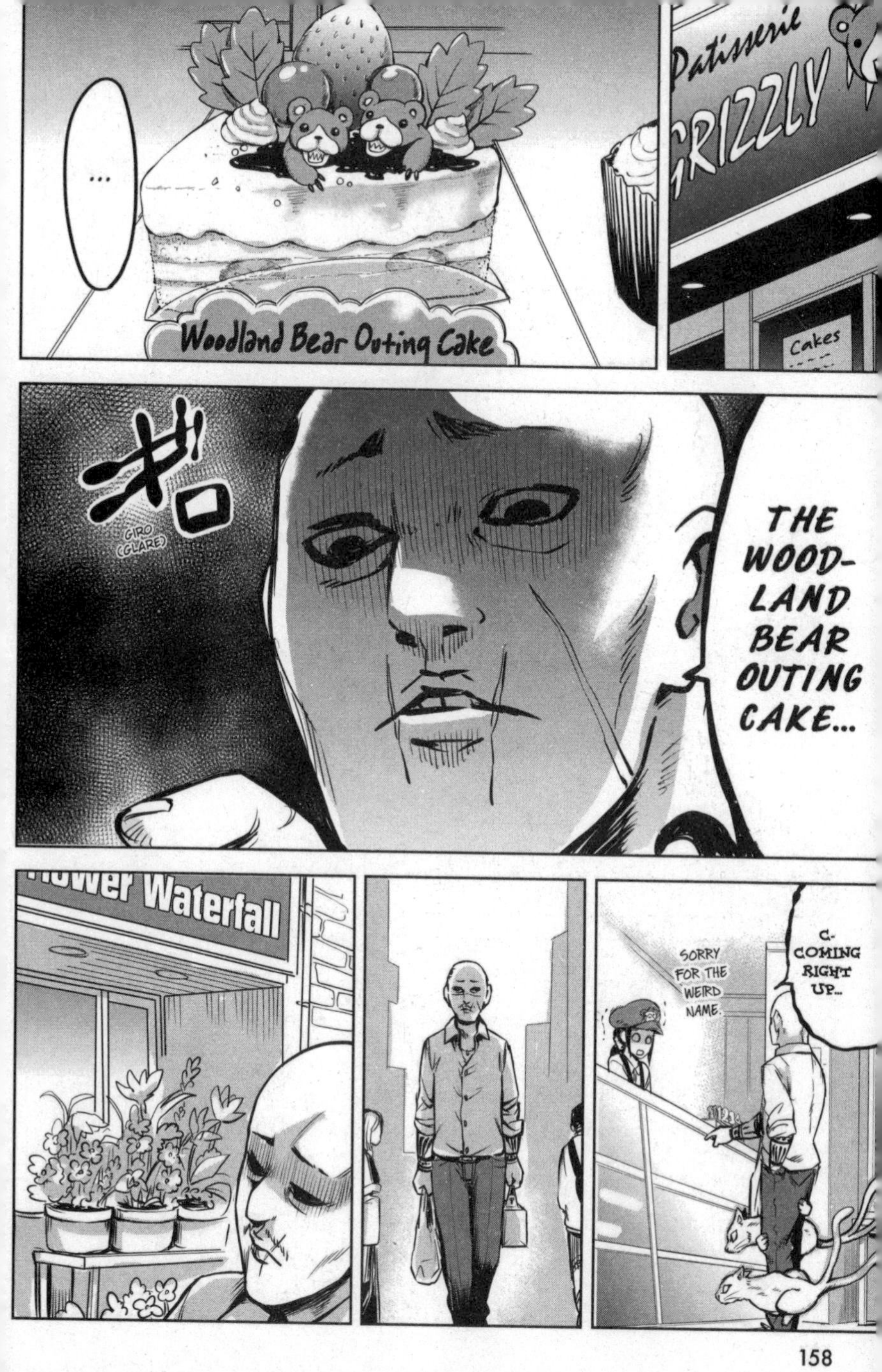
Patisserie GRIZZLY
Cakes
...
Woodland Bear Outing Cake
THE WOOD-LAND BEAR OUTING CAKE...
ギロ
GIRO (GLARE)
C- COMING RIGHT UP...
SORRY FOR THE WEIRD NAME.
Waterfall

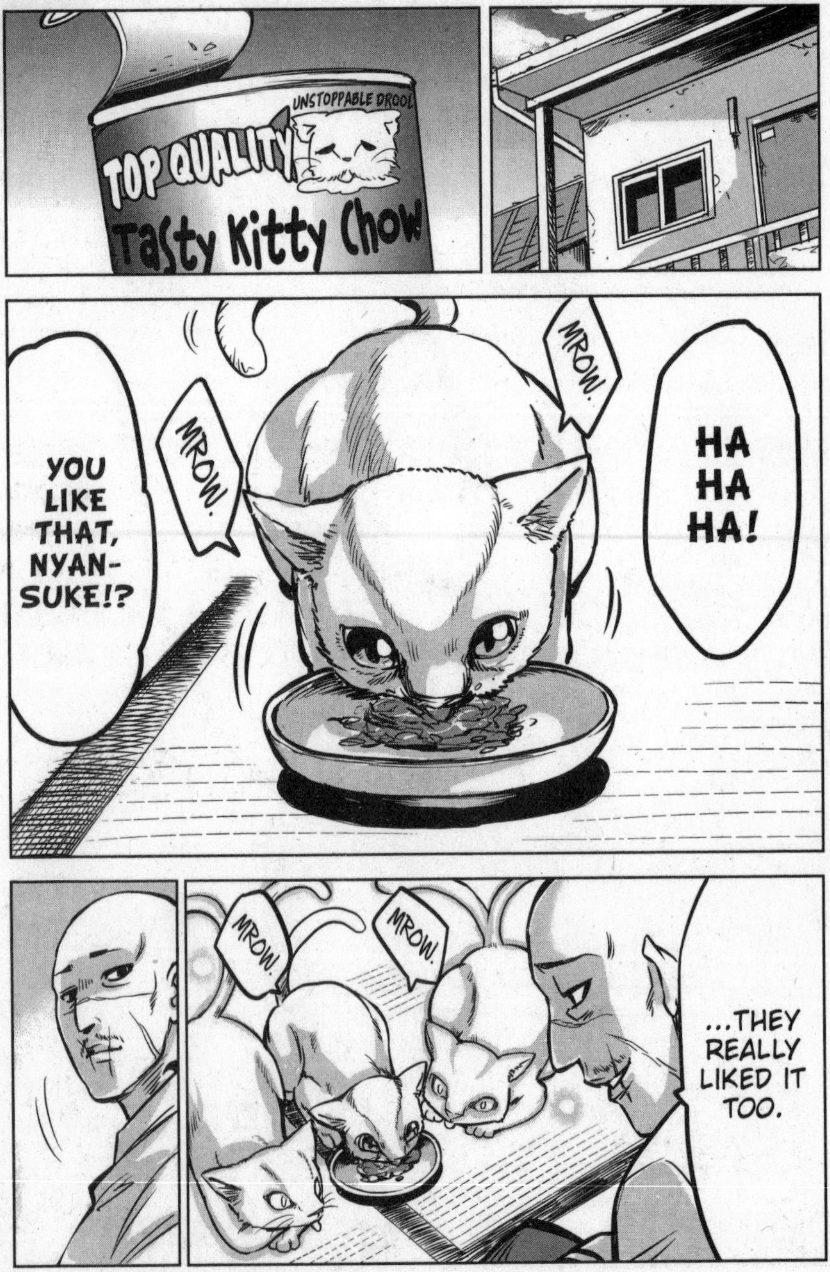
UNSTOPPABLE DROOL
TOP QUALITY
Tasty Kitty Chow
MROW.
HA HA HA!
MROW.
YOU LIKE THAT, NYAN-SUKE!?
...THEY REALLY LIKED IT TOO.
MROW.
MROW.

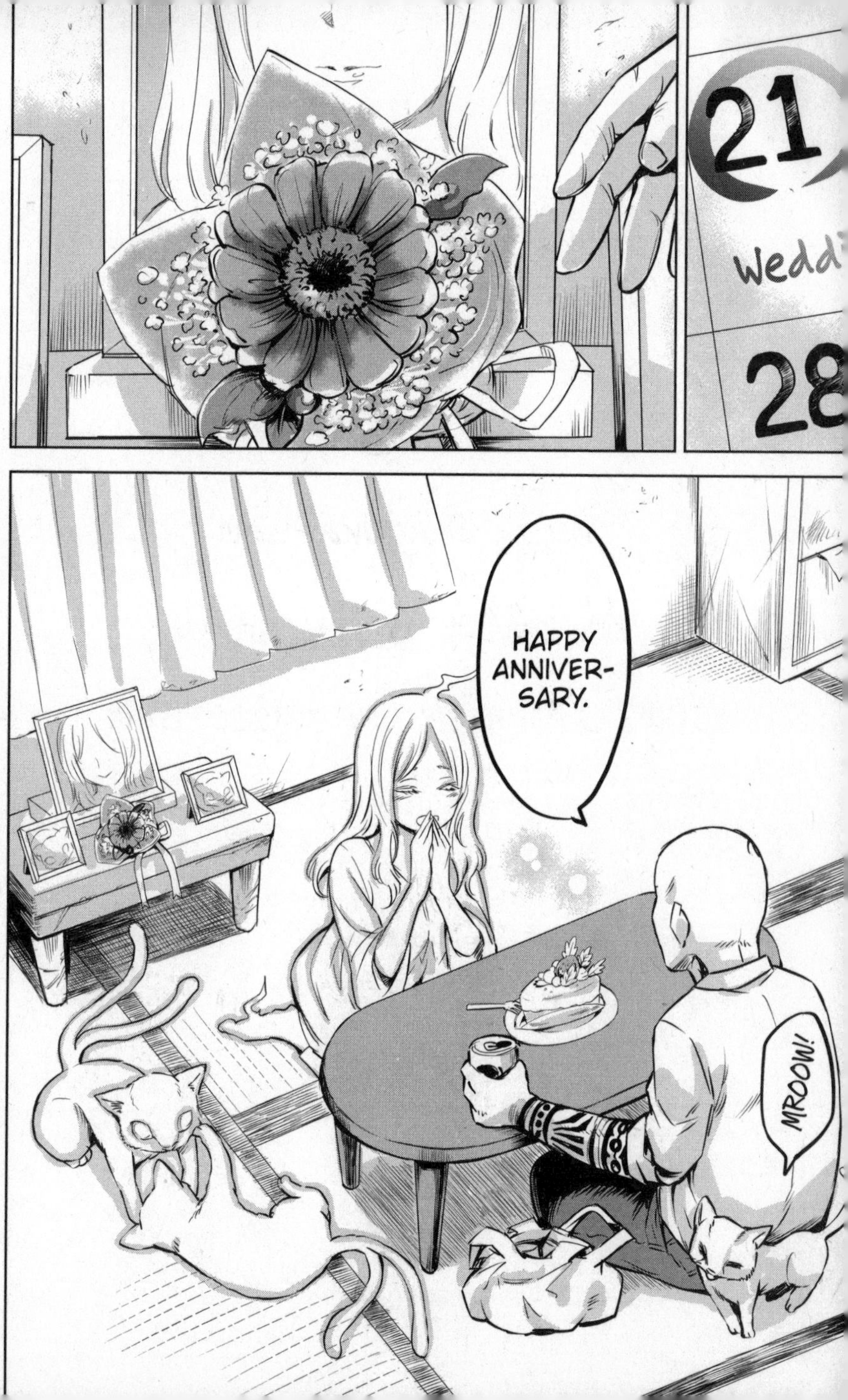
21
Wedd
28
HAPPY ANNIVER-SARY.
MROOW!

Special Thanks

Emo Izumi

Ryou Sugiura-san

My editor A-Mura-shi

The designer Sugimoto-san

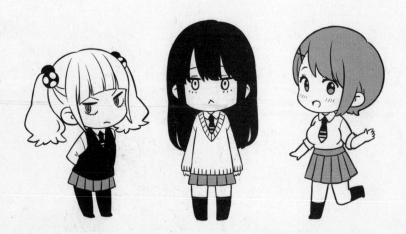

MIERUKO CHAN 2

Tomoki Izumi

Translation: LEIGHANN HARVEY   Lettering: ALEXIS ECKERMAN

MIERUKO-CHAN vol. 2
© Tomoki Izumi 2019
First published in Japan in 2019 by KADOKAWA CORPORATION, Tokyo.
English translation rights arranged with KADOKAWA CORPORATION, Tokyo, and Yen Press, LLC
through Tuttle-Mori Agency, Inc.

English translation © 2021 by Yen Press, LLC.

Yen Press
150 West 30th Street, 19th Floor
New York, NY 10001

Visit us at yenpress.com • facebook.com/yenpress • twitter.com/yenpress • yenpress.tumblr.com

First Yen Press Edition: February 2021

Yen Press is an imprint of Yen Press, LLC.
The Yen Press name and logo are trademarks of Yen Press, LLC.

The publisher is not responsible for websites (or their content) that are not owned by the publisher.

Library of Congress Control Number: 2020944845

ISBNs: 978-1-9753-1759-1 (paperback)
        978-1-9753-1760-7 (ebook)

10 9 8 7 6 5 4 3 2 1

WOR

Printed in the United States of America

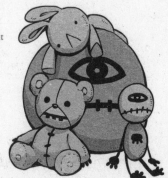